0144081

KT-486-211

RAA
(AIf)

on or before the la

03000595'82

Group Psychology and Political Theory

C. FRED ALFORD

Group Psychology
and
Political ❖
Theory

YALE UNIVERSITY PRESS
NEW HAVEN AND LONDON

Designed by Sally Harris/Summer Hill Books.
Set in Meridien type by Marathon Typography Service,
Durham, North Carolina.

Printed in the United States of America by
BookCrafters, Inc., Chelsea, Michigan.

Library of Congress Cataloging-in-Publication Data

Alford, C. Fred.
   Group psychology and political theory / C. Fred Alford.
      p.   cm.
   Includes bibliographical references and index.
   ISBN 0-300-05958-2 (alk. paper)
   1. Small groups.   2. Political psychology.   I. Title.
HM133.A45   1994
302.3'4—dc20   94-6774
                                              CIP

A catalogue record for this book is available
from the British Library.

The paper in this book meets the guidelines for
permanence and durability of the Committee on
Production Guidelines for Book Longevity
of the Council on Library Resources.

10 9 8 7 6 5 4 3 2 1

To the students in my graduate seminar in group psychology—
one of my favorite small groups

The individual is a group animal at war, not simply with the group, but with him-self for being a group animal and with those aspects of his personality that constitute his "groupishness." —*Wilfred Bion,* Experiences in Groups

Contents

Preface

This book is a report from the front, an argument that small study groups (sometimes called Tavistock groups, after the Institute in England where this method of group study originated) are the closest thing to the state of nature that political theorists write about—closer than any laboratory study, closer than any formal model. Of course I understand that the state of nature is metaphor, not history. My argument is that it is a misleading metaphor unless we understand that the group comes first. Before a man or woman is an individual or citizen, he or she is a group member, at war with his or her "groupishness." None of the familiar traditions in political theory—modern state-of-nature theory, liberalism, communitarianism, postmodernism, even feminist theory—helped me to make sense of this experience, this insight. Not even Aristotle's famous *zoon politikon*. So I have developed my own, based upon my experience with groups, applying it to political theories. The application is eclectic, not systematic. My goal is not so much to develop an alternative theory as to argue that political theory ignores the reality of groups, the most fundamental reality there is about society. It's not an oversight, but the result of ideological intention.

Hundreds of hours as member of, and consultant to, various Tavistock-type groups is the basis of my study. Several years ago Georgia Sorenson, director of the Center for Political Leadership and Participation at the University of Maryland, nominated me for membership in the A. K. Rice Institute, affiliated with the Tavistock Institute in London. We've had lots of interesting talks about it. Nancy Adams, director of several group relations conferences for the Washington–Baltimore Center, invited me to participate, first in the Advanced Study of the Small Group, then on the conference staff.

The experience has been invaluable—not just the opportunity to serve as a staff member, but to learn by her example another way of thinking and being, more about articulated feeling than theory. A. K. Rice is not a perfect organization, but it is tolerant and tolerable. Ernest Frugé, consultant to my small group at the first residential conference I attended, is one of several from whom I learned more than I knew at the time.

Jerrold Post's invitation to serve on the staff of his Workshop on International Conflict and Cooperation, a version of the Tavistock approach, opened new doors for me. Elliott Jaques, who with Wilfred Bion helped found this method of group study, but who no longer finds it very useful, has taken the time to explain why. Though we do not agree, his comments on the importance of role have had their influence. His 1955 case study of Glacier Metal, "Social Systems as Defense against Persecutory and Depressive Anxiety," remains one of the finest applications of group theory that I know. For my part, I've found Freud's *Group Psychology and the Analysis of the Ego* the most fruitful work of all, in part because it grasps the importance of leaders and their sacrifice by the group. For years I wondered why Freud would combine a work on group psychology with an analysis of the ego (the German title is *Massenpsychologie und Ich-Analyse*). Now I think I know. One sees the parts of the ego divided up and acted out in the group.

I became acquainted with *Lost in Familiar Places,* by Edward R. Shapiro and A. Wesley Carr, only after completing this book. Mine is a work in political theory, not organization theory, a big difference. Nonetheless, I'm pleased that my work, the work of Shapiro and Carr, and of several others in organization theory have developed along parallel lines, analyzing large organizations in terms of the psychology of the small group. Whether the small group is a good model for the large organization will continue to be debated. My theory does not entirely depend on this debate, as it is as much about reading texts as studying organizations. Texts that are already, I argue, a type of group.

To protect and respect the confidentiality of the small group and its members, I have altered the identifying characteristics, such as occupation, of every group member to whom I refer, as well as every name. None are made up, and none are composites. For several years I took extensive notes during each conference, and I rely on these. Nor have I changed the age or sex of any member, as this would mislead the reader.

Several colleagues have been most helpful. Victor Wolfenstein read the entire book in manuscript, making lots of suggestions, particularly about its tone. My compatriot Jim Glass also found the manuscript a little stringent. I've not done much to change the tone, though. I wrote the book as an argument with political theory as currently practiced, and that's what it remains. Steve Elkin, my colleague, read the whole manuscript, arguing that my theory is unnecessarily fancy, that it's not necessary for political theory to go so deep. The late Judith Shklar's "The Liberalism of Fear" better captures the proper concerns of political theory, protecting individuals from systematic fear. I disagree, but it's an important argument, addressed in chapter 6. Roger Lewin's influence is difficult to categorize, more subtle than I know how to put into words. My wife, Elly, encouraged my work on the epilogue.

The epilogue on the Wolini helped me better understand what I could only feel. I hope that it will do the same for some readers.

A Note on Sex, Gender, and Grammar

For grammatical purposes I generally use the masculine gender, except when referring to the reader, who is always he or she. I do this not just for reasons of stylistic ease, though that is important, but because an implication of group theory is that sexual difference matters, and that groups frequently seek to repress their knowledge of this difference. Since my argument is that a text in political theory is like a group, I do not wish to reproduce this tendency in my writing. When I say she, or he and she, I mean it. That is, I mean to call attention to the difference, not to pretend that there is none.

Group Psychology and Political Theory

1 ✳ In the Beginning Was the Group

In the beginning was the group. This is the fundamental truth about human nature and politics, and neither modern nor contemporary political theory has yet come to terms with it. It is an empirical truth. As far as we know, male and female humans have always lived together in groups. All the anthropological evidence supports this conclusion, and none refutes it, however much anthropologists differ on the details.[1] The state of nature that Hobbes and Rousseau write about, a bunch of isolated individuals running around either killing each other or ignoring each other, is pure fiction. Yet mine would not be a very interesting argument if all it said was that the state-of-nature theorists are historically inaccurate about the origins of human society. They know this. Rousseau starts his *Second Discourse* with that marvelous statement, "Let us therefore begin by setting all the facts aside, for they do not affect the question." Mine is also a critique of ideology. The way in which the traditional state-of-nature theorists, as well as many contemporary political theorists, set aside the facts about man's groupishness makes their theories ideologies: systems of ideas that defend against knowledge of social reality. Not empirical reality versus fiction, but whether one uses stories to get at the truth—or escape it—is the issue.

This book stems from my experience, hundreds of hours as consultant to, and member of, small, unstructured, leaderless groups, sometimes called Tavistock groups after the Tavistock Institute of Human Relations in London, where this method of group study originated. Founded in the years

---

1. Richard Leakey and Roger Lewin, *People of the Lake: Mankind and its Beginnings* (New York: Avon Books, 1978). Stephen A. Marglin, review of *Stone-Age Economics*, by Marshall Stahlins, *New York Review of Books*, 19 July 1984.

after World War II by Wilfred Bion, Elliott Jaques, and others, this method was brought to America by the A. K. Rice Institute and is explained in chapter 2. Sometime during the first small group in which I participated I had an idea, and I have pursued it since. It is the basis of this book. It is that the small, unstructured, leaderless group is a model of the state of nature. It is my version of the experiment that Rousseau proposes to know natural man. "What experiments would be necessary to achieve knowledge of natural man? And what are the means for making these experiments in the midst of society?," he asks.[2] Rousseau answers by bracketing reason and performing a thought experiment in which he imagines what a being might be like who does not possess reason. The result is natural man.

My experiment is different, using the Tavistock group as a model of the state of nature. But mine too is a thought experiment, not just an experiment. It assumes, for example, that a cutting remark is akin to a cut with a knife, a willingness to scapegoat a member akin to a blood sacrifice. Yet, my approach has an advantage. Because it assumes that man is first of all a group animal, it need not imagine what a being would be who had no group, as Rousseau must. The continuity between then and now can be emphasized, not denied. "Then" is not some place and some time in the distant past. "Then" is present in every group, in the most primitive levels of experience, levels normally concealed (but by no means buried) by bureaucracy, formal leadership, and designated task. It is the absence of all three in the Tavistock group that allows us to see these primitive levels more clearly.

Employing the Tavistock group as a model of the state of nature has advantages and disadvantages, or rather limits. I discuss the limits shortly. The advantage is not so much that it suggests a particular theory, though I have developed one on the basis of my experience. The advantage is that it keeps one close to experience, making it more difficult to ignore the obvious: that the members of small groups are scared to death of each other, especially at first; that they desperately desire to be led and are deeply humiliated and shamed by this desire, so much so that they make leadership impossible; that members want to be known by other members but are deeply afraid of being intruded upon, rendered transparent as one member put it; that members want to work, the work of learning about group process, but are so concerned with security that the work often gets left behind; that the relationship between member and group is funda-

2. Jean-Jacques Rousseau, "Discourse on the Origin and Foundations of Inequality among Men" (Second Discourse), in *The First and Second Discourses,* trans. Roger Masters and Judith Masters (New York: St. Martin's Press, 1964), 78–228, p. 93.

mentally unstable, the member oscillating between isolate and submerged groupie; that groups get depressed, and members frequently create little dramas to distract them from their despair, confusing these dramas with group development.

What If We Put Experience First?

These are the things that have impressed me most about groups. What if one were to build a political theory from the ground up, so to speak, so as to take these experiences into account? What would this theory say about modern and contemporary political theory? This is the question that guides this book. One might call mine an inductive approach to political theory, but I would put it differently. Mine is an approach that takes simple things seriously, that grants to the experiences I have enumerated the importance they deserve. Experiences that are, after all, available not merely to those who study Tavistock groups, but to any who would open their eyes and look at human life in groups. A story by Václav Havel will help to explain the spirit that animates my approach, one that attempts to avoid the split between thought and reality that Havel calls "evasive thinking." The story takes place a number of years before the velvet revolution.

It seems that a stone window ledge in Prague came loose, falling to the street and killing a pedestrian. Soon after, another ledge fell, resulting in another death. The public was outraged, and a columnist for *Literární noviny* assured the public that their outrage was proper. Nevertheless, he continued, the public's outrage should be properly directed. Falling window ledges are a danger, but the public should really concern itself with issues more worthy of the dignity of the human experience and more appropriate to the humanistic ideal of man and the challenges of socialism. Literature too, he said, should free itself from petty, local, and municipal matters and begin at last to deal with the proper future of mankind. With noble simplicity Havel calls this "evasive thinking."

Evasive thinking occurs when thought and reality become too much separated.

Notice, for example, how often the words we use these days are more important than what we are talking about. The word—as such—has ceased to be a sign for a category, and has gained a kind of occult power to transform one reality into another. Arguments are not carried on through ideas, but through concepts. . . . A typical example is how reality can be liquidated with the help of false "contextualization": the praiseworthy attempt to see things in their wider context becomes so formalized that . . .

it becomes a single and widely used model of thinking with a special capacity to dissolve—in the vagueness of all the possible wider contexts—everything particular in that reality.[3]

The solution is to see, really see, individual, specific things. If we can't see them, if we can't see the window ledges that fall off and kill people but must transform them into abstract concepts, then we can't really see anything at all. The individual, specific things I have chosen to see are the conflicts that occur in small self-study groups. Or rather, these conflicts have so impressed themselves on me, so imprinted themselves on my soul, that I cannot avoid them. This book is an attempt to generalize these conflicts to political entities and political theory. But it starts with individual, specific things, puzzling and startling occurrences in these groups, such as why everyone seems so scared.

Just think about it for a minute. Think about what the world really looks like when it reverts to a state of nature, humans as they really are in the absence of established political authority. It is never Hobbes's war of all against all, of individual against individual. In the former Yugoslavia, Somalia, Angola, and countless other places it is always tribe against tribe, group against group, in seemingly infinite and endless permutations and combinations. I think this individual specific thing is terribly important and that political theory has never fully confronted it: that the group is the original state of nature. Ironically, it is traditional state-of-nature theory that comes closest, knowing itself to be an ideology of individualism.

Most contemporary political theory is evasive thinking, dissolving the tragic reality of human life in groups into this or that concept or parade of adjectives. Chapter 5 is devoted to showing how liberalism, communitarianism, participationism, and postmodernism all liquidate reality through false contextualization, as Havel calls it. What is this reality? Not merely—and it would be enough—that human life in groups is tragic, as group members destroy the one entity, a developed group, that could help them realize their identity. *But that there is no solution.* Group members oscillate between isolation and submersion in the group in such a way that no possible arrangement of the group could prevent it; because the conflict is not just within the group, but within each member, his war with his own groupishness, as Bion puts it.

Not only is there no solution, but attempts to realize one generally result in making the problem worse. Solutions solve the problem by splitting off half of it, driving it underground, where it exerts its influence in

3. Václav Havel, "On Evasive Thinking," in *Open Letters: Selected Writings, 1965–1990,* ed. Paul Wilson (New York: Vintage Books, 1992), 10–24, pp. 11–13.

even more perverse ways. Liberalism ignores and devalues man's groupishness, whereas participationism and communitarianism systematically downplay man's war with his own groupishness, his tendency to destroy the community he depends upon. Postmodernism knows both these things but analyzes them at such a high level of abstraction that it obliterates the reality of both individual and group. All are evasive thinking. What is necessary is to live with the reality of no solution, which means to accept that within each individual is the desire to be an autonomous individual, the desire to submerge oneself in the group, and a perpetual conflict between these two desires. It is a conflict so intense that it frequently leads the individual to try to do both at once, the "schizoid compromise." Analyzed in chapter 3, the schizoid compromise is the tragedy of human life in groups, in which members split themselves in such a way as to make impossible either the contentment of genuine belonging or the satisfaction of individual autonomy. The attempt to achieve a solution results not in the best, but generally the worst, of two worlds.

While there are no solutions, some resolutions and compromises are better than others. It is possible to minimize members' oscillations between isolate and groupie and so create a relatively stable group that finds a place for the individual member, one who can find his boundary at the skin of his neighbor, as one group theorist puts it, instead of deep inside his neighbor (a groupie) or a thousand miles away (an isolate). This, though, takes good leadership, an almost taboo topic in political theory. In fact, this is probably the most important single thing I have learned from small groups. *Group development requires leadership, a fact that political theory has worked hard to ignore, evidently because the need for leadership is experienced as humiliating and dangerous.* Humiliating, because the need for leadership questions the autonomy and freedom of individuals, and dangerous, because leadership so often seems to connote the *Führerprinzip.* In fact, the real danger is the pretense that leadership is unnecessary, that the subjects of political theory are already autonomous and free. Such an assumption not only fails to appreciate the dangers of group psychology; it fails at the proper task of political theory, which is to promote individual and group development, which means to bring groups of individuals to the point where they can be individuals in a group, members who retain their individuality. Most political theory has failed to address this developmental task, writing as though the task were already complete, as though its subjects were already the individuals they might become if group development were addressed. The social contract proposed in chapter 5 accepts this developmental task.

The reasons why political theory has ignored this issue are complex, but one is surely the fear of overburdening politics, of making it the realm of self-fulfillment, and so bringing into the political realm needs that politics cannot properly address while respecting the freedom of citizens. Making politics the realm of personal and group development is, many fear, an invitation to totalitarianism. Certainly one might read Plato's *Republic* this way. To make soulcraft the proper realm of statecraft is to make even the souls of citizens the subject of the regime. This fear is real and legitimate. But just as there is no solution to the problem of individual and group, so excluding the realm of individual and group development from politics is no solution to the dangers of totalitarianism. *On the contrary, isolating politics from issues of individual and group development only makes politics more vulnerable to totalitarian pressures.* Reality is whole, which means that defining politics as properly about this but not that doesn't automatically make it so. Scared and isolated citizens, even (or perhaps particularly) in a liberal regime, are vulnerable to illiberal demagogues. The Weimar Republic is the most dramatic example, but there are others. Chapter 6 returns to this issue by way of a discussion of Judith Shklar's "The Liberalism of Fear."

Another reason why political theorists have ignored these issues is that they interfere with the theorist's control of the material, his ability to make his subject be any way he wants it to be—at least on paper, in texts. Not only have political theorists traditionally asked their questions in ways that make psychology irrelevant, but they have formulated their questions so as to subsume psychology in epistemology, the theory of knowledge. The *de facto* transformation of political theory into epistemology, so that the question becomes what man can know (Plato's forms, Hobbes's science of man in motion, Locke's natural law, Habermas's universal pragmatics), assumes that if we can figure this out, we can figure out how to convince the subject of political theory of its truth. Then he, and more recently she, will offer up his or her rational assent. Seen from the ivory tower of epistemology, the specifics of individual and group psychology are details: not facts that determine the limits of any regime, but contingencies subject to transcendence via new epistemologies. It's called jumping over your own shadow. Since Nietzsche, the strategy of epistemological transcendence has been less than compelling.

Postmodern political theory dances on the grave of epistemological political theory, showing each transcendent leap to be one more leap of bad faith, one more grand narrative pretending to be more than just another story. In place of the "philosophy of the subject," postmodern political theory deconstructs the pretensions of subjectivity itself, the claim of man to know anything or be anything. So different from traditional political theory, postmodern political theory is no friend of psychology either, insofar as psychology says that men and women are this way, not that. "You are essentializing human nature," the postmodern political theorist maintains. As though the existence of human nature were strictly a philosophical, rather than empirical, issue. In this respect, at least, traditional and postmodern political theory are identical. Both utilize philosophical abstraction to overcome psychology. To dance on the grave of epistemology turns out not to be so different from practicing it. I shall be returning to these issues again and again throughout the book. They are the political-theoretical version of what Havel calls evasive thinking, a refusal to see individual, specific things.

Although traditional state-of-nature theory shares in the strategy of epistemological transformation (Hobbes and Locke were mentioned above), the figure of a state of nature is not so much epistemological as utopian: how specific things might be or might have been. While traditional state-of-nature theory is mistaken about these specific things, this turns out to be a far more interesting and fruitful error, an error of substance rather than denial. The thesis that the group comes first implies that Pufendorf, Hobbes, Locke, and Rousseau are not only mistaken but have it backwards. The task of government and civil society is not, as they would have it, to socialize autonomous individuals. The task is to individualize an overly social animal, a groupie. Liberal individualism is an achievement, not a given. The task, in other words, is to help group members individuate themselves from the group, so that they may come to live freely and critically, while knowing themselves to be social creatures, bound in relationships with others from birth to death. In many ways an impossible task, some ways of failing at it are better than others.

State-of-nature theorists write as if they know that this is the proper task of government but believe that it can be approached only indirectly, via a noble lie. One like the following: "We know that it is not individuals but groups that launch crusades, make war, and commit genocide. It is man's willingness to follow, his eagerness to belong, that makes these horrors possible. If, however, we write about the members of these groups as though they were autonomous individuals, perhaps they will begin to think like ones. If so, then they would be so much easier to control, as they might respond to reason, or at least to appeals to individual interest." It is this that makes traditional state-of-nature theory an ideology. It would not be an ideology were these theorists to design their accounts so as to help men and women become more autonomous and free, instead of convincing them that they already are. The social contract proposed in chapter 5 is not ideology. It aims not to convince men and women of their freedom but to characterize genuine freedom and autonomy in a life shared with others in groups, so as to pose it as a developmental task, a goal, not an achievement.

Chapter 4 analyzes traditional state-of-nature theory as an ideology that almost, but not quite, knows itself to be one. It is a transitional chapter. Chapters 2 and 3 develop a group psychology with special reference to politics. Chapter 4 is in effect an immanent critique, arguing that the state-of-nature theorists know of man's groupishness, which means his war with his own groupishness, but organize their theories as a defense against this insight. *Chapter 5 is the payoff, applying the group theory of chapters 2 and 3 and the critique of chapter 4 to contemporary political theory.* Chapter 6 turns to the question of leadership, so important in groups and so ignored by traditional and contemporary political theory. In the Epilogue I tell a story about a state of nature, intended to capture with images and tropes something of the complexity of my experience of the small group. Referred to only infrequently, the Epilogue runs parallel to the argument of chapters 2–6. It comes last, but might just as well have come first or along the way, as it contains everything I want to say, albeit in a different form.

It will come as no surprise that a group-psychological perspective is critical of the liberal individualism of traditional state-of-nature theory. One might think that communitarian and participationist critics of liberal individualism would come closer to the mark from a group-psychological perspective. They don't. The way these approaches to political theory idealize community and participation denies the second half of Wilfred Bion's statement that serves as the epigraph to this book. Man is not only a group animal. He is at war with his own groupishness, which means with his own group. *It is to this tendency that the term "groupie" refers:* not merely man's desire to abandon himself to groups but his tendency to declare war on his own group, as though destroying the group with which he wants to merge could save his individuality. Man could be a group animal, Aristotle's zoon politikon, without being a groupie. It's logically possible: it's just not empirically the case.

Generally seeking to undermine the effectiveness of the group to which he belongs, man soon finds that the undermined group is inadequate to support his own individuality. This is the tragedy of human life in groups. In order to protect their individuality, individuals destroy the one entity that could, if properly organized, help them realize it. Postmodern political theory comes closest to understanding the way in which groups threaten individual identity, while grasping that individual identity is always identity in relationship to a group. William Connolly calls this the "paradox of politics," making it central to his analysis in *Identity\Difference*. Yet, postmodern political theory generally proceeds at such an abstract level of analysis that it transforms the real conflict between individuals and groups into a conflict between the ideas of identity and difference. In so doing, postmodernism abandons its potential as ideology critique.

Most political theory operates with a model of man and woman too simple to capture adequately the phenomena experienced in small groups. While this book refers to human nature, this is not intended to suggest that this nature is fixed or given, but only that it is not unitary, not just one thing. Nor is human nature merely protean, fluid, and mutable, as many postmoderns would have it. This puts it too nicely. Human nature has many parts, and the parts are at war with each other, the insight of Plato over two millennia ago when he wrote of the three-part *psyche* divided against itself (*Republic*, 439d–441c). The debate between liberals and communitarians, for example, is not just a debate between two perspectives on the human psyche. It is an attempt by each party to split the psyche in two, so as to solve the conflict by pretending the other parties don't exist or make no valid claim. It would be more accurate to say that liberalism and communitarianism are both right, at the same time, which means—since they are not saying the same thing—that the individual subject is a liberal at war with his communitarianism and a communitarian at war with his liberalism.

My Experience, Readers' Experiences, and My Conclusion

In *The Self in Social Theory* I showed how political theorists split the self in various ways to make it more tractable, more amenable to society. The present book is in many ways the second half of that project, beginning from the ground up; not from what political theorists write about but from the experiences of myself in others in small groups. Unlike *Self*, in this book references to the secondary literature are minimal. This book states the results of an ongoing experiment with groups. I don't believe that anyone has done anything quite like it, and my argument aims to highlight its experiential quality, my attempt to connect life and texts. I might have proceeded otherwise, reviewing the huge secondary literature on traditional state-of-nature theory while drawing upon many more examples of contemporary political theory. This would have diluted the experience.

What about those without this experience, it might be asked? What about the 99 percent of readers of this book who will not have participated in Tavistock groups? They will have participated in similar groups, for that is what it is to be human: families, groups at school, work, and the like, all the associations of which Americans are so fond, according to Tocqueville.

Most will have read political theorists who write about groups: from Aristotle's zoon politikon to the traditional state-of-nature theorists to contemporary debates between liberal individualists and communitarians. Tavistock groups are not magic. There is no experience that occurs in a Tavistock group that is not available in countless other groups. The Tavistock group brings these experiences from background to foreground by interpreting them. *But it reveals nothing that two millennia of thoughtful observers have not known or intuited.* Unfortunately, these observers have generally concluded (often tacitly) that these experiences are too threatening and disturbing to be acknowledged, so they construct their theories to defend against them. Chapters 4 and 5 are concerned with just this. Not suppressed quite so easily, reality comes back to haunt groups and individuals. Not suppression but interpretation is the answer.

Perhaps the reader is a good liberal, concerned, as any thoughtful liberal must be, that liberalism fails to acknowledge fully man's need for community. Perhaps the reader is a good communitarian, concerned, as any thoughtful communitarian must be, that communitarianism risks sacrificing the individual to the group. The reader is already a group theorist, concerned with the fundamental issue of this book, the tension between individual and group. What I add is that every individual is both liberal and communitarian, a liberal at war with his communitarianism, a communitarian at war with his liberalism. The struggle between liberal and communitarian is fought out within every individual and within every group, frequently leading the individual to destroy the group and the group to destroy the individual: the worst of both worlds. *For the reader who has any sense of this conflict within himself or herself the experience that I report should be readily comprehensible.* I have chosen the Tavistock group as my model not just because it is about groups, but because it highlights an experience that is universal, not requiring a lot of psychoanalytic theory to interpret. Not psychoanalytic theory, but dramas of conflict, despair, terror, hope, and revenge are the stuff of Tavistock groups—and, I presume, the lives of readers as well.

Instead of experience, I might have turned to history, analyzing the different ways in which members of groups have conceived of themselves, as citizens of the *polis,* link in the Great Chain of Being, mass man, economic man, and so forth. Certainly it remains an open question whether the Tavistock groups with which I have worked capture "man's groupishness" or just the particular form in which men and women express their groupishness in Western, postmodern, late capitalist mass societies. Had I done this, I'm sure that I would have found that in different societies, cultures, and epochs men and women have conceived of their groupishness quite differently. The dynamics of a Tavistock group in a feudal, tribal, or polis-based society (if that can even be imagined) would presumably be different from those in contemporary liberal democracies. I did not employ this approach for several reasons, primarily because it would have diluted the experiential quality of my report: what it's like to be in a Tavistock group (the topic of chapter 2) and what this experience of the state of nature says about political theory. A report on experience must, by its very nature, be a report of a *particular* experience, not every possible experience of man's groupishness. Mine is reportage, not history.

I have not ignored history, however. The traditional state-of-nature theorists wrote several hundred years ago (Hobbes published *Leviathan* in 1651) about societies almost as feudal as they were modern. I have had no difficulty finding the fundamental experiences of the Tavistock group in their accounts—which raises an issue discussed in detail shortly. How men and women conceive of their groupishness may be less important, but far more variable, than how they act in groups. Had I taken a historical approach, I would have been looking not at actual, different groups in various cultures and epochs but at intellectuals' *ideas* about groups and individuals—not the same thing. Again, I have sought to stay close to experience, finding in Tavistock groups the closest thing to the experiment that Rousseau writes of. It is this experiment that has captivated me.

Beginning within the state-of-nature–social-contract tradition, this book also ends there, albeit in a unique way. I don't believe my starting point has determined the end point, but I can hardly deny the influence. Mine is not a survey of man's groupishness, but an argument about it. I conclude that constitutional liberalism coupled with strong leadership (what I call interpretive leadership) is the best way to contain man's groupishness: his tendency to destroy the groups upon which he depends for his self-realization. Most who write of constitutional liberalism, such as Shklar and Michael Oakeshott, place little value on leadership; nor do most communitarians and participationists. Many who value leadership devalue individualism. Yet, it is the combination of the two, constitutional liberalism plus strong leadership, that best captures the lesson of Tavistock: that individual and group development don't just happen. They depend on each other and must be fostered.

My hope is that by the time the reader has finished the book he or she will say, "Of course this is the implication of the Tavistock group for political theory. He hardly needed to mention it, as it's implicit in everything he said, and quite a logical combination really." Indeed it is, yet constitutional liberalism plus strong (interpretive) leadership is not a combination that gets much attention, leadership being anathema to most liberals. Yet it is really this unfamiliar but hardly illogical combination that best respects man's war with his own groupishness, constitutional liberalism protecting his individuality, leadership developing his ability to be an individual group member, not merely an alienated groupie. However, it is not this solution that I stress, but the social contract that goes with it, a social contract that states that the relationships it describes and the institutions upon which they are based *not primarily serve to allow one or more parties to locate disowned parts of themselves in others.* The social contract is a series of institutions, arrangements, and practices by which citizens come to reclaim parts of themselves previously lost to the group. Such a contract is not so much a condition of constitutional liberalism and strong leadership as it is a result, another way in which my account differs from traditional social-contract theory.

Groups and Grouplike Entities:
The Relation is Empirical not Methodological

Before commencing the argument, two preliminary but fundamental issues remain. First, I shall show that it makes sound conceptual sense to apply the experience of the small group to large grouplike entities, as I shall call them, like nation-states. It is not obvious that small groups illuminate the fundamental processes of large collectivities, and an argument that they do is necessary. Second, I argue that the experience of the small group is enough like a textual experience (a fancy way of saying "reading a book about political theory") that the former may illuminate the latter. Small groups are not texts, but they are enough like texts that it makes sense to read one in order to better read the other.

Since Freud's *Group Psychology and the Analysis of the Ego* (1921), group psychology has used the term "group" loosely. It doesn't cover a crowd at a beach, unless that crowd is organized in some way, such as to observe the rescue of a drowning man. But it does cover the army and the Catholic church, Freud's two examples, entities spread out all over the globe and hierarchically organized. This is not how I employ the term "group." Civil societies, cultures, and nation-states are not groups. A group is individuals occupying space and time together in contiguous, but possibly mediated, interaction in an entity small enough that the members might come to know each other as individuals even if they do not. The Catholic church by this definition is no group, but the priest and parishioners of a church are.

An army is no group, but a platoon is. A New England township is probably not a group, but the citizens who attend a town meeting on a cold winter night are. A large corporation, such as IBM or General Motors, is no group, but the design section of the Chevrolet division may be. A university is no group, but an academic department or class is.

Contiguous interaction is not unmediated interaction. Each member need not be in contact with every other member, but each member must be in contact with someone, usually a leader, who is in contact with every other. A group occupies space and time, but this need not be interpreted literally. The parishioners of a church or the members of an academic department share space and time, even if they do not do so all at once at every moment. Level of organization is not part of this definition, primarily because even the ostensibly unstructured and unorganized Tavistock group quickly develops an elaborate, albeit informal, structure as compelling as any formal one. All groups have structures and hierarchies and division of labor. The only question is whether they are formal or not, which turns out not to be the most important question.

GROUPLIKE ENTITIES. Cultures, civil societies, and nation-states are not groups. They are grouplike entities, a term that is not a cop-out. A grouplike entity is one in which basic patterns of relationships among members or citizens resemble the patterns found in small groups. For example, chapter 5 discusses the phenomenon of civil privatism, as it is called by Jürgen Habermas and others, in which citizens expect that government efficiently administer the economy but leave them alone. Questions of legitimation or opportunities for self-governance are considered little more than a nuisance. This orientation is, I argue, comparable to and illuminated by a phenomenon frequently seen in the small group, schizoid individualism. Human relations are varied but not infinitely so. Or if the variations are infinite, basic patterns recur, patterns observed in the smallest groups and the largest nations. By studying these patterns in the small group we may understand them better in grouplike entities.

Whether an entity, such as a culture or society, is a grouplike entity is not an analytic question, not a question of definition. It is a question of empirical reality. Whether a particular society, culture, or nation-state is a grouplike entity depends upon whether in fact the basic pattern of social relations in the entity resembles the pattern in small groups. This is not an issue that can be resolved in the abstract—except to say that should it be the case that factors emerging as a result of size, scope, and level of organization (for example, presence of mass media) transform the pattern of small group relations in large entities, then the large entity would not be a group-like one. Whether I have been successful in using group psychology to illuminate large-scale grouplike entities, such as nation-states and civic cultures, will depend upon just one thing: whether the experiences and processes identified in small groups do, in fact, illuminate larger entities, as the experiences and processes turn out to be similar, though not necessarily identical. In the end, the reader will be the judge of this. Group process is not the only thing that matters, but it is important and has been neglected.

Methodological Individualism and Emergence

If the relationship of the small group to large grouplike entities is an empirical, rather than conceptual or philosophical, issue, then it will not be settled by a priori arguments. A review of the issues of methodological individualism and emergence will support my position. "The psychology of groups," says Freud, "is the oldest human psychology; what we have isolated as individual psychology, by neglecting all traces of the group, has only since come into prominence out of the old group psychology."[4] While group psychology comes first, Freud understands that this has nothing to do with a group mind or any other emergent property of groups. It means that because men and women are born and reared in groups, those aspects of their psychologies that respond to the presence of others in groups will be of paramount importance. Individuals behave as they do in groups because the presence of the group releases latent potentials in the individuals. But perhaps this isn't quite right. Because man is a group animal to begin with, these potentials are actually more likely to be manifest. The latent potentials have more to do with being an autonomous individual, which has been my point all along. It is also Freud's.

Wilfred Bion, founder of the psychoanalytic study of small groups, writes of a "group mentality," but his position is much the same as Freud's. The group mentality is the way in which members attribute to the group impulses and desires for which they do not wish to take responsibility.[5] The reification of the group is a defense against individual responsibility. While members may talk about the group as though it were a single entity, it is important for the observer not to buy into this illusion. Rather, the observer must understand that

there are characteristics in the individual whose real significance cannot be understood unless it is realized that they are part of his equipment as a herd

4. Sigmund Freud, *Group Psychology and the Analysis of the Ego*, trans. James Strachey (New York: W. W. Norton, 1959), p. 55.
5. Wilfred Bion, *Experiences in Groups* (New York: Basic Books, 1961), pp. 50–53.

animal and their operation cannot be seen unless it is looked for in the intelligible field of study—which in this instance is the group. . . . The apparent difference between group psychology and individual psychology is an illusion produced by the fact that the group provides an intelligible field of study for certain aspects of individual psychology, and in so doing brings into prominence phenomena that appear alien to an observer unaccustomed to using the group.[6]

This differs from Freud's position, closer to my own, in which individual psychology is the exception, group psychology the norm. But that hardly matters here. Both founders of the psychoanalytic study of the group are deeply aware of the risk of postulating mysterious explanatory entities, such as the group mind, which in the end explain nothing but only reify the group. Groups are collections of individuals in interaction. To forget this is itself regressive.

This may seem obvious, but it is sometimes argued against group psychology that it violates the principle of methodological individualism and as such runs counter to empiricism. It doesn't. Methodological individualism holds that all terms defining the properties of groups—for example, "The group is angry at its leader"—are in principle definable in terms of the behavior of individuals in them. "X is angry, Y is angry, and their anger makes Z angry too." The nemesis of methodological individualism is holism, the assertion that there are group properties "over and above the individuals making up the group, their properties, *and the relations among them.*"[7] Freud and Bion are methodological individualists. So am I. The entities with which we are concerned are individuals, their properties, and the relationships among these individuals in groups. What else is there?

Sometimes methodological individualism is confused with explanatory individualism, an empirical issue. The belief that there exist no emergent group *properties,* ones not definable in terms of individuals and their relationships, is a statement about what exists in the world, a philosophical commitment to empiricism. There may, however, be laws of group behavior that are emergent with respect to laws about individuals. This means that we could know all about the individuals in a group, including all about how they are transformed in their relationships with others, and still be unable to explain the behavior of the group. "X is angry, Y is angry, and this makes Z angry, but somehow the group (defined in terms of its individual mem-

6. Ibid., pp. 133–134.
7. May Brodbeck, "Methodological Individualisms: Definition and Reduction," in *Readings in the Philosophy of the Social Sciences,* ed. Brodbeck (New York: Macmillan, 1968), 280–303, p. 283, my emphasis. I draw heavily on Brodbeck here.

bers, X, Y, and Z) is not angry." If this were so, we could not reduce our explanations of group *behavior* to statements about individuals, their relationships, and the composition laws, as they are called, that predict what happens when, for example, the number of relationships reaches a certain size or complexity. Whether this is the case is not a methodological issue and not a philosophical one, but an empirical one. It remains to be seen, if and when we ever have a group science of sufficient precision for the problem to arise.

We don't, and there is no need to worry about it now, except to point out that the battle against a group-psychological approach to politics or anything else will have to be fought at an empirical level, not a methodological one. There is nothing methodologically or philosophically problematic about stating that "the group does this, or the group thinks that." It is shorthand for "X, Y, Z . . . , all members of the group, in their roles as group members and influenced by the fears and desires of other group members, perhaps in ways they are hardly aware of, did this and think that." Nor is this shorthand unusual. We use it everyday when we say things like, "It is the policy of the United States not to pay ransom for hostages," or "Industrial production fell in the last quarter." The statement about the group may, of course, be empirically wrong, but it is not logically suspect.

Most who study groups, such as Freud and Bion, are more aware of the risks of reifying the group and so forgetting that the group is its members than those who don't. Freud and Bion understand that the experience of the group as an entity in itself, distinct from the members, is itself a sign of regressive deindividuation. As Bion puts it, the

belief that a group exists, as distinct from an aggregate of individuals, is an essential part of this regression. . . . Substance is given to the phantasy that the group exists by the fact that the regression involves the individual in the loss of his "individual distinctiveness" (Freud). . . . It follows that if the observer judges a group to be in existence, the individuals composing it must have experienced this regression.[8]

This does not seem quite right, as it leaves no room for anything between an aggregate of individuals and the regressed group. Individual members in interaction with each other is the ideal. Should the observer of the group experience merely an aggregate of individuals, he may well be experiencing the individuals' extreme reaction against the deindividuating forces of the group. Nevertheless, this reaction is itself a response of individuals, and that is my point. Group psychology is no alternative to individual psychology, individuals, or individualism, but rather the most sophisticated state-

8. Bion, *Experiences in Groups,* p. 142.

ment of what it is to explain and understand individual action in a world of others.

Traditional state-of-nature theory is liberal and individualistic (Rousseau may be the exception), concerned with how autonomous individuals might come together under a social contract to create a decent society. In arguing that the group comes first, this book might be seen as reversing the traditional order. It does, at least empirically: not just in arguing that the proper task of society and government is to individualize the overly socialized groupie but also in arguing that individual and group development require each other. The tragedy of groups is an individual tragedy. Out of fear of the group, individuals undermine its effectiveness and so destroy the one arena in which they might truly realize their individuality. From a normative or value-based perspective, however, my approach remains liberal and individualistic. The goal is not group development for its own sake, but group development for the sake of the development of the individuals in it. The goal, the standard, is individual unfolding. If it could be achieved in some other way, I might encourage it. It can't. Individual and group development go hand in hand.

Sometimes liberal individualism and methodological individualism are confused. Even Brodbeck, whose account I have drawn on to explain methodological individualism, suggests this equation.[9] In fact, there is no necessary connection between the two. One could, for example, hold that the group is the highest standard of value, to which the individual should be sacrificed, and quite consistently define the group in terms of its members and their relationships, which is the only issue as far as methodological individualism is concerned. Nevertheless, methodological individualism draws our attention to the individuals who constitute the group. In this way it dramatizes my point: that it makes perfect sense to focus on the group even, or especially, when one values above all else the development of the individuals in it.

Group Psychological Materialism: The Origins of Concepts in Real Relationships

This book is not just about groups and grouplike entities. It is about political theories, texts that embody concepts and ideas about grouplike entities. Yet, my argument is more ambitious than that political theory is about grouplike entities. Not only are political theories *about* grouplike entities, but one can analyze political theories as though the theories themselves

9. Brodbeck, "Methodological Individualisms," p. 283.

were groups. The key ideas and concepts of political theories concerning relationships among people (and almost all the concepts of political theory are about this) may fruitfully be interpreted as though they were relationships observed in a small group. This is because concepts and ideas are a type of relationship. *Otherwise expressed, political theory is itself a type of grouplike entity, embodying in its ideas and concepts relationships akin to those in the small group. Political theory may thus be read and interpreted as though it were a small group, using our knowledge of small group relations to explain, and sometimes undermine and reinterpret (deconstruct in the jargon of the day) the theory itself.* The rest of this chapter is devoted to explaining this statement, which is an epistemological one about the origins of our ideas and concepts in material relationships with others. Group-psychological materialism I call it, the foundation of my approach to reading texts in political theory.

Arthur Bentley, the first political scientist to call himself a group theorist, understood that groups are not merely political entities. They are epistemological ones as well, structuring the way in which we have ideas. In *The Process of Government* (1908), Bentley holds that groups are the fundamental reality of social life, more fundamental than any "ideas" men may have of them. His group-psychological materialism is an inspiration for my own, even if his conclusions are not. Groups, says Bentley,

are vastly more real than a man's reflection of them in his "ideas" . . .
which, as speech activity, help to reconcile him with the groups he deserts,
and which help to establish him firmly with the group he finally cleaves to.
Indeed the only reality of the ideas is their reflection of the groups, only that
and nothing more. The ideas can be stated in terms of the groups; the
groups never in terms of ideas.[10]

I would put Bentley's insight this way. Human existence is about relations with others: other humans, other things, other ideas than our own. In deference to Freud, who wrote of the object of a drive, psychoanalysts call these others "objects." Before we have ideas, or at least before we have ideas that can be expressed in language as concepts, we have relationships with objects. Long before. It is out of these primordial relationships that ideas and concepts are born, abstractions that retain their rootedness in these original relationships, even as the concepts appear to live a life of their own. Groups such as the Tavistock group are so unstructured, so regressive in their pull, that they reproduce relationships that are psychologically similar to these original relationships. By studying these relation-

10. Arthur Bentley, *The Process of Government* (Chicago: University of Chicago Press, 1908), pp. 205-206.

ships in Tavistock groups, particularly the way in which members of these groups use abstract ideas and concepts as though they were things, one can better understand not merely the original relationship, but concepts and ideas, no matter how abstract, that reflect this original relationship, reborn in the Tavistock group.

Consider, for example, the idea of what it means to "belong to a group." The experience of belonging echoes the earliest experiences in which the infant "belongs" in a relationship with the mother and the mother with the infant. This experience, so primitive that it is felt rather than thought, is the material out of which every concept of belonging, to self as well as other, is built. Liberalism, republicanism, communitarianism, participationism, Hegel's dialectic of mutual recognition: each of these concepts reflects a different experience of belonging, a different balance of the experiences of separateness and connectedness. Each of these concepts reflects a different resolution of the *conflict* between the desire to individuate and the desire to be one with the group. Which is the same thing as saying that each of these concepts reflects a different resolution of the conflict to which Bion refers, that man is a group animal at war with his own groupishness, at war with his own desire to abandon himself to the group. The concepts of liberalism, republicanism, and communitarianism are attempts to strike this balance and so realize a *modus vivendi,* a way of living with the conflict.

Every concept—or at least every concept of political theory—is an attempt to contain this conflict. Fusion versus separation, connection versus disconnection, attachment versus loss, belonging versus alienation, introjection (put everything in me) versus projection (put everything outside me), wholeness versus splitting into parts, self defined in relation to other to whom I belong versus self defined in opposition to other, holding versus crushing versus dropping, claustrophobia versus agoraphobia: these are the polarities of human existence. They are the tensions in any relationship, with mother, with parents, with small group, with every grouplike entity from civil society to nation-state. Not only does every concept in political theory, such as liberalism, participationism, communitarianism, republicanism, and even postmodernism, situate itself within these polarities, but most do so in a way that would resolve the tension by denying one of the extremes, as though it weren't there or could be finessed in some way. Reality is both, at once. There is no solution to reality, though some ways of living with it are better than others.

One sees a glimpse of this in words like *cleave* and *suture,* which capture both poles at once. *Cleave* means to separate and to join, as does *suture.* "Primal words," Freud called them, as they capture the ultimate psychic reality:

the desire to do both at once.[11] Individuals in groups seek the same thing, to be a complete individual and a total groupie, what chapter 3 terms the "schizoid compromise." It doesn't work and causes no end of trouble. But it is not solved by approaches, concepts, and theories that pretend the other half, the other pole, doesn't exist and doesn't attract. For then the other pole is driven underground, where it exerts its influence in ever more powerful and destructive ways. Communitarians seek to destroy their community so as to be free of it, while liberal individuals seek to fuse with others whom they pretend hardly exist. The only solution is to take both poles seriously—which means that there is no solution, but only resolutions, though some resolutions are better than others. Studying how small groups frequently fail, but occasionally succeed, in arriving at decent resolutions, ones that respect both poles, will clarify not merely how grouplike entities might do this but also how political theorists might best conceptualize the result—and the process.

My view is incompatible with perspectives widely held, albeit frequently unreflectively, by social theorists. In *The Idea of a Social Science*, Peter Winch applies the philosophy of Ludwig Wittgenstein, the founder of linguistic philosophy, to social theory. For Wittgenstein, meaning = use. To understand the meaning of a term, just look at how it is used. The meaning of justice, for example, is explained and exhausted by cataloging its different uses in forms of life. Winch turns the doctrine around. Or rather, he reads the equation from right to left. Use = meaning. If one wants to understand how ideas are used, look to the meaning of them—which means, according to Winch, that if one wants to understand a social relationship, understand the idea behind it. Social relations embody ideas. Understand the idea of demonical possession, for example, and then and only then can one understand the relationship between witch doctor and patient.[12]

Winch's view has been most influential, or at least his way of thinking has. It deeply influences John Pocock's classic study of republicanism, *The Machiavellian Moment*. Understand the ideas of republicanism, corruption, and virtue held by various grouplike entities, and one understands their relationship, Pocock in effect argues. Without these ideas the group members could not relate to each other, just as two people could not engage in a banking transaction, to use Winch's example, without understanding the idea of a bank, a financial exchange, and so forth. As Pocock puts it in "Virtue and

11. Sigmund Freud, "The Antithetical Meaning of Primal Words," in *The Standard Edition of the Complete Psychological Works of Sigmund Freud*, ed. James Strachey, 24 vols. (London: Hogarth Press, 1953–1974), 11:155–161.
12. Peter Winch, *The Idea of a Social Science* (London: Routledge and Kegan Paul, 1958).

Commerce in the Eighteenth Century," "men cannot do what they have no means of saying they have done, and what they do must in part be what they can say and conceive it is." About this statement Joyce Appleby says, "We sense that this must be true."[13]

I don't believe that it is true at all. In fact, it is quite misleading. Another example will show why. Romantic love is such a powerful emotional experience that one might assume it to be universal. But in fact, romantic love is historically and culturally specific, emerging in the early Middle Ages in the West (but not just there; Sappho wrote of romantic love in the seventh century B.C.). Or, at least, the *idea* of romantic love is historically and culturally specific. Writing of the Trobriand Islanders, the anthropologist Bronislaw Malinowski has shown that the idea of romantic love is quite missing in their accounts of human relationships. But does this mean that they did not experience what we call romantic love? The answer is not so simple, for the Trobrianders also told of experiences of strong attachments, emotional dependence, and jealousy—experiences that are central to, that indeed define, our idea of romantic love. Why not conclude that they had the experience but not the concept? Pocock, Winch, and others tell us that the idea comes first; but they make this assertion from the perspective of linguistic philosophy, not experience. What if we put the experience first?[14]

In fact, it's not so simple as experience versus idea. One may have an experience without the idea, term, or concept to make sense of it. Otherwise we would have to conclude that infants and children didn't have experiences. Nevertheless, ideas, terms, and concepts are not neutral labels. They don't create the experience or the relationship that it reflects, but they give it form and structure, allowing us to represent the experience more fully to ourselves and others—and also to misrepresent it, deceiving ourselves and others. My experience of groups is that members are generally struggling to name an experience, so as to know it, control it, and defend against it. Leadership in these groups is largely concerned with helping the members define their experiences more adequately, pointing out the defensive use of concepts and suggesting more subtle concepts that might better reflect the experiences of the members—or sometimes not so subtle concepts. Members frequently use psycho-babble (clinical psychological terms employed in

13. John Pocock, "Virtue and Commerce in the Eighteenth Century," *Journal of Interdisciplinary History* 3, no. 2 (1972), p. 122. Joyce Appleby, *Liberalism and Republicanism in the Historical Imagination* (Cambridge, Mass.: Harvard University Press, 1992), p. 334.

14. Irving Singer, Introduction to *The Nature of Love*, vol. 1, in *The Philosophy of (Erotic) Love*, ed. Robert Solomon and Kathleen Higgins (Lawrence: University Press of Kansas, 1991), 259–278, pp. 259–261.

a vague and misleading manner) to express themselves, as in "I cannot validate that experience and wish you would own that projection." The consultant leader might interpret this statement as "Shut up or I'll punch you in the nose." The idea doesn't create the experience, and the experience is effective without the idea, sometimes too effective. Lacking an idea of his experience, the member is at the mercy of it, unable to make sense of it, find a place for it, or integrate it. Winch and Pocock have it backwards, or at least sideways, confusing the sense of intellectual control (which may be real or misleading: itself a defense) that stems from naming an experience with the experience itself.

Not all historians of ideas get it backward. In *The Radicalism of the American Revolution* Gordon Wood argues that the American Revolution was not "essentially an intellectual event." It was instead a "transformation of the relationships that bound people to each other."[15] Only I would say the same about every historical event and every intellectual summary thereof—what we call concepts. This is so even as those who use these concepts frequently forget their rootedness in experience and so write of the experience as though it belonged strictly to the world of ideas, such as "revolution" or "republicanism" or "liberalism." My view is similar to that of Michael Oakeshott, who writes that an ideology is "an abbreviation of some manner of concrete activity."[16] Which is fine, he continues, as long as the origins of the idea in experience are not forgotten, as long as the idea serves merely as shorthand among those who share a tradition. Origins forgotten, the idea is bound to be employed in a crude and one-dimensional fashion, as all the subtleties of the practice that gave it sharpness and outline and set its limits are forgotten. Here is the proper context for political theory: not the context that pits one abstract concept against another but one that recalls the origins of political ideas in experience, tracing the experience of revolution, for example, back to simpler and more fundamental experiences, such as separation from parents.

Does this sound farfetched? It didn't to the American revolutionaries. Nor does it to Wood, who states that

scarcely a piece of American writing, whig or tory, did not involve the parent–child image to describe the . . . [colonial] relationship. The king was the "father" and Great Britain was the "mother country" and the colonists their "children." Because the image was so powerful, so suggestive of the

15. Gordon S. Wood, *The Radicalism of the American Revolution* (New York: Knopf, 1992), pp. 4–6.
16. Michael Oakeshott, *Rationalism in Politics and Other Essays,* new expanded ed., ed. Timothy Fuller (Indianapolis: Liberty Press, 1962), p. 54.

personal traditional world in which most colonists still lived, almost the entire . . . debate was inevitably carried on within its conflicts. At times the polemics between whigs and tories appeared to be little more than a quarrel over the proper method of child-rearing.[17]

My argument is not that we must study child-rearing to understand revolution. Rather, revolution is a particular type of separation, radical, principled, and generally undertaken in the name of freedom. Frequently the results are disappointing, new chains being substituted for old. Similar separations occur in the small group. Studying these separations there may help us understand revolution—not so much the actual practice of revolution, which involves numerous historical and institutional factors not present in the small group, but the idea of revolution and so the concept of revolution about which political theorists write.

One might argue that even if Pocock and Winch put the cart before the horse, the idea before the relationship, my view is still compatible with that of Wittgenstein, who argues that use = meaning. Use just comes to characterize the way in which a term is employed to embody and express a relationship, frequently unconscious, a broader sense of use. Such a response would not be mistaken, but it is not so simple either. In the tradition of Wittgenstein what we know about use is restricted to what an ideal native informant, as he is sometimes called, could tell us. "Sociological knowledge is the kind of knowledge possessed in implicit and partial form by the members of a society rendered explicit and complete."[18] Otherwise, it is held, we are imposing our understanding, our form of life, on another, interpreting their use in terms of our own, our meaning in place of theirs.

The trouble with this position is that group members generally have little idea of what they are doing, at least at first. Using words to act out psychologically primitive dramas of separation, connection, and loss, they often think they are doing something else entirely, such as discussing current events. They think they are discussing the prospects of Bush and Clinton, using terms such as "electability," "high negatives," and "charisma." In fact, they are longing for someone to lead their group, right now. Words have depths of meaning of which those who use them, the so-called ideal native informants, are frequently unaware. Taking the member's account as gospel, or even as roughly accurate, is tantamount to abandoning critical thought, substituting ideology for analysis and theory. Alasdair MacIntyre has made

17. Wood, *Radicalism of the American Revolution*, p. 165.
18. Alasdair MacIntyre, "The Idea of a Social Science," in *The Philosophy of Social Explanation*, ed. Alan Ryan (Oxford: Oxford University Press, 1973), 15–32, pp. 15–16.

this argument against Winch, but it has more general application, fitting much of the political theory criticized in chapter 5 of this book.

If group members are frequently deceived about what they are doing, they can be brought to awareness by the interpretations of the consultant. A follower of Wittgenstein might well regard this as the imposition of one form of life, that of Tavistock, on another. And perhaps it is. But consider that by the conclusion of a group relations conference many members come to hold that their previous understanding was faulty, that the interpretations of the consultant have helped them understand their own experiences, as well as the behavior of the group, in new ways that are both frightening and liberating. Is this really intellectual imperialism and brainwashing? If so, then all teaching has this quality. People generally misunderstand what they are doing, especially in groups, and this misunderstanding is not merely the result of ignorance. It is also due to the operation of defenses against intolerable conflicts, particularly that identified by Bion in the epigraph to this book. If, however, these defenses can be interpreted, and members can come to recognize themselves in this interpretation, then growth, development, individuation, and increased freedom are possible. This way of looking at the world is also part of a distinguished philosophical tradition, going back to Socrates, who held that self-knowledge was a difficult thing, requiring teachers willing to challenge cherished assumptions (forms of life) and students with the courage to learn. To pose this challenge well is the task not only of the group consultant but of political leadership as well, the topic with which this book concludes. Few political theorists have understood this point.

The way in which these considerations direct my reading of political theory should be apparent. Interpreting the ideas of political theory as abstract relationships, I look to the small group for more primitive expressions of comparable relationships, in order to understand the way in which political theorists really *use* these relationships-in-ideas—as opposed to how they *say* they use them. My assumption is that all accounts of human relationships confront the basic polarities listed above, polarities that may be summarized under the rubric separation and connection. In a word, political theorists write about relationships. In reading a text in political theory I ask myself, "What if I heard someone talking like this in a small group? What group forces would I presume to be at play? What conflicts are these ideas about relations defending against?" Then I would try to answer these questions based on my knowledge of groups, just as I do in this book.

Not only is political theory a type of group relationship, but the corollary also holds: the Tavistock group is itself a type of political theory. It is this political theory that I use to read and reinterpret traditional political theory. Both are concerned with trying to have it all, separation and connection. Both generally do this by denying half the conflict, driving it underground, where it doesn't disappear but just acts out its desires in more insistent and primitive ways. Unlike political theorists, however, the members of the Tavistock group are constrained by reality, the reality of the group. I place some of these constraints on political theory in order to mitigate its worst tendency, particularly among contemporary theorists—the magical use of words, as if saying it just right could make it so. Havel calls this evasive thinking. So do I.

2 ❋ The Experience of the Small Group

Sheppard–Pratt Mental Hospital in Baltimore, one of the most advanced institutions in the world in its treatment of borderline personality disorders, might seem an especially appropriate place to experience the state of nature, as expressed in the temporary institution of the Tavistock group. Vassar College in the summer seems less appropriate in this regard, as does Catholic University of America in Washington, D.C., with a glimpse of the Shrine of the Immaculate Conception from the classroom windows. In the end, however, the physical location hardly matters. The state of nature is now, already within the 25–50 men and women who come to these and similar locations to participate in a group relations conference sponsored by the A. K. Rice Institute. Some conferences last as few as three days; the conference at Vassar lasted nine. At the heart of the group relations conference is the unstructured small group of about ten members and one consultant, as he or she is called.

Picture this. Five men and five women from their late twenties to early fifties enter the room and take seats arranged in a tight circle. The group is remarkably heterogeneous, though it takes the members some time to figure this out: a female Black dean of a school of social work, a White male rabbi, and a male WASP professor, all three in their mid-forties; a female psychiatric social worker of Egyptian heritage, a male Lithuanian doctor, a female Jewish civil rights activist, and an accountant with strong connections to her German heritage, all in their thirties. An ex-nun in her early fifties and a strikingly handsome Black-Hispanic lawyer in his early forties round out the group. The consultant, as he is called, comes into the room on the hour, closes the door, and sits down. He will not speak for some time, and then mostly in riddles, koans, and oracles. Or so it seems. That's it: no leadership, no formal structure, and no apparent task, other than that the group is to study itself, whatever that means exactly.

Difficult to convey is the level of anxiety this experience evokes in the members. The sense of threat is palpable, and there is no simpler but more important question in all of group life than why this should be so. Why do presumably mature, not especially disturbed (at least for the most part), and frequently quite accomplished men and women become so terribly anxious in these first few minutes of the group? What is the threat that the silence, the rituals ("Let us go around the group and introduce ourselves"—simple facts about each other that are quickly forgotten and must be repeated many times over the course of the next nine days), the jokes, the nervous laughter, the anxious breathing ("Why is it so hot in here all of a sudden?"), the foot tapping, and so forth express or defend against? Way down deep do the members fear that they will kill each other? Have violent and exploitative sex with each other? Do they fear that some will have sex and leave others out? Will the group sacrifice one of its members, perhaps causing a psychological or physical breakdown in the member? Or will they perhaps humiliate and reject their consultant leader? Perhaps all will leave the group in nine days feeling devalued and demoralized.

Five Dramas

The theoretical possibilities, and explanations, are various and are explored in the next chapter. For now the key point is that Bion seems quite right when he states that the group seeks first of all its own security.[1] The creation of a less threatening environment is the group's paramount task. Everything else, including the recognition of its individual members, is subordinated to it. Security in the face of what, it may be asked? Where does the threat come from? The answer will take time to develop, and it is with this goal in mind that this chapter first elucidates five dramas central to all the small groups of which I have been a member:

1. The sacrificial leader
2. Despair, deadness, and hopelessness in the group
3. Sex and death
4. Leadership and individuality
5. Tribal warfare and superficial ideologies.

These are empirical themes, so to speak—patterns of events that I have observed in groups. First I characterize them, drawing upon various theo-

1. Bion, *Experiences in Groups,* pp. 94–95.

ries to do so, but stressing the experience, trying to convey some sense of what it is like to participate in these dramas. Next the status of these dramas is explained, how they are organized, whose fantasies they represent. Chapter 3 develops a theoretical explanation of the dramas. Each drama is a way of acting out the missing leader in the life of the group. It is from this perspective that chapter 3 returns to the dramas, reinterpreting them from this theoretical perspective. How is each an acting out of the missing leader? Chapter 3 concludes with a consideration of what is required for group development. The depressing thing about these dramas is that they generally don't lead anywhere—they just go on and on.

The Sacrificial Leader

Among the most profound fears of the group members, a fear that emerges early and lessens only slowly is the fear of being "it," the scapegoat, the one sacrificed by the group. A variant fear is that one member will psychologically terrorize another and that no one will step in to stop the mugging. Comments to the effect that "I feel so exposed and vulnerable," "Let somebody else be 'it' for a change," or "It's so easy to get hurt in here" are frequent. When an intimidated member fails to return to the group, someone will almost always say something to the effect that "we have killed him off." Not entirely untrue, such a comment overlooks the self-sacrifice involved. In such a hostile and threatening environment, members seek desperately a leader who will bring order to the group. Ordinarily this would be the consultant, the authorized and official leader. The "consultant-leader" I shall call him. Only the consultant refuses to take this role, generally saying almost nothing in the first sessions of the group, offering little guidance and no protection. This leads to a desperate desire for a leader within the group, one who will protect the members from each other. It also leads to a fierce competitiveness, which only heightens the fear of being "it," the "scapegoat," as the emerging leader becomes the most inviting target. Comments such as "I would try to make some order out of this mess, if only I felt you would not cut me off at the knees" are common. Freud writes that the mythical (whether Freud always regarded him as mythical is another question) primal father is killed and eaten not only because he monopolizes the women, but because he serves as a group sacrifice. In killing the father, the group acts out its violence in a limited fashion, transforming the violence that might destroy the entire group into a ritual that sacrifices only one.[2]

2. Freud, *Civilization and its Discontents,* trans. James Strachey (New York: W. W. Norton, 1961), pp. 87–89. Idem, *Totem and Taboo,* trans. James Strachey (New York: W. W. Norton, 1950), pp. 141–145.

In the earliest stages of its development the small group is in what the psychoanalyst Thomas Ogden calls the autistic-contiguous position. Applied to groups (Ogden refers only to individuals) the term suggests that the group is so undeveloped, disorganized, and incoherent that it is unable to use the leadership and guidance of the consultant, as it cannot make sustained contact with him. It cannot yet listen and learn from anyone, because it is so overwhelmed with the task of preserving itself against dissolution in the face of internal and external threats. Ogden argues that the characteristic autistic-contiguous anxiety is that of leakage through holes in the self: the boundaries of the entity will not hold. The modal defense against this anxiety is the creation of a hard, given, rigid boundary that protects the unstable entity within, albeit at the cost of learning from without: from experience and from the consultant.[3]

In the study group this is expressed in the practice of dedifferentiation and exclusion. The group masses together as a dedifferentiated entity. Individuals and their differences, the attributes each brings to the group, are studiously ignored. The group has no history, every member is just like every other member, as the members huddle together to protect the fragile cohesion of the group. Comments such as "There's really no difference between us," "We are all in the same boat now," or "It's like we are lost in time and space, cast together on a distant planet and forced to get along" are common. So too are comments such as "Black or White, man or woman, young or old, it really doesn't matter, does it? We are all newborns as far as this group is concerned." Such willful deindividualization, the massification of the group, is enforced by the members' unwillingness to listen to individual stories or even remember individual's names. The last thing the group wants to know is who its members are, where they come from, what their histories are, and so forth. Generally, however, such dedifferentiation is insufficient to quell the anxiety, and the group must find a sacrifice, a scapegoat, frequently a member who stands out in some way. Sometimes this member stands out by attempting to lead the group, but frequently he simply refuses to give up his individuality in some way, perhaps by talking about his life outside the group.

A major function performed by the sacrifice of a member is to bring the remaining members closer together. To exclude, ridicule, ignore, belittle, or criticize an outsider is a time-honored way of creating cohesion within a group. Shared guilt, as well as each member's fear that if he does not go along he might be next, is the glue that binds many groups, from families to nations. The unspoken knowledge that a family member is an alcoholic

3. Thomas Ogden, *The Primitive Edge of Experience* (Northvale, N.J.: Jason Aronson, 1989), pp. 47–82.

or that a nation's prosperity depends upon its exploitation of an underclass may be a powerful unifying force. A conspiracy of silence creates co-conspirators, which means that it creates a group. But this is not the whole story, and perhaps not even the main story. Groups sacrifice a member in order to at once protect the leader and attack him, a schizoid strategy about which I shall have much to say later on.

The sacrifice is not merely a sacrifice, however. The sacrifice is a sacrificial leader, one who stands out in some way, like the consultant-leader, and so must be destroyed "in the name of the leader." The sacrifice is destroyed both to protect the consultant-leader from the pretender and as a way of destroying the consultant-leader in effigy. Both are undertaken in the name of the leader—that is, for his sake and for the sake of the group in its relationship to the leader. If the group could do everything it wished, it would preserve the leader and destroy him at the same time. It would have its leader and eat him too.

Bion argues that the pair represents the locus of hope in the group, the group acting as if it believes that the pair might produce a child who will save it.[4] I would locate the locus of hope in the pair that is the consultant-leader and the sacrificial leader, the latter sacrificing himself to preserve the group's hope for the future, its hope that a leader might one day reemerge from the realm of the dead, or dying to save the group from itself. Different from Bion's account in important respects, mine nonetheless preserves—even extends—Bion's Christian thematics of birth, death, and resurrection.

Bion argues that the group will frequently exploit its sickest member in the hope that the consultant leader will come to this member's rescue and so be forced to lead the group. This occurs. However, it is my impression that in the early stages of its development the group is enacting an even more primitive psychodrama, whose script runs something like this: "The reason the consultant-leader does not help us is because our badness (anger, aggression, and so forth) has made him sick. Let us sacrifice those in the group who would pretend to be leaders. This will divert our aggression from the leader and also give him some nourishment, in the form [and here the most primitive level of psychological development segues into more sophisticated levels, as it so often does] of something dramatic and interesting to interpret. Perhaps this will be enough to entice him to save us; or at least keep him alive until we can figure out how to do so."

While this interpretation is, of course, speculation, it is supported by empirical and theoretical evidence. Comments that relate the sacrifice of a member to giving the consultant-leader "something to chew on" are com-

4. Bion, *Experiences in Groups,* pp. 61–63.

mon. Frequent too are comments such as "I think we must have made our consultant sick" or "We are enough to drive any consultant crazy." Theoretically, this interpretation fits the Kleinian account of the origins of depressive anxiety in the fear that one has irreparably damaged the good object and so will forever lack its goodness and support. This interpretation also fits recent work in the social psychology of blood ritual, such as René Girard's *Violence and the Sacred,* probably the single most famous work on this topic. Girard argues that ritual blood sacrifice emerges early in human history as a way to redirect a group's violence away from the group itself and so break the cycle of violence and retaliation that threatens to destroy the community, much like the civil war in Corcyra about which Thucydides writes (*History,* III. 69–85).

Ritual sacrifice serves as what Girard calls generative violence, which substitutes a single victim for the entire community, so allowing the community to live. For this to work, the surrogate must be close enough to the natural, actually intended target of the violence to satisfy the aggression and distant enough for his death not to plunge the community into a renewed cycle of violence.[5] The way in which a small group member is ostracized before being sacrificed—or rather, the way in which ostracism from the group really *is* the sacrifice of the small group member—fits this requirement nicely. Freud's argument in *Totem and Taboo* is similar, emphasizing how the ritual killing of the father-leader also acts to set limits on the group members' aggression, as the members internalize the father's strictures as their own, the origins of the superego.[6]

In *The Golden Bough,* the most famous anthropological work ever, Sir James Frazer writes of a golden bough that represents the leader's vitality. The bough can be broken only by the man who would be king, the one who kills the old leader when he begins to show signs of age and decay, lest his enfeeblement be transferred to the new king. It turns out that the golden bough is actually mistletoe, a parasite. An ancient drama with a thousand variants (Frazer explores hundreds), it may be interpreted in group-theoretical terms as follows. Feeling that they themselves are parasites on the leader whom they must destroy with their needs, the members would kill him quickly—before they can suck all the life out of him, and before they are forced to confront their shame and their need. Dividing the leader up, akin to the new king breaking the golden bough, the members work feverishly to keep the spirit of the leader alive in the group until another appears

5. René Girard, *Violence and the Sacred,* trans. Patrick Gregory (Baltimore: Johns Hopkins University Press, 1977), pp. 266, 99.
6. Freud, *Totem and Taboo,* p. 146.

to embody his immortal soul. Then the drama begins all over again. Not just a drama of the succession of leaders, it is about the desperate need of members to destroy their leader in order to save him, giving new meaning to the motto "The king is dead, long live the king." It is no wonder that one can read group psychology in terms of the rituals studied by anthropologists. In ritual, group members express their dread and desire without having to talk about it. More than anything else, my group study is an interpretation of ritual, putting words to what group members act out.

For the ancient Greeks, who understood full well the origins of animal sacrifice in its human counterpart, it was terribly important that the sacrificial animal show his willingness to be sacrificed, usually by a nod of the head, which might be induced by offering him drink or food. Members of the group are sometimes tricked to sacrifice themselves in a similar fashion. The group appears to accept a member's leadership, only to turn on him with criticism, rejection, psychological abuse, and a tacit refusal to cooperate, causing the member-leader's humiliating failure and withdrawal. It is not uncommon, however, for individuals to willingly sacrifice themselves for the consultant-leader, often by psychologically sacrificing any opportunity they might have had to use the group to explore and develop their own individuality. In the final meeting of one small study group, the consultant referred to the men sitting opposite him as "three shades." One member reminded the group that the term "shade" is a translation of the Greek term psyche, by which Homer means that part of a man that remains after his body has died. A shade lacks will or power, while remaining everlastingly conscious of its wounds, never losing its rancor. Another member referred to the three men as three blind mice, while still another called them "See no evil, speak no evil, hear no evil." What had happened, apparently, was that these men could figure out no way of challenging the male consultant that would not, they feared, lead to his destruction (if not physically, then to his humiliated withdrawal) or their own. They sacrificed themselves— which means their opportunity to use the group as a medium of self-development and discovery—with the tacit cooperation of the group. The sacrificial leader is not always one who stands up and is cut down. He may be one who refuses to stand up in the first place, sacrificing his developmental potential to the group. Often he seems to do so out of desperate love for the leader, a type of *Liebestod,* fusing with the leader in self-sacrifice.

Despair, Deadness, and Hopelessness in the Group

So central to the small group, as well as group life at large, the shared experience of deadness, despair, and hopelessness in the group is granted far too little attention. Comments such as "This group feels like it's dead and buried and beginning to stink" are not infrequent, as are comments like "Bringing this group to life is tougher than raising the dead" or "This group needs a jumpstart, an electric shock or something." Group despair and deadness are as central as anxiety, and while the group seems to oscillate between rage and despair, much of the rage is actually a defense against despair. "Rage, rage against the dying of the light," says Dylan Thomas. Rage is about doing something, it allows action; whereas despair is experienced passively, as something merely to be suffered. Rage is revivifying, or at least so it seems. Despair over what? Here it is useful to distinguish between the goals of the individual members and the group goal. The goal of the group, at least ostensibly, is to study its own group process and so learn about groups. The inability of the group, after several sessions, to make any sense of this goal, to have any idea of what it might mean to make progress toward it, leads to despair, as a group of frequently quite accomplished adults cannot even begin to make sense of their collective task.

Individual members despair for more private and personal reasons as well, as they come to recognize that the group is not going to save them, at least not in the way they had originally hoped. It is my experience that most individuals come to these group conferences (this statement is most true of the nine-day residential conference, where members understand what they are getting into) in order to be healed, revivified, and made whole in some way. One member of the group wants the group to teach her how to separate herself from groups, so that she is not so crushed and paranoid when, in the political arena, she loses an important fight. Another wants to learn how to feel and so become less bored with himself. Still another wants to learn how to make contact with the emotional life of the group and so feel more alive, while not sacrificing his individuality. Yet another wants to get in touch with his anger, and another to be relieved of his loneliness. But perhaps all want this. One might conclude that all this makes the membership of these conferences uniquely needy, but I don't think so. Around the world billions of Christians, Moslems, Jews, and others devote a goodly portion of their lives to being saved. One might argue about whether the members of the group relations conference are looking in the wrong place, but that's a different story.

The centrality of confession in the group is best seen from this perspective. "I really wish I could be the leader, kill the leader, marry the leader," or "I get so envious of attractive women," or "I'm deeply attracted to so and so," or "I hate you for that," or "I feel fat and ugly, and that no one listens to me," or "I'm afraid that I'll be left without a man or woman," or "I just have to acknowledge my homosexual feelings toward so-and-so," or "I joined the homosexual panic," or. . . . The list goes on. While such confessions are frequently couched in psycho-babble, psycho-babble is simply the coin of the realm in such groups and should not cause us to dismiss the phenomenon. Rather, the psycho-babble needs to be interpreted, albeit not in its own terms. Originally I had thought that the frequent resort to confession was akin to a dog's rolling on its back and exposing its throat and stomach to placate the aggressor: confession as ritual supplication.

After having seen many more confessions when the group is in despair than when it is filled with free-floating rage, I have changed my mind and now believe that confession serves primarily as a plea for salvation. This is not unknown in religious circles. In confessing one's sins one is somehow in a better position to receive grace or love. In fact, it may be that these two functions of confession are related. One confesses one's hostile, hateful, aggressive, selfish thoughts to the group, in the hope that if all do so, then the group can somehow be purged of its badness and get on with its task. Confession is another version of ritual sacrifice, in which members offer to sacrifice themselves to the group, but only if others do likewise. In the *Social Contract* (para. 43) Rousseau argues that a society may be legitimate only if each gives himself up to all, with no reservations. Only then can the "union [be] . . . as perfect as it can be." Here, perhaps, is the truth behind this insight. For the group not to destroy itself (or so the members think), each individual must sacrifice himself to the group, exposing to all his vulnerabilities and weaknesses, his predilection to commit the seven deadly sins and more.

If individuals seek salvation in the group and so to be made whole, vital, alive, and real, then they seek to love and be loved by the group. It's the same thing. In giving himself up to the group in confessional self-sacrifice, the member shows love for the group, abandoning his individuality out of love for its members, "ihnen zu liebe" as Freud puts it. To be sure, confession is not necessarily an abandonment of individuality, but the way it is practiced in the group generally is, as the member confesses his thought crimes in order to be absorbed back into the bosom of the group. We cannot understand the group without understanding the role of love in it: how members come to love the group and its leader; how desperately members wish to be loved by the group; and, most particularly, the price members are willing to pay for love. Freud tells us the price.

A group is clearly held together by a power of some kind: and to what power could this feat be better ascribed than to Eros, which holds together everything in the world. . . . If an individual gives up his distinctiveness in a group and lets its other members influence him by suggestion, it gives one the impression that he does it because he feels the need of being in harmony with them rather than in opposition to them—so that perhaps after all he does it "ihnen zu Liebe" [for love of them].[7]

"If you want to be loved and recognized by the group," the group seems to say to its members, "then you must give up your individual distinctiveness. Furthermore, you must do so willingly, for love of the group." Most members pay the price and are doubly disappointed, as it doesn't work. They sacrifice a part of their individuality to the group and fail to receive the recognition from the group upon which love depends. Silent rage, tacit withdrawal, sabotage of the group, aggression against other group members—these are just some of the common responses to this bargain that is bound to fail. Love requires mutual recognition, and it is this that the group cannot offer.

Sex and Death

Just as the small group oscillates between rage and despair, so too it oscillates between themes of sex and death—for much the same reason. Sex serves as a defense against deadness in the group, and group deadness serves as a defense against the potential violent explosiveness and pain of sex. Which is not to say that sex and death serve only as defenses. Each has a stark reality of its own in the group. Contrary to Bion's account of the pairing group, it is not my experience that the group dotes on the pair whom it fantasizes will produce a child to save it. Instead, lots of pairing goes on—many pairs, shifting pairs, and jealous triangles. Lots of mutual attraction takes place and lots of fear that in the final pairing up someone will be left out or paired with someone undesirable. A related fear is that sex will lead to violence. One form of violence commonly feared is that of men against women: rape. In addition, women frequently resent the fact that men in the group do not seem prepared to protect them against other men. Rape itself never occurs in the group. But terms like "mindfucking," "psychological rape," and "psychological assault" are common. So too are terms referring to incestuous relationships, as though the members were siblings, so that any sexual desire present among the members must be taboo. As common, and actually more disturbing, is the experience of so many women in the group that the price of intimacy with men—almost any man—is violation, gross intrusion into their dignity and privacy: incest, abuse, psychological domination, and so forth.

Sex threatens the group not only when it threatens to break out in vio-

7. Freud, *Civilization and its Discontents*, p. 24.

lence but also when it threatens to break out in love. As Freud recognized, the romantic pair is sufficient unto itself, so that a group of pairs is almost an oxymoron. The pair doesn't need the group and doesn't want it, their love being a religion of two. But if both the violent and the loving aspects of sexuality threaten to destroy the group, sexuality is also essential to the life of the group. In the larger society, sex is literally the way in which death is transcended, procreating new human beings who will carry on when the previous generation becomes worn out and finally dies. But, as with so much, perhaps everything, in human existence, the literal meaning of sex is less important than its symbolism, so that sex comes to signify life itself; creativity, progress, worthwhile activity, realizing goals, and sharing purposes come to express and partake in sexuality, understood as the conjunction of desire and creation. "Sublimation" is the term Freud used to characterize this conjunction.

The creativity of desire drives the small group too. In fact, it represents the one realistic way in which the group might heal its members, allowing them to do something worthwhile collectively that they could not do as individuals. In this sense at least, group sex is both possible and desirable. Indeed, the existence of the group is validated only to the degree that it helps its members create themselves. This is not so much a normative statement, though it is that too, as it is an empirical one. Deep in their hearts and minds, the members hold to this too, which is why despair is so rampant in the group. Members despair over the inability of the group to perform its task in a creative manner. In this despair, the members turn to sex, in the hope that it might revivify the group. This is expressed in so-called humorous comments such as "Well, if we can't work together, maybe we can fuck together," or "At least we could have an orgy; I think we could at least figure out how to do that," or (and this theme is most frequent), "Why don't you two get it on, and the rest of us can watch. That will at least give us something to do." It is no accident that the small group experience is frequently referred to as though it were bad sex, as in "It was tantalizing, frustrating, and then it was over," or "Was it bad for you too?" The group experience *is* like bad sex, in the sense that it seems to promise wholeness and fulfillment via participation in something larger than oneself and ends up being an experience in which one is intruded upon or invaded in an insensitive fashion. The group does not multiply the member's individuality but diminishes it.

In order to get its work done, the group will have to turn to sex in some way. This means that it will have to come to terms with the threat posed by sexuality, jealousy, and fear of sexual violence, as well as figure out some way that pairs might be recognized so as not to dilute the group. In fact, this rarely happens. What happens is that the pair becomes an alternative to the deadness, hopelessness, and stasis of the group, so that individuals pair up or have fantasies about pairing up or watch others pair up, as an alternative to stasis of the group. Rather than contributing to the group, pairs and fantasies about them become an alternative to the group. It is for this reason that Freud advocated sexual repression. Only this could assure that there might be enough eros left over to bind the group in the face of its own aggression. It is not so easy. (Or perhaps Freud didn't think it was so easy anyway; just that there was no alternative.) Repression of the pair and of the creativity represented by the desire of the couple for each other will deprive the group of the only source of vitality capable of overcoming its stasis and hopelessness. Somehow the group must find a place for the pair, so that the pair may remain part of the group yet separate from it. To do this, the group must first be prepared to recognize its members as individuals, probably the group's most difficult and important challenge.

Leadership and Individuality

One should not conclude from the apparent competition for leadership among members that everyone wants to be leader. It is more useful to focus on what members don't want. Most of all, what members don't want is to be in a position of weakness, humiliation, and incompetence (even this claim requires qualification). Yet, this is just the position one finds oneself in as a group member. Without effective leadership the group itself is incompetent; so too are the members qua members. Furthermore, individuals are expected by the group to give up a large measure of their individuality to be a member of the group. In this position, the autonomy of the leader is especially humiliating, evoking large amounts of envy, rage, and resentment, as his individuality is a constant reminder of the member's sacrifice. Ignoring the consultant-leader or seeking to identify with him and his power become dominant strategies. In fact, they become a single strategy: to ignore the consultant-leader in reality, so as to more completely identify with him in fantasy. This theme, part of the schizoid compromise, is developed in the theoretical section. There is no more important group phenomenon than this, as it unites and explains so many others.

Members' identification with the consultant-leader is difficult to see at first, as the leader is studiously ignored. So studiously, in fact, that it is this that aroused my suspicion. Could he really be so unimportant, a fifth wheel? The best evidence for the leader's importance is what is not talked about, the secret that everyone knows and none dare whisper: that every communication is aimed, in one way or another, at the consultant-leader. If this is even hypothesized by one member, the group will work mightily to deny it—virtually to deny that the leader even exists. Similarly, if a member should challenge the consultant-leader in some way, the group will labor mightily to ignore it. Not by attacking the member who challenged the leader. That would require recognizing the leader too, as someone worth defending. Rather, group members will frequently start attacking each other, with one exception. He who has challenged the leader becomes as inviolable and invisible as the leader himself, as the group is willing to sacrifice itself, member by member, rather than confront this challenge which would mean confronting the existence of the consultant-leader. This displacement of members' emotions regarding the leader into the group itself, so that members come to act out among themselves their emotional relationships to the missing leader, is a key aspect of group life, one which will be much discussed in the theoretical section of this chapter.

Why is direct confrontation with the consultant-leader so threatening? One reason is that it becomes more difficult to hold onto the archaic fantasy of fusion with the leader when the leader is actually recognized and confronted. Another reason, actually a version of this reason, is that all wish to be loved and cared for by the leader, and conflict with him threatens this relationship. More than this, each member wishes to be loved most of all by the leader, a relationship that is threatened not only by conflict with the leader, but by other group members as well, who stand in competition for this love. It is for this reason, argues Freud, that members agree upon codes of law and justice, which result in each member denying himself the exclusive love of the leader, so that other members will not get more.[8] Jealousy, it seems, is more painful than mere deprivation, as it is in jealousy that our deprivation becomes most apparent in contrast to another's fulfillment.

Yet, love is not all that members want from their leader. Or rather, members want not merely to stand in a dependent love relationship with the leader. They also want to be recognized as individuals, a point acknowledged by Freud but not fully developed by him. In the group, says Freud, the leader is the only real individual. Only he has an individual psychology. The group members have only a group psychology, which means, of course, that they are not real individuals. "From the first there were two kinds of psychologies, that of the individual members of the group and that of the father, chief, or leader. The members of the group were subject to ties just as we see them to-day, but the father of the primal horde was free."[9] What makes the father the only free man, the leader the only individual? Because the leader was able to fall in love (Freud says have sex) with another indi-

8. Ibid., p. 47.
9. Freud, *Group Psychology and the Analysis of the Ego,* p. 55.

vidual, while the rest of the members could only relate to the group qua group. This is what Freud means when he says that the father "forced them [the sons], so to speak, into group psychology," via his domination of the women of the group.[10]

Seen from this perspective, it may well be that what the members of the group want most of all is not to usurp the leader or possess all the women (or men) for themselves, but to be individuals themselves, not just groupies. The trouble is that this seems to require that the leader be killed and eaten, just as the primal father was—albeit for somewhat different reasons, reasons of self and identity, not just sexual desire. As Mikkel Borch-Jacobsen puts it in "The Freudian Subject,"

> In this light, then, the murder of the Father is far less a mere animal struggle than it is the Freudian version of Hegel's 'struggle for pure prestige.' If desire leads to murder and devouring, it is because it is a desire to take unto oneself the other's being, a desire to assimilate his power (Macht), his strength (Staerke), in short, his mastery. . . . My being is in the other, and it is for that reason that I can become 'me,' an ego, only by devouring him— *that* is what the Freudian myth is telling us.[11]

Behind the desire to lead, to dominate and control others, including all the members of the sex to which one is most attracted, lies the desire to be recognized as an individual. Which does not, unfortunately, obviate conflict but only intensifies it. This is, of course, the insight of Hegel in his dialectic of master and slave, in which Ego wishes to affirm itself as absolute and free, utterly independent of Alter's will. Yet, to know oneself as absolute and free requires the recognition of Alter, who of course also wishes to be absolute and free, independent of Ego's recognition. Alter withholds his recognition, so as not to be a mere instrument of Ego's will. And the struggle continues, becoming more and more ironic, as Ego seeks to force Alter to do what Ego should be able to do for himself were he truly free and independent: to recognize himself, self-recognition. Eventually Ego may force Alter to recognize him, so that instead of mutually recognizing each other, Ego becomes Alter's master. Yet, even this victory must be a hollow one, as it reveals Ego's dependence upon Alter's recognition, quite the opposite of Ego's intended goal of demonstrating his absolute freedom.[12]

A similar struggle occurs in the group, albeit with a different resolution,

10. Ibid., p. 56.
11. Mikkel Borch-Jacobsen, "The Freudian Subject," in *Who Comes After the Subject?*, ed. Eduardo Cadava, Peter Connor, and Jean-Luc Nancy (New York: Routledge, 1991), 61–78, pp. 74–75.
12. G. W. F. Hegel, *Phänomenologie des Geistes* (Hamburg: Felix Meiner Verlag, 1952), p. 143.

because no single group member is powerful enough to force all the others to recognize him. The result is generally stalemate, in which no member is powerful enough to force all others to recognize him, but each member is powerful enough to withhold his recognition. If all cannot be individuals, then none shall be, as the pain of deindividuation is lessened when the deindividuated member is not forced to confront genuine individuals. The situation is analogous to Freud's comment on the source of law and justice in the envy and jealousy of members who fear that the leader might love some more than others.[13]

To be an individual in the group and to know oneself as such requires a subtle and difficult balance of merger and differentiation, in which the individual is at once part of the group, merged with it, and at the same time valued and recognized for his or her difference. An "individual member" Pierre Turquet calls him, a simple but noble ideal to which I shall refer throughout the book.[14] This is a difficult but not impossible balance in intimate relationships between couples and friends. It occurs in groups. I have seen it, but it is such a difficult and tenuous balance that it is almost impossible to maintain for long. It is also painful, in part because one is reminded so dramatically by its occasional, fleeting presence that it is so rare. Despair and rage are frequent reactions to this painful reminder. Nonetheless, a group of individual members is an ideal, the standard by which political theory should be judged. Does political theory acquaint us with this ideal, a society of individual member-citizens? Does political theory tell us of the obstacles to this ideal, making suggestions as to how we might move a little closer to it? Almost always the answer will be no. Political theory, be it liberal social-contract theory or its contemporary communitarian and developmental alternatives, generally fails to address these questions. Instead, political theory constructs ideal accounts of the relationship of individual and group that refuse to face the difficulties involved. Most political theory is ideology, the ideology of the individual or the ideology of the group. Almost never does it tell the truth, that man is a group animal at war with his own groupishness.

Tribal Warfare and Superficial Ideologies:
The Narcissism of Small Differences

Before it does almost anything else, the small study group polarizes itself in some way. Men versus women; young versus old; Black versus White; Jew versus Gentile, are only some of the more frequent divisions. No single move in the life of the group is more important than this. To be sure,

13. Freud, *Civilization and its Discontents,* p. 47.
14. Pierre Turquet, "Threats to Identity in the Large Group," in *The Large Group: Dynamics and Therapy,* ed. L. Kreeger (London: Maresfield Reprints, 1975), pp. 94–115.

these divisions are real. To ignore the differences that these polarities represent would be unrealistic. Furthermore, a member's sex, age, ethnicity, religion, are surely all central to what it is to be an individual. Nevertheless, the search for polarities and divisions around which to organize the group frequently takes on a desperate, superficial quality, as if it hardly matters *what* principle of division is adopted just as long as some is. In one group the principle of division was between those who sat in chairs with little writing-desks attached and those who sat in plain chairs. The former tribe was labeled the passive student group.

In "The Need to Have Enemies and Allies: A Developmental Approach," Vamık Volkan argues that people need their enemies as much as their allies. His perspective is roughly Kleinian. The young child develops mental images of himself and the world in a bipolar fashion, so that he originally experiences himself as virtually a different person when sad and hungry than when he is happy and fulfilled. Emotional development is about putting these experiences together. Both are me. The task, however, is never complete. The more absolute and saturated with primitive feeling the original experience, the more incomplete the integration. So that his development will not be stymied by conflict, the child puts these unintegrated experiences into "reservoirs" in the real world.

At first these reservoirs are private and personal, but soon the child comes to share them with others, what Volkan calls "suitable targets of externalization." Examples of suitable targets for good feelings would be my church, the smells of home cooking, the appearance of my family, the sound of my language and dialect. Examples of suitable targets for bad feelings would be an alien religion, the smells of foreign cooking, a family that looks and acts differently. "And although they are actually part of the environment rather than part of the child, the child will invest something of himself in them accompanied by *raw* feelings of love and hate." Suitable targets are shared, the culture in effect saying to the individual, "Put your unintegrated and intolerable fear and hate into this group, that symbol. This will relieve your anxiety by allowing you to disown bad parts of yourself, while at the same time allowing you to bond more securely with the good group that is us." Shared targets bind groups. It is their glue. "It is these 'suitable targets,'" says Volkan, "that bridge the distance between individual and group psychology." Without external enemies, shared targets, the group would fall apart into warring tribes, and the members would go crazy. In fact, insanity may be defined as the individual's inability to use shared targets of externalization.[15]

15. Vamık Volkan, "The Need to have Enemies and Allies: A Developmental Approach," *Political Psychology* 6, no. 2 (1985): 219–247, pp. 231–236.

The group does not provide this psychological service gratis. On the contrary, the group generally demands as payment that the individual give up his uniqueness to the group, which means that he not express his individuality in the group. In return, the individual is offered a group identity, a self-definition based upon the group-sanctioned suitable target. Not only is this trade no bargain, but it suggests an important point insufficiently emphasized by Volkan. The real threat to the individual is his *own* group, the way in which it demands that the individual suppress his own unique individuality to be a member. It is this threat that is projected into the suitable target and fought there. From Freud onward, critics have noted how similar enemies frequently are. "The narcissism of small differences" Freud called it, be it between Jew and Arab, both Semites, or Protestant and Catholic, both Christians. Now we see the reason for this phenomenon. Enemies are similar because the real enemy is really one's own group, the demands it makes on the individual in order to be a member. Finding a similar enemy is a way of belonging to one's own group and fighting it at the same time, another version of the schizoid compromise.

The narcissism of small differences makes real but subtle and complex distinctions between groups massive and one-dimensional. The same can be said about most ideologies, the rhetoric of group difference. Ideologies follow the fault lines within groups, which means that they explain, justify, and legitimate differences. Particularly noticeable in this regard is the way in which the small group has trouble handling more than simple binary distinctions, a sure sign that the splitting involved is primitive and profound. One small group of which I was a member, which had already spent a number of hours together, had great difficulty with the idea that someone could be both culturally Jewish and a Zen master at the same time. That this person could be female, Jewish, and a Zen master seemed beyond the realm of human comprehension. This sounds almost ludicrous, but anyone who has worked with small groups like this will know what I mean. Regressed groups simply can't think, which means that members of groups lose their critical faculties when they are acting and thinking qua members of the regressed group, as their critical faculties are overwhelmed and paralyzed by the anxiety circulating in the group. That, or the members are so heavily defended against the group, so repressed, that they cannot let themselves think—about anything. As Freud puts it, "The feelings of a group are always very simple and very exaggerated. So that a group knows neither doubt nor uncertainty."[16]

16. Freud, *Group Psychology and the Analysis of the Ego,* p. 10.

From birth on, my experience of my own otherness will be expressed in my attempt to grasp both the otherness and the similarity of another. Which is why, I suspect, it was so difficult for the group to come to terms with the idea of a member who was a minority twice over, Black and Hispanic, a concept with which the group struggled mightly for some time, as though it were the most difficult and abstract concept in the world. It was, because it confused the attempt to define self by similarity and contrast to another, as the other did not seem identical with himself, at least to the simplistic thinking of the regressed group. In still another group an original confusion as to who was the rabbi, who the fundamentalist Christian (the Christian looked like a stereotype of an Old Testament patriarch), persisted throughout the life of the group, even though the clarifying information was presented in the first minutes of the group's life. Not only could the group not think except in the most primitive and exclusive binary categories, but it did not assimilate new information. These deficits are, of course, hardly absent in more sophisticated ideologies as well.

Originally the question of whom I can trust and rely upon is answered by answering the question "Who is like me?" Evidently this reflects the massive role played by identification in the earliest love relationships. At first, to love another is to want to be just like him. Love of difference comes later. "Identification," says Freud, "is known to psycho-analysis as the earliest expression of an emotional tie with another person."[17] It is because love, trust, and identification are so closely linked that the group seems to divide up into tribes, as though this would provide an answer to the need for security and individuality at the same time. Of course, it rarely works this way, tribes generally being about as tolerant of individuality as the group, which is to say, not very. Rather, one gets "pseudo-speciation" as Erik Erikson calls it, identities based upon categories that are insufficiently rich and manifold to sustain genuine individuality. For the group to progress, tribes must give way to individuals.

Sex, age, ethnicity, religion, sexual orientation, social class—all these and more are central to identity, connecting the deepest levels of experience with social categories around which the group divides itself. As such, these categories help the group member to answer the question "Who am I in this group?" One division, however, seems more central than any other: sex, male versus female. This claim is an empirical rather than a theoretical one, which means that I have seen it but cannot fully explain it. To many members it appears that it is their race or religion that is at least as important as their sex to their self-understanding. Nor is it the case that differences organized

17. Ibid., pp. 39–40.

according to age, religion, and race are somehow really about sex, for they are not, and in any case all these conflicts occur among members of the same sex.

Nevertheless, there is something especially fundamental about sexual difference, which is to say perhaps no more than that sex generally colors all the other differences more than they color sexual difference. From a developmental perspective we are aware of the otherness and difference of other bodies long before we are aware of the sexual difference embodied in them. Yet, sexual difference is so deeply physical and real, so bound to the desire to cross the boundary and possess the otherness that it represents, that it readily becomes the paradigm of all difference. Certainly an awareness of sexual difference precedes that of racial difference by several years.[18] However, I do not fully understand the primacy of sexual difference, and my explanation remains speculative. What is not speculation, but observation and experience, is that of all the tribal distinctions with which the group must deal, it is the difference between male and female tribes that is in some ways the most intransigent and the most difficult, in part perhaps because it is also the most rewarding. It is particularly disappointing that traditional state-of-nature theory has done so little with this reality.

What Explains These Dramas?

In *What Happens in Groups,* R. D. Hinshelwood writes of group dramatization, in which the group acts out its fantasies rather than verbalizing them. It is this, he suggests, that accounts for the stubborn persistence of such dramas. Unlike verbalization, which contributes to awareness and insight, dramatization is unconscious all the way through, the members not fully understanding what they are doing and so condemned to repeat it.[19] In dramatization, the group does not so much share a common fantasy as act out the fantasies of individual members, who regard the group as a stage. Here is real political power: the power to persuade the group to act out one's fantasies, which means to persuade the group to act as if its members were little more than symbols of the persuader's internal objects.

18. Actually it's not so simple. In *Us and Them: The Psychology of Ethnonationalism* (New York: Brunner/Mazel, 1987), the Group for the Advancement of Psychiatry (GAP) concludes that while racial awareness (at first simply as skin color) generally begins at around three or four, some children seem aware of racial difference as early as ten months, accepting strangers of their parents' skin color but rejecting strangers of a different color. It depends, GAP speculates, on the importance of ethnicity to the parents. GAP reviews a number of studies on the topic, pp. 58–64.

19. R. D. Hinshelwood, *What Happens in Groups* (London: Free Association Books, 1987), pp. 31–33.

Hinshelwood is onto something important. The concept of a shared group fantasy, acted out in little dramas, is not really an explanation of the phenomenon but a description. What is required is an explanation of where the fantasy comes from and how it comes to be shared. Hinshelwood's is such an explanation, one that runs counter to the A. K. Rice position that members simply hold parts in the group's fantasy, enacting the roles the group impresses them into. On the contrary, the group is extraordinarily vulnerable to the aggressive imaginer, able to impress his fantasy on the group. Not only does the Rice position not explain where the fantasy comes from, but its "group-as-a-whole" perspective fails to appreciate the power of the individual to impose his fantasy on the group. The group-as-a-whole perspective is itself a reification of the group, a sign that the theorist is participating in the group's regression. Furthermore, in addressing the group as though it were a whole, not a group of individuals, the consultant may actually foster the group's regression, leading it to become the regressed group he treats it as being.[20]

In one group Sarah persisted in treating the older members as her despised parents, akin to the aggressive, intrusive leader, who lacks all care and understanding. As is often the case, however, she became the mirror image of those she despised, tormenting the older members like the leader she so feared (and admired—at least she admired the power of leaders). Eventually things became so hot and uncomfortable that Sarah left the group, the members predictably responding that they had "killed her off." As predictably, the consultant spoke about Sarah as "holding the group's fear and anger," as though she were merely a part of the group. She was, and she did hold the group's fear and anger. But Sarah was not merely part of the group. Through the force of her personality she directed the group to play her drama and no one else's. And she kept it playing her drama until, having had her fill, she left the group. And when she left, the group was bereft, lacking any idea of what drama to play next, having developed no understudies waiting in the wings. There was a reality to Sarah and the power of her fantasies that the Rice perspective downplays. So too, the Rice perspective downplays the vulnerability of the group to the fantasies of the most aggressive and powerful member.

But if there is a reality to the individual and his fantasies that the Rice perspective ignores, it is well to recall Marx's dictum in the *Eighteenth Bru-*

20. Leroy Wells Jr., "The Group-as-a-Whole Perspective and its Theoretical Roots," in *Group Relations Reader,* vol. 2, ed. Arthur Colman and Marvin Geller (Washington, D.C.: A. K. Rice Institute, 1985), 109–126. There is no official A. K. Rice position on any theoretical issue, only general agreement or general disagreement.

maire that while man makes history, he does not make it anyway he wants or under conditions of his own choosing. The situation of the group is structured in such a way that not any fantasy will play, and only certain fantasies will play at certain times. Sarah's was a fantasy of polarization and tribal warfare, probably the easiest fantasy of all to direct and produce, generally the first fantasy drama a group enacts. She kept the group locked into this particular drama, but she would not have had the power, no matter how persuasive her imagination, to get the members to, for example, confront the reality of the leader. That item is simply not on the agenda so early in the members' lives together. When the group shifts from dramas of sacrifice to dramas of despair may well depend on the fantasies of a member particularly well suited to lead the dramas of sacrifice or despair. That the group will shift when it becomes apparent, sooner or later, that sacrifice doesn't solve its problems is beyond the fantasies of any member. Not because the group has a life of its own independent of the members, but because there is a reality of group life together, particularly the way in which various solutions or dramas are bound to fail, that impresses itself on all the members.

3 ✳ Theoretical Perspectives on the Small Group: Acting Out the Missing Leader

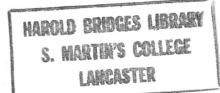
What remains to be explained is how group members like Sarah communicate their fantasies to other group members, persuading them to act them out. The answer is projective identification, a relationship that will be explained in this chapter. Not, however, simply in terms of each of the five dramas, but in terms of the larger drama of which each is a part: the drama in which group members enact the missing leader. If meta-ethics, metaphysics, and meta-theories exist, as they do, can there be meta-dramas? In any case, that is what I am writing about. Not only is the missing leader the totem for whose sake all things are done, for whom all these dramatic rituals are performed, either to revive him or kill him or both. He himself is acted out in the group, as members come to take on aspects of his personality, acting them out in relationship to the group. According to his predilection (what Bion calls "valence," or the quality of his personality), each member acts out an aspect of the missing leader: one member becomes the hostile aggressive aspect of the leader; another the maternal and caring aspect; still another the sick, withdrawn leader, too ill to care for the group. One member is the persecutory leader, another is the good leader, one the insightful leader, one the dumb leader.

Which parts are acted out will depend upon who the leader actually is, upon how well the group knows the leader, and most of all upon whether the group possesses members who have a predilection for the available roles. Good leader, bad leader; caring leader, persecutory leader: these roles will almost always find a player, as they are so central. Whether others are acted out, and the sophistication of the drama, will depend upon leader and group. Why does the group enact the leader? To tear the leader into bits, eat him up, and still possess him. Out of rage, longing, and desire. To replace the missing leader, to contain him within the group so that he can't escape, to identify with him and so love him and be loved in return. Because the group is scared to death of the leader and desperately in need of him.

How It Works: Projective Identification and Schizoid Compromise

Acting out the missing leader is made possible by two tendencies of group life: projective identification and the schizoid compromise. Those familiar with the psychoanalytic theory of Melanie Klein will see a connection with her paranoid-schizoid position: paranoia is projection (of terror), and the schizoid compromise, like Klein's schizoid position, involves a split in the self. Nevertheless, my account of the group in terms of projective identification and the schizoid compromise is not identical to Klein's. No matter how regressed, the group members are adults, and the terror they experience is more subtle than the infant's. The members fear for their identities as individual selves. Projective identification and the schizoid compromise go together: projective identification is the mechanism of the schizoid compromise, indeed of all the little dramas of the group. Nevertheless, I shall explain them separately.

Projective Identification

The concept of projective identification was developed by Melanie Klein, though Elizabeth Spillius gets it just right when she states that there is not a vast difference between Freud's concept of projection and projective identification.

I do not think it useful to distinguish projection from projective identification. What Klein did, in my view, was to add depth and meaning to Freud's concept of projection by emphasizing that one cannot project impulses without projecting part of the ego, which involves splitting, and, further, that impulses do not just vanish when projected: they go into an object, and they distort the perception of the object.[1]

Though strict Kleinians reject its status as an interpersonal phenomenon, in which the projected impulses influence the other, it is this aspect of projective identification that has received so much attention in recent years by analysts of all theoretical stripes. As Thomas Ogden puts it in *Projective Identification and Psychotherapeutic Technique*, projective identification concerns the

1. R. D. Hinshelwood, *A Dictionary of Kleinian Thought* (London: Free Association Books, 1989), quoting Spillius, "Some Developments from the Work of Melanie Klein," *International Journal of Psycho-Analysis* 64 (1983), p. 322.

way in which feeling-states corresponding to the unconscious fantasies of one person (the projector) are engendered in another (the recipient). In other words, projective identification is concerned with how one person makes use of another to experience and contain aspects of himself. The projector generally desires to get rid of an unwanted or endangered part of himself, depositing it with another so as to better control it by controlling the other. A familiar example is when an angry man says "I'm not angry at you; it's you who are angry with me."

Closely associated with the unconscious fantasies of projective identification is an interpersonal interaction by means of which the recipient is "pressured to think, feel, and behave in a manner congruent with the ejected feelings and the self- and object-representations embodied in the projective fantasy. In other words, the recipient is pressured to engage in an identification with a specific, disowned aspect of the projector."[2] It is the conjunction of fantasy and interpersonal pressure on the recipient to act in accord with the fantasy that makes the concept of projective identification so useful. If the angry man in the previous example manages to get the other to be angry at him, he will have succeeded in using interpersonal pressure to get the other to hold his anger, at which point he may well become the epitome of calm, asking sweetly "Why are you angry at me?" Any psychoanalytic theory that makes projective identification central is *already* a group theory, insofar as it is concerned not only with an individual's mental state but with the way that state is communicated to others, causing them either to act out the projector's fantasy or reject it.

Projective identification brings the intrapsychic together with the interpersonal. Though Ogden is writing strictly about patient and analyst, he writes of the operation of projective identification in dramaturgical terms that are useful in the study of the group. Indeed, from Ogden's perspective, the analytic setting is simply a very small group. "If we imagine for a moment that the patient is both the director and one of the principal actors in the interpersonal enactment of an internal . . . [fantasy], and that the therapist is an unwitting actor in the same drama, then projective identification is the process whereby the therapist is given stage directions for a particular role."[3] Projective identification is the medium of group commerce, the way group members communicate with each other and so unconsciously coordinate their activities, particularly the way they act out the missing leader among themselves, each taking as his role an aspect of the missing

2. Thomas Ogden, *Projective Identification and Psychotherapeutic Technique* (Northvale, N.J.: Jason Aronson, 1982), pp. 1–2.
3. Ibid., p. 4.

leader. It is through projective identification that Sarah communicated her fantasies about authority (the only way to combat a hostile and malevolent leader is to become like him, only more so) to other group members, using her charm and anger and the members' fear of both to get them to play along.

Projective identification is the vehicle of a "role suction," as it is called, in which various group members are pressured into playing the aggressive leader, the good leader, the sick leader, and the sacrificial leader. Among intimates, interpersonal cues necessary for such coordination are often remarkably subtle, a slight shift in body position, a change in the tone of voice. In small groups, where the members don't know each other very well, the interpersonal cues are less subtle. But the principle is the same in either case: the recipient of projective identification is pressured to play the role assigned to him by a type of rhythm, in which the members respond only to those aspects of his behavior and personality that fit the role, ignoring or rejecting others. A simple example may help. In one group in which I participated there was an engaged and engaging, passionate, intense, and deeply emotional man of about fifty, the oldest member of the group, the rest of whom, apart from one, were women in college and graduate school. The group, however, needed someone different, a benign but remote father figure, and there were few other candidates. So how did the group get the father it needed? By criticizing this member for being what he was so obviously not, at least at first: abstract, theoretical, remote but fatherly, kindly but not very understanding. Soon enough, however, the man was offering long, abstract, rather obscure theoretical explanations of the group's behavior, which the members could then dismiss, as though to say, "We don't need to listen to our leader; he's a kindly father, but he's just not with it, and so very dry." The group had succeeded in getting this member to help it contain and dispose of an aspect of the missing leader.

The rhythm by which the group responds to its members, so as to encourage them to play certain roles, is akin to the rhythm by which a mother responds to her baby. It's a subtle and complicated dance. "Attunement" it is sometimes called, in which the mother's responsiveness to aspects of the baby's personality leads to the development of these aspects, and her ignorance and neglect of others allows these aspects to fall into desuetude, or at least be put into cold storage. While the baby is neither unlimited nor strictly reactive in his developmental potential, which aspects of his personality are developed will depend in good measure on which aspects the mother, and later the father, respond to. It is in this context, I believe, that we should read Bion's statement that the task of establishing emotional contact with the life of the group "would appear to be as formidable to the adult as the relationship with the breast appears to be to the infant."[4] But the emotional life of the group is far less satisfying than the breast, being largely a matter of fitting people into roles in which essential aspects of the individual's identity are obliterated. In the case of the man mentioned above, it was only he who dared cry in the group. But the group couldn't even see it, criticizing his unemotional behavior as tears were streaming down his face, so strong was the group's need for the remote father whom it could reject. The group's behavior was harshly aggressive, even violent, the type of threat to a member's identity that makes the group such a terrifying place, as it refuses to recognize individuals who don't fit in, which means don't play their role. It's Hegel's dialectic of mutual recognition, in which the group simply won't recognize the individual unless he plays along. Often, of course, individuals take to their roles like a duck to water. But only in the short run is the result less violent. In the long run even those who take readily to their roles are damaged, as the demand of the role restricts the display, unfolding, and development of other aspects of the self in the group.

Projective identification can be benign, even richly rewarding, allowing people to share their innermost feelings. It is the medium of almost infinite closeness, how one can feel what it is like to be another person. In the group, however, its effects are generally deleterious, as the individuality and creativity of each member is constrained by the role he is suctioned into and not permitted to leave. Projective identification is bad not merely because members use it to deny responsibility for their own fear, hatred, and aggression, loading it upon another, the scapegoat or sacrifice. Projective identification is bad because members generally disown their own competence and creativity as well, locating it in the missing leader, who, it is fantasized, will save them if only the group can act him out just right, so as to bring him to life by some sort of primitive mimetic ritual. In the end, however, this is why the group's acting out of the missing leader is so problematic: acted out is an empty leader, whose creativity and competence remains forever outside the group. Group development requires that members come to reclaim lost parts of themselves, parts projectively located in other members or the missing leader. While self-aware members can make some progress in this regard on their own, redemption is really a group activity, in which each member comes to play a wider variety of roles, responding to others who do likewise. A role, like its medium of projective identification, is not really an individ-

4. Bion, *Experiences in Groups*, pp. 141–142.

ual part (even if it is played by an individual), but a part in a group drama. For an individual to play a richer role, the group must act out a richer drama, one that has a richer repertoire of roles. This, in turn, requires that the group somehow come to terms with its missing leader. Which means learning how to relate to its real one.

Schizoid Compromise

Projective identification involves splitting, as Spillius points out. For a person to projectively identify with another, he must split off part of himself in order to locate it in another. The schizoid compromise is the most important split, at least as far as group life is concerned. The term is Harry Guntrip's, but it is Howard Bacal and Kenneth Newman's definition of it that I adapt.[5] In the schizoid compromise:

1. One part of the self sees itself as instrument of the other's malevolent or careless will. The other may be group or leader; generally (I have argued) the primary fear is of the group, displaced onto the leader.

2. Another part of the self imagines itself to be in an ideal relationship with the other, so that the other's power, beauty, and so forth becomes an extension of one's own.

3. Still a third part of the self is isolated and withdrawn, a result of not being able to fully invest the self in any real relationship.

The schizoid compromise is, I believe, the fundamental psychological event in the group. What marks it as a schizoid compromise is, of course, the fact that the member tries to have his cake and eat it too: to give himself over to the group, while being separate and independent of it. Groups recall the earliest stage of individual development, in which the member is desperately in need of attunement and harmony with the other. At this stage, harmony is tantamount to survival. If my theory of the schizoid compromise is correct, every group member will experience unconscious fantasies of being in a close, loving, possibly merged relationship with the leader, while splitting off into the group the rage, resentment, and hurt he or she feels against the leader who fails to lead.

The schizoid compromise doesn't work. Not only does the group recreate in itself the lack of harmony (indeed, the terror) that it seeks to escape, but the cost is great for both individual and group. The split self is not enough for either the group or the individual. Each is impoverished, and

5. Harry Guntrip, *Schizoid Phenomena, Object Relations and the Self* (Madison, Conn.: International Universities Press, 1992), pp. 288–310. Howard Bacal and Kenneth Newman, *Theories of Object Relations: Bridges to Self-Psychology* (New York: Columbia University Press, 1990), pp. 240, 168.

each impoverishes the other, as the group provides insufficient recognition of the individual, causing him to withdraw further from the group, impoverishing both individual and group. Bion states that "the individual has to resort to splitting to isolate himself from the group, and his own essential 'groupishness.'"[6] Isolation from the group *and* from large parts of oneself: Is there a better recipe for loneliness? The result is that group life becomes increasingly empty and sterile, members alienated from self and others. In desperation members turn to the leader for signs of life and revivification, which, when not forthcoming, leads to still more rage and despair. The group cycles downward as it lacks the resources, potentially available to it in the members, to overcome its frozen development.

An example may help to clarify this point and develop another. In one group a member stated that when she entered the group she tried to "leave all this baggage of mine outside the group, at the door." She was referring to her feelings about Whites and about race relations in general, but her point has a more general validity. Each member of the group tries to leave his baggage outside, which means those parts of the self that might interfere with the member's attunement with the group, that might make the member an outsider or sacrifice. The trouble is that it is not really the baggage of the self that is left outside but the experiences and history of the self that get left: the self itself. What get brought in are the contents of the baggage, so to speak: fear, rage, and desire uncontained by the experiencing and historical self. Without the baggage that is the self to contain it, these contents start flying around the room, propelled by projective identification unconstrained by the interests of the self. The reason that the self gets left at the door is because the group is too threatening to it. Leaving the self at the door is part of the schizoid compromise, as in "I will participate in the group, be a good group member, but only with a part of myself, and not a terribly important part at that." Part of the problem with such a compromise is that it deprives the group of the real selves of real members, the only thing that might contribute to the vitality and reality of the group.

The other problem with this compromise is that without the self to contain its fear, rage, and desire, these emotions get released into the group in a terrifying fashion. To be sure, the group has a way of dealing with these emotions: they are structured according to the split-off functions of the failed leader, so that one member may become the fearful leader, another the enraged leader, still another the desiring leader, and so forth. The trouble is that this solution guarantees that these emotions will never be put

6. Bion, *Experiences in Groups*, p. 95.

together again, which means that the group will never become a collection of whole members. Finally, it is now apparent that while the group is structured according to the split-off attributes of its leader, the origin of the fear that leads to this structure is within, in the fear that the member can't take his full self into the group, lest it be destroyed or damaged in some way. The fear of the malevolent authority of the leader segues into the fear that the group itself, which has split the leader into pieces and incorporated him in the group, is the malevolent authority.

The schizoid compromise plays such a central role in the chapters that follow that it may be useful to explore its theoretical origins. The schizoid compromise is a strategy by which the group member seeks to protect his true self from the group, which is not interested in knowing, protecting, or understanding individual identity. With the term "true self" I am, of course, drawing upon the psychoanalytic theory of D. W. Winnicott. Guntrip, who coined the term "schizoid compromise," was an analysand of Winnicott and a devotee of the idea of a true self. It is no joining incommensurables to draw upon Winnicott to explore a concept, the schizoid compromise, developed by Guntrip. Nevertheless, it is not the purity of the conceptual line that I am interested in, but the fact that Winnicott's account of the endangered self seems best to explain why and how the schizoid compromise is such a popular strategy in groups.

Winnicott argues that in the face of a nonfacilitating environment, an unresponsive or intrusive mother, the child splits its self in two, relating with one half of himself to his environment in a false and compliant manner, in order to receive whatever recognition he can. At the same time, the child withholds the other half of himself, the more spontaneous, authentic, vital part, so that it will be less damaged by misunderstanding, intrusiveness, carelessness, or neglect. This part harbors the child's deepest desire, to be known for who he truly is, even before he knows it. The deepest danger to the self, says Winnicott, is precocious adaptation to an environment that does not recognize the individual qua individual but only as he meets the demands of his environment. As I read Winnicott, the true self is not a location or function or structure, like the ego, but a type of object relationship, to self as well as others, in which one feels most real and alive.[7] When the

7. For Winnicott, the narcissistic hallucination of perfect responsiveness is the core of the true self. Consequently, the true self's deepest desire is that it be left untouched. As I see it, the true self is the self as it would be were it responded to perfectly by its caretakers, so as to maximize its pure potential. These positions are not identical, as mine makes the true self a relational entity. I believe that my view comes closer to the way Christopher Bollas has reinterpreted the true self in terms of the unthought known in *The Shadow of the Object: Psychoanalysis of the Unthought Known* (New York: Columbia University Press, 1987), p. 278.

self finds itself in relationships that exploit or ignore it, it splits in two in order to protect and preserve the true self by putting it into cold storage, as Guntrip expresses it; for the alternative is death, death of the soul or true self.

Bion argues, and I have too, that the small group is experienced much like the mother was originally experienced—except that groups are always bad mothers, nonfacilitating mothers, not good enough mothers, in the sense that they always fail to recognize the individual, always demanding adaptation to the group above all else. If the members of the group have had good mothering as children, then the split that Winnicott writes of need not be as deep and wide as it is in the infant who has grown up in a nonfacilitating environment. Adults are not children. Nevertheless, insofar as he is a group member and involved in the life of the group, the member will tend to respond to this nonfacilitating environment by splitting, just as the young child does. This is more than enough to spoil the life of the group. All children and all adults split in some degree in order to protect their true selves. It is always and just a matter of degree. Here, by the way, we see that it takes no doctrine of emergence or group mind to explain group behavior. The behavior of the group is explained by the tendency of its members to split in the face of the threat posed by the nonfacilitating group itself. The behavior of the group is fully explained when the pattern of these splits, the way the parts and pieces are enacted in little dramas, is known.

The key terror of life, according to Winnicott, is total dependence, because total dependence requires total compliance and attunement to the other and hence the murder of the true self, the source of spontaneity, creativity, wonder, and above all vitality.[8] Splitting off the true self is an alternative to suicide (or, in the group, offering oneself up as a willing sacrifice), a way to preserve the true self, albeit in a way that is unavailable to member or group. Imagine what happens to the life of the group when each member splits off and withholds these parts not just from the group, but from himself qua group member. One thing he does is to seek them in others, especially the leader, which is why the split looks a little more complicated in the group than in the mother–infant dyad that Winnicott writes of. The group is actually a triad—individual, group, and leader—which is why the schizoid compromise has three parts. But if the group is not mother, it is nonetheless an environment upon which the member is deeply dependent, not just for recognition but for safety. The fact that the gravest threat to the member's safety stems from the group itself, its willingness to sacrifice the nonconformist, only heightens this dependence.

8. D. W. Winnicott, "Primary Maternal Preoccupation," in *Collected Papers: Through Paediatrics to Psycho-Analysis* (New York: Basic Books, 1958), pp. 304–305.

"Feeling real," says Winnicott, "is more than existing; it is finding a way to exist as oneself, and to relate to objects as oneself, and to have a self into which to retreat for relaxation."[9] The group fails on each of these three counts to help its members feel real. Probably the most striking experience of being in the small group has to do with the third, the loss of a sense of self to retreat into. As a result of being bombarded with the projective identifications of other members, the self in the group comes to lack dimensionality and depth, as the member feels himself unable to connect with those parts of himself that don't fit the role he has been assigned. Frequently this experience takes the form of being unable to think in the group, unable to get in touch with what one knows—for example, that one is acting in a way that seems forced, unnatural, a part in someone else's drama. This does not mean, of course, that the rest of the self has disappeared. The member has split it off in order to protect it, with the result that it is not available to him or to the group, both of which desperately need it to be whole.

The task of group development is to recover the lost vitality and reality of its members, including their reality-testing ability, so that the group can draw upon the members' creativity, talents, and knowledge of reality without treating these attributes as mere manna for the group. This is terribly difficult, and most groups don't do it well; most don't do it at all. Much of what goes on in groups, including the aggression and the sacrifices, as well as the other little dramas, is an attempt to restore the vitality, creativity, and hope lost to the group when the members withhold themselves from it. Most of what is tragic about group life stems from these strategies, which not only are bound to fail but are bound to make life in the group even scarier and more miserable, to which the members respond with more splitting and hence further loss of vitality.

Acting Out the Missing Leader versus Bion's Basic Assumptions

Projective identification, coupled with the schizoid compromise, makes available to the group aspects of the personalities of the members for various group dramas, all of which have the same title: acting out the missing leader. Which particular drama is playing depends upon the emotional constellation of the group: the dramas follow and enact these emotions, rather than cause them, even though the dramas may perpetuate these emotional states or make them worse. For example, when rage at the missing consul-

9. D. W. Winnicott, "Mirror-Role of Mother and Family in Child Development," in *Playing and Reality* (London: Routledge, 1971), p. 117.

tant-leader dominates, members best able to characterize the bad aspects of the leader, such as his self-contained arrogance and refusal of support, will take the lead, attacking group members and being attacked in return. If, however, this rage threatens to get out of control, the group may invite the member who represents, for example, the sick leader, so enfeebled and disabled that he cannot, rather than will not, lead to take center stage, so that the member representing the caring leader can care for him in some way. And so it goes, one drama segueing into another.

In one group in which I served as consultant-leader, the man cast in the role of aggressive group prosecutor in a previous drama sat to my immediate left, the man cast in the role of "conscience of the group" on my immediate right. As the new drama developed, the first man came to play the intrusive, marauding leader who would take all the women for himself, forcing the men into homosexual submission in order to receive any attention. The second man came to play the caring, fatherly leader, who loved all his children equally. And they fought across my body for my soul for hours. Unfortunately, the result was stalemate, as this is not an especially productive conflict. What is necessary for group development is that this conflict for the soul of the leader be interpreted as an expression of the group's inability to see the leader as a whole, real person.

There is an irony to the conflict among members over the soul of the consultant-leader. It is in reality frequently a conflict over who shall be sacrificed first. Why? Because in the end the group, including the contestants for sacrificial leader, is waiting for the reemergence and rebirth of the consultant-leader, whole and in charge, the murderous aggression that might have torn him to pieces having been displaced into the group itself in order to save him. In *Totem and Taboo,* Freud argues that after killing and eating the primal father, the sons, scared to death of their own violence and guilty too, because they loved the father, establish within themselves his harsh regime, the origin of the superego. Only now we see the addition of a Christian coda, so to speak, the members acting as if they believe that if they are harsh enough on themselves, the primal father will himself be reborn, as he wasn't really killed and eaten, just put into cold storage for a while.

While I have referred to various dramas played out in the group, the term could be misleading, suggesting more organization and coherence to the events than they possess. The way it works is in fact remarkably chaotic and fragmented, as the group jumps from one little drama to another, minute by minute. The overall experience is not one of a smoothly unfolding plot but of fragmentation and chaos, as if many dramas were being played on the same stage at the same time or in a sequence that is almost indecipherable. In this regard it is interesting to compare my account with that of Bion. Bion too stresses the way in which "basic assumption groups," as he calls them, are remarkably unstable, metamorphosing from one to another in the blink of an eye. My experience is that while Bion captures the unstable quality of the emotional life of the group, his notion of basic assumptions is misleading, because it suggests that the group is whole, moving from assumption to assumption, state to state, as a single entity.

This is no small criticism. In their introduction to *Group Relations Reader 2*, published by the A. K. Rice Institute, Marvin Geller and James Krantz state that the group-as-a-whole perspective is the single most important principle in group study, an implication of Bion's view of the "group-as-mother," as another contributor puts it.[10] On the contrary, the group is never whole but always fragmented, its members acting out an image of the leader who is never whole but always broken into pieces, the result of the group's own rage and fear, ultimately of itself. There is, to be sure, a certain wholeness to this experience, as each little drama has a cast of characters and script. It is only this that makes it meaningful to refer to the group as a whole, which means to the group as its members play roles in a larger drama. However, the group is not whole in the sense that each member is feeling the same emotion at the same time, what Bion calls a basic assumption. On the contrary, the group is generally divided against itself, some members projecting their rage at the unsupportive consultant into another member or members, while the recipients of this rage generally feel themselves filled up with an anger and fear they can barely comprehend. The result, for most members, is an experience of being vaguely, or not so vaguely, out of control, playing a part in somebody else's drama. Which it is. But it is also each member's own drama, acted out with alienated and split-off parts of himself.

To be sure, the group-as-a-whole perspective does not deny the splitting that occurs in groups, particularly the way in which members come to serve as receptacles in which others deposit split-off parts of themselves. On the contrary, the group-as-a-whole approach emphasizes splitting—albeit from a particular perspective, in which splitting is a defense against the enforced unity of the group, the threat to individual identity generated by the group's regression to the whole. Behind all the splits the members unconsciously fantasize that they are a single, unified body, the group as a whole. But what if behind this fantasy of unity and wholeness there lies a deeper chaos, confusion, and conflict? A reign of terror of part-objects and

10. M. Geller and J. Krantz, Introduction to *Group Relations Reader*, vol. 2, ed. A. Colman and M. Geller (Washington, D.C.: A. K. Rice Institute, 1985), p. 1, and Wells, Jr., "Group-as-a-Whole Perspective," pp. 113–115.

their relationships, as members rend and mend parts of themselves and others in a desperate attempt to create order out of chaos, swapping parts as though nothing was real and stable. If this is so, then we should want to know if there are any patterns to this reign of terror. Not only is the group-as-a-whole perspective not helpful in this regard; it confuses the defense with the anxiety, the desperate attempt to create a whole with the part-object terror behind it.

Bion understands basic assumptions as basic defenses against psychotic anxiety. "Basic assumptions now emerge as formations secondary to an extremely early *primal scene* worked out on a level of part objects, and associated with psychotic anxiety and mechanisms of splitting and projective identification such as Melanie Klein has described as characteristic of the paranoid-schizoid and depressive positions."[11] Bion knows all about the part-object terrors that run loose in groups, but his theory (not just basic assumptions, but the group-as-a-whole perspective) doesn't give them room to move around. Instead, it encysts these terrors in a reified whole. What's needed is a theory that can better capture the way in which members act out primitive part-object fantasies. Acting out the missing leader is such a theory, one that opens up the terrors so that they may be more readily confronted and interpreted.

From the perspective of acting out the missing leader, the leading metaphor is not the primal scene of parental intercourse to which Bion refers, but the *primal horde* that Freud writes of in *Totem and Taboo*. In the primal horde, as in the drama of acting out the missing leader, the group wants to have its leader and eat him too. The advantage of the primal horde over the primal scene is that it is a more open drama, with more parts, pieces, roles, variations, and mythic elements to draw upon, particularly the theme of ritual sacrifice. It is a looser container, moving from the claustrophobic parental bedroom to the plains of Asia and Africa where civilization was born. A dramatic formulation, but group life is drama, the group acting out its fantasies instead of verbalizing them. Acting out the missing leader is the primal horde.

Why Does the Group Act Out the Missing Leader?

For several reasons. The members are enraged at the leader who fails to lead and so tear him to pieces and incorporate the pieces in the group. There he lives on as a sort of Dr. Frankenstein's monster, aspects of the original leader that don't fit together as they are played out by a dozen group members. The members also love and need the leader, wishing to be so close

11. Bion, *Experiences in Groups*, p. 164.

to him that they identify with him, as though to become him. Probably most important, the members enact the leader in order to perform his functions for themselves and so survive without him. Acting out the missing leader is an attempt to contain the part-object chaos of the group. It doesn't work very well, at least not as practiced in regressed and undeveloped groups, for the same reason that individuals cannot "hold" themselves very well, as D. W. Winnicott points out. With the term "holding," Winnicott refers to all aspects of maternal responsiveness to the infant's needs, from secure cradling in the mother's arms to her attunement to the infant's emotions. Holding not only provides security but allows the infant to simply be, freely experiencing his world, without having to put all the pieces together too soon into what Winnicott calls a "false self."[12] Conversely, when the infant must hold himself, he can never simply be. His creativity and spontaneity are stifled in rigid, stereotyped behavior, designed to hold the pieces of his experience together in the absence of a developed self and in the face of his rage. In fact, the pieces never fit together very well, so that the world comes to be experienced as more chaotic and random than need be.

Something similar happens when the group must hold itself in the absence of leadership. It internalizes the missing and failed consultant-leader and so creates a pattern, giving meaning and boundaries to its members' life together. But the pattern is rigid and stereotyped, a defense against rage and fear that ends in stalemate, rapidly shifting and unstable little dramas that contribute nothing to group development. As with the inadequately held individual, the member's "true self," as Winnicott calls it, the source of creativity, spontaneity, and growth, is withheld from the group, so group life becomes arid and meaningless. Like individual development, group development requires a leader who can hold the group for a while, until the members are in a position to relate to the leader and each other in a more realistic fashion.

The ritual of enacting the leader is in the end about enacting a primitive and punitive superego powerful enough to contain and control the group's aggression, which is why it is the so-called bad leader who is most frequently acted out. Because, the group seems to believe, only the severest aggression by the leader is capable of controlling the members' terrifying aggression. The logic is almost pure *lex talionis*, like the psycho-logic of the primitive superego that Freud writes of, which directs back against the self the aggression that it would vent on others. In Freud's account too the father is rent and eaten by the group. What I add is that the fight is over

12. D. W. Winnicott, *Holding and Interpretation* (New York: Grove Press, 1986).

identity, not just the possession of women. Sons and daughters both kill and eat the father. Both are equally concerned with possessing an identity. But each son and daughter eats a different piece of father, so to speak, becoming the part or member he or she consumes, according to his or her valence for the role. It is this that makes group life a much more differentiated drama than Freud or Bion ever recognized. But if the drama is more differentiated and sophisticated than these pioneers recognized, the outcome is much the same, as the group remains stuck in a type of perpetual civil war. Necessary for group development is a leader who can interpret to the members the way in which each projectively alienates large parts of himself in others, including the leader. This too is holding, what leaders are for. Only then is group development possible—possible, but not probable, and certainly not guaranteed. Here we see the real advantage of my account over that of Bion or Freud. While my account does not make group development more likely, its more differentiated explication of group drama generates a more sophisticated explanation of what makes group development possible.

The Five Dramas All Act Out the Relationship to the Missing Leader

The five group dramas are simply the titles of the most popular plays that the group members act out in relationship to the missing leader. Each of the five dramas is actually but an act in this larger drama of acting out the missing leader. For each drama the question to ask is which aspect of the missing leader is dominating. This helps identify the theme and explain it more fully. But there is a fly in the ointment; it's really not so simple. Frequently two aspects of the leader are present at the same time, fighting each other, not unlike what Bion calls the "dual" of the basic assumption group. It is this conflict between two aspects of the missing leader that characterizes most dramas. Bion, for example, writes of the dual of the dependency basic assumption group, in which the group turns from seeking to be nourished by the leader to nourishing him instead.[13] In the drama of the sacrificial leader, the most aggressive members, those directing the ritual sacrifice, are acting out the role of the greedy, bellicose, intrusive leader who demands the blood of his subjects. At the same time, those directing the sacrifice frequently become scapegoats themselves, a willingness to do so being part of the role description.

THE SACRIFICIAL LEADER. In this drama the group is enacting the conflict between its fantasy of the consultant-leader as aggressive, intrusive sadist to whom all must submit (a view not without its attractions, apparently)

13. Bion, *Experiences in Groups,* pp. 119–121.

and its fantasy of the consultant-leader as one whom the group must destroy in order to save itself. Or perhaps this won't be necessary: the leader may offer himself up willingly. In analyzing this drama (or any drama), the trick is to figure out who is playing what role at a particular time. Three roles dominate: the aggressive, sadistic leader; the leader who is to be sacrificed or who will go willingly; and the group member who will be fed to the aggressive leader or will lead the revolt against him. It's complicated, as one member may play all three roles, or different members may play each role, as one member is benched to be replaced by a substitute. But while it's complex, it's not incomprehensible. On the contrary, the drama itself is quite simple, once the basic principle is grasped: that the group is fighting for the soul of its consultant-leader, engaging in a titanic conflict over which fantasy of the leader is to dominate. While I have written of the group as acting out different and conflicting aspects of the missing leader, this is not quite right. The group acts out its *fantasies* of the different aspects of the missing leader. Or rather, it acts out its *conflicting fantasies* of the missing leader: that he demands blood from the group, that the group will destroy him as he would destroy them, or that the missing leader will give himself up willingly for the group.

DESPAIR, DEADNESS, AND HOPELESSNESS. This is an easier drama to interpret, as the cast is more limited. In it the group enacts the dead leader, the one whom it has sacrificed. Within the group there will be a modest division of labor, some acting as mourners, some as murderers, and others as the dead consultant-leader himself. Still others may seek to raise the dead. In general, however, the tone of this drama is dominated by the experience of deadness, the group's identification with the dead leader. But not always. Sometimes rage, frequently individual or tribal conflict within the group, is employed to revivify the group and so cover over the sadness. When this occurs, it is important to determine whether the rage is primary, a response to the terror that is the group, or secondary, orchestrated by the group to keep itself alive. In general, the larger the group, the more likely it will turn to rage; the smaller the group, the more likely it will mourn, even as it usually gets stuck in its mourning. Probably this is because mourning is a more sophisticated emotion, one that the small group is somewhat more likely to develop than the large.

SEX AND DEATH. While I have treated the *drama of sex and death* as a separate one, it is in many (but not all) respects the double of despair, deadness, and hopelessness. In the drama of sex and death the question is whether the sexuality of the consultant-leader, acted out in the group, can be used in a creative fashion to bring life to the group or whether sexuality must be an instrument of fear, power, and control, by which some dominate others, as the group fears (and often desires) that the leader will do. In the face of this, death sometimes seems preferable. The key roles are as one would expect: the lover, who offers to pair with others (frequently more than one) in order to create something new and beautiful; the sexual predator, who will use sex to dominate and control others; and various group members who are receptive to neither, one, or both. Generally, the members fall into the roles of the chaste, beloved, or abused, in order to complete the drama. Each role, in my experience, is gender-neutral, so to speak, played equally well by either man or woman. Certainly men play the abused, and women the sexual predator. Nevertheless, cultural stereotypes and influences die hard. In the groups in which I have participated, men are more likely to be the abusers, women the abused, and both sexes about equally likely to be chaste, lovers, and beloved.

LEADERSHIP AND IDENTITY. In this drama the question is whether one can be an individual without being the consultant-leader—that is, without sacrificing him. Can leaders and individuals coexist? Which means, can the group members retain their individuality in the presence of a leader? Or must the leader be sacrificed, ignored, or transformed into a god? In this drama the roles are distributed according to Hegel's dialectic of mutual recognition. One member, acting the part of master (leader), will generally seek to force others to recognize him. Other members will sacrifice their individuality to do so, while still other members will resist. This is, in my experience, a particularly dynamic drama, with the roles rapidly shifting, the master-leader quickly becoming the slave and vice versa. In fact, this is just what one would expect from Hegel's account, in which the slave is actually playing with more trumps than the master, the one who needs recognition generally being in a weaker position than he who grants it. But, while the role-changing in this drama has a dynamic quality, in another sense the drama is (like all the dramas) quite static. The result is stalemate, as no one recognizes anyone. If all can't be leader, then none shall be an individual.

TRIBAL WARFARE AND SUPERFICIAL IDEOLOGIES. This last drama is the longest-running show in town, the most ancient drama, the one to which groups return when all else fails. Perhaps because the rules and the roles are so simple: us and them, allies and enemies, good guys and bad guys. It might seem that in this drama there is no room for a leader at all, that it is not really a matter of acting out the missing leader. Quite the opposite is the case. The identification with the leader by each side is total, complete, as in

God is on our side. The other side is the Antichrist. In this drama each side claims the leader for itself, totally and unreservedly. Actually, not quite unreservedly. Recall that the real enemy is one's own group and the demands on the member's individuality that it makes. To claim the leader for one's own side is not simply an act of possession, or even consumption. It is an act of war, in which a part of the member's self is fighting with the other tribe against the leader in himself and his tribe. This is why tribes have so much difficulty living side by side: the conflict is not incidental to the relationship but central, the way the members take revenge on their own group, their own leader, by identifying with the enemy. Which is why anti-Communists in the United States in the 1950s so often acted like the enemy, avowing the same tactics as Communists. The real enemies of many anti-Communists were the United States, capitalism, and democracy and the way these entities failed to meet their own needs for order, security, and community. As in the drama of the sacrificial leader which it so closely resembles, warring tribes are not just fighting each other; they are fighting each other to sacrifice themselves. It is this that gives tribal warfare its fratricidal quality, as though each side will accept nothing less than the destruction of both. They won't.

Group Development

The depressing thing about these dramas is that they just go on and on, the group moving from one to another. To be sure, some dramas reflect more group development than others. Tribal warfare and the sacrificial leader express what Klein calls paranoid-schizoid thinking, whereas group despair and the attempt to use sex as a paradigm of creativity express the depressive position, in which the world is no longer divided into Manichaean dualities.[14] The dispute over leadership and identity is in many ways more developed still, at least insofar as issues of identity and differentiation come to the fore. Nevertheless, it would be quite mistaken to rank these dramas in developmental terms. All reflect a refusal to confront the reality of the leader and the apparent inability of the group to lead itself. Groups do develop, however, though generally not on their own. On their own, groups cycle through the various dramas. With leadership, groups have a chance of developing, something one wouldn't know from reading most political theory, which assumes either that development is impossible or that it is reached

14. In *Melanie Klein and Critical Social Theory* (New Haven: Yale University Press, 1989), pp. 23–56, I explore the relationship between the paranoid-schizoid and depressive positions.

when the social contract is signed. In fact, the social contract is just the beginning.

It is useful to characterize three positions in group development. The term "positions" is drawn from Klein and is used in lieu of stages to suggest that the group may move from one to the other and back again, as it usually does. Group development is not so much about the group achieving the developed stage as it is about the group acting in a developed fashion more often than not. It might be argued that a normative judgment is implicit in any scheme of development (at least where humans are concerned). I would respond that the normative judgment is and should be explicit. As argued in chapter 1, group development is good because, and only because, it allows for individual development. It is individual development that is the highest standard, the sine qua non by which group development is judged. This is not to say that individual and group are not in conflict, for they are. But group development and individual development are not in conflict. Only group development allows even the possibility of individual development. Little dramas occur in all three positions, but their quality changes from the regressed to the undeveloped to the developed group.

The Regressed Group

In *The Primitive Edge of Experience,* Ogden writes of the autistic-contiguous position, arguing that it precedes even the paranoid-schizoid position. Discussed earlier, it will be useful to expand upon it. In the autistic-contiguous position the struggle is to make emotional contact with an entity to which one is already joined at the skin, the mother. "Contiguity of surfaces . . . generate[s] the experience of a sensory surface rather than the feeling of two surfaces coming together. . . . There is practically no sense of inside and outside, or self and other; rather, what is important is the pattern, boundedness, shape, rhythm, texture, hardness, softness, warmth, coldness, and so on."[15] When the rhythm falls, tantamount to what Winnicott calls the failure of maternal holding, the experience is one of being violated and intruded, the inability to regulate and control one's boundaries. Characteristic defenses are the creation of hard, rigid edges that delineate and protect the vulnerable surface. Terms like "armor," "shell," "crust," "rigidity," and "impenetrability" characterize these defenses, which have much in common with the rigid self-holding that is required when maternal holding fails. As with his account of projective identification, Ogden is writing about his experience of another in therapy, not about groups. But it is often the case that the deepest insights into groups come from the smallest group of all,

15. Ogden, *Primitive Edge of Experience,* p. 33.

the group of two that is analyst and analysand or mother and child. Ogden calls it the autistic-contiguous position because it is connection, contiguity, without awareness of connection, or autism. It is this lack of awareness that makes differentiation impossible in this position.

The regressed group is in the autistic-contiguous position, in both the relationship of the members to each other and the relationship of the members to the consultant-leader. The members of the regressed group are, one by one (recall that this is not a group fantasy but an individual one, albeit of each individual), in an unconscious symbiotic relationship with the consultant-leader, so they cannot recognize his separate existence in reality and confront it. Similarly, the members are so scared of each other that they can make no real contact. The schizoid compromise runs wide and deep. Words and rituals are used not to convey information or foster understanding but to create an atmosphere that possesses rhythm, warmth, and soothing comfort. It is striking, for example, how often the environment of the room is referred to in the regressed group. It's too cold, too hot; the chairs are too hard, too small; there are too few windows; and so forth. In such an atmosphere a certain comfort may be achieved, albeit at the expense of individuality. In the autistic-contiguous position the reality of both other group members and the leader is ignored, as the group members are, in unconscious fantasy, united with both, so closely that they can gain no perspective on the reality of either. It is in the autistic-contiguous position that group members are most emphatic in denying the importance of differences, such as sex, race, age, and class. Yet tribal dramas occur, largely to secure the shaky boundaries of the group by fighting another: fusion is reinforced by fission so as to defend the boundary. Any boundary. Sacrificial leaders emerge, but the group seems most interested in simply getting rid of anyone who disrupts its rhythm or calls attention to the leader. Thus it ignores the consultant-leader or consumes him, treating him as if he were just one more group member. The strategies are dissimilar, even opposite, but the goal is identical: to make the leader disappear. Somewhat more developmentally advanced, the dramas of despair, sex and death, and leadership and identity do not appear in the regressed group.

The regressed group is a theoretical construct, and it would be mistaken to assume that members experience life in the regressed group in theoretical terms. On the contrary, the members experience the group as a bunch of isolated individuals, but only because the members are in such a state of dedifferentiation that all they can know of the other is that he is other, his otherness constituting the threat that dedifferentiation defends against. Not autonomy but isolation is how individuality is experienced in the regressed group, as members avoid knowing each other as real individuals, so as to more readily fuse with the group in fantasy. More precisely put, in the regressed group autonomy and isolation are confused, as if autonomy could only be experienced as withdrawal. This insight will prove especially useful in interpreting Rousseau's state of nature.

The paranoid-schizoid position is not simply one in which the individual or group finds and fights enemies, persecutors. The key mark of the paranoid-schizoid position is that there is no history. It is this that the paranoid-schizoid position and the even more primitive autistic-contiguous position of the regressed group share. Things happen . . . first one thing and then another, with no apparent connection between them. "All of a sudden we were fighting; then everyone was sad. I don't know what happened," is a typical statement that one hears in this position. Experience is chaotic, seemingly random. Individuals are not agents but are acted upon by experience. The group can construct no coherent narrative of its experiences. It cannot even begin to tell a story about itself. Not simply because it has very little history. It is not my experience that the regressed group is where all groups begin. On the contrary, most groups begin as undeveloped groups and regress to the regressed group under the pressure of fear and failure. In the regressed group there are no individuals. But there is really no group either. In the autistic-contiguous position this difference makes no sense, as it assumes a distinction between individual and group in the first place, one the members cannot make in this position.

The Undeveloped Group

In the undeveloped group, which is where most groups spend most of their time, little dramas are at their peak. The group does almost nothing else, and the dramas are increasingly sophisticated, with more players and more roles. Dramas are so central because self-holding is at its peak, as the group tries to lead itself by incorporating its missing leader in various ways, all the ways that the little dramas reflect. Individuation occurs but is limited to the roles offered in the little dramas. Aspects of the reality of the missing leader may be recognized, but these aspects are never integrated into a realistic perception. Instead, they are organized into various dramaturgical patterns and fought over by surrogates, as though only one aspect of the consultant-leader, such as the good or bad leader, can be allowed to exist. The drama of the sacrificial leader is at its peak in this stage, as the group recognizes its need for leadership but is unable to figure out how to use the leader, other than to kill him, eat him, or become him. The schizoid compromise still dominates at this stage, even if individuals sometimes peek out from behind the mask the group has assigned to them, if only to try to make real individual contact with the leader. In one group Joe said simply, "Gee, our consultant looked at me for a moment as though I were a human being."

The undeveloped group has a history, the history of its dramas. But its history is essentially meaningless, sequences without meaningful connection, the raw empiricism of events. "First we sacrificed Helen, then we all got sad. Then Chris started making sexual jokes which livened us all up a bit, until Ann called him a sexist pig, at which point the men and women really went at it" is how the narrative unity of the life of the group would be constructed in the undeveloped group. Connections are recognized, but the group itself has no goal, meaning, or purpose. It acts, one thing causes another, but to no end. In other words, the group's history stops dead in the present, having no meaning when projected into the future, because the group itself has no future, only the promise that one drama will follow another. In its despair the group will frequently organize itself into tribes, as though creating new groups through fission might somehow create life out of death. Amoeba strategy. In fact, what this usually does is to heighten autistic-contiguous anxiety, the fear that the group itself will disappear, fragmenting into a thousand pieces. It is this fear that leads the developed group to become a regressed one. And so it goes, in the small study group and in real life, particularly in ideological groups so filled with rage that constant schism seems the only alternative to group suicide.

The Developed Group

Not only is the developed group a rare achievement, but it is rarer still for the group to remain this way for very long. Nevertheless, development occurs, and good leadership can cause it to occur more often and last longer. In the developed group the members still act out the missing leader. But just as the child learns by imitation, so this acting out takes on a quality of acting like a consultant-leader, as the members learn to perform some leadership functions for themselves. For example, the member who directed the sacrifice of another member may come to direct the group in its dealings with the consultant-leader, a key task. As one member put it, "At first we didn't acknowledge your [the consultant's] existence, then we tried to destroy you. Now maybe we can learn something from you, but maybe not everything. Maybe we still need to learn some things for ourselves." Similarly, the member who acted out the depressed and failed leader may come to help the group mourn its own realistic failures and limits. Members who act like this are acting as role leaders rather than simply acting out the role of leader. As role leader, the member combines his individuality, his personality, and his unique gifts with work that needs to be performed in the group. When the work of the group changes, one role leader will give way to another in the developed group. In one group, Martin took on the task of negotiating with the consultant-leader, then stepped aside as Mary took over the task of mourning the group's failure to learn more from its leader. The group needed to do both, and it needed leadership to do it, but it didn't need the same leader for both. It just needed the leadership function performed by the man or woman best able to do it, which varied with the task.

Developed groups have a history, a story about the group that connects past, present, and future. "Once all we did is fight among ourselves. Now we seem able to listen to each other. Maybe in the future we can learn from each other too" would be a simple, but not simplistic, expression of this sense of history. By a sense of its history I do not mean that the developed group is optimistic or utopian. On the contrary, it is just as historical for a member to say something like, "This group began last week with its members at each other's throats, and even today, in our last session, we are still cutting each other up. Still, look at all we have been through together, Ron's attack on Sally, John's despair that seemed to infect the entire group, our consultant getting so disgusted with us that he walked out. Boy, I'll never forget that!" Such insights may not be the stuff of history as progress in enlightenment, but they are still history. The group is responsible for itself, causing things to happen which its members regret and will not have a chance to rectify. Still, it happened, it's real, and it tells a story, even if it's a story of lost opportunities and tragic conflicts.

There is no history, says Emerson, only biography. In the developed group there is both. The group's history is rightly told in terms of things that individuals did, as when Ron attacked Sally or John despaired. But the developed history of the group isn't just an account of what its members did It's also an account of a shared experience, a journey taken together, not perhaps for the pleasure of each other's company but because certain journeys cannot be taken alone. Learning about group dynamics is one such journey. With the exception of Rousseau, who idealizes the regressed group, traditional state-of-nature–social-contract theory idealizes the undeveloped group. One reason to be concerned with group development is so that we don't confuse failed group development with the epitome of individual development. Not merely traditional state-of-nature theory, but most contemporary political theory, makes this mistake.

Why is the developed group so difficult to realize and even more difficult to maintain? Because members must abandon the schizoid compromise and the security it offers for an unstable, slippery, transitional relationship with the group. With the term "transitional relationship" I mean to invoke Winnicott's idea of the transitional object, such as a favorite blanket or teddy bear, that is at once mother and not-mother, self and not-self. Transitional objects ease the pain of separation, preserving the illusion (but only the illusion: the child knows the reality but prefers not to acknowledge it just yet) of connectedness to the comforting and soothing mother when the mother is absent. One way transitional objects do this is via their constant availability. Unlike the mother, the transitional object does not have a life of its own. While I intend to invoke Winnicott's idea with the term "transitional relationship to the group," the group is no teddy bear. On the contrary, it is beyond the control of any member. Which is just what makes the developed group so difficult to achieve and maintain. The group is a transitional object in the sense that it is at once self and other, self and non-self. The small group is quite literally not the same group with a member missing. The member is part of the group. Still, he is not the group. He does not control the group, at least not fully, and the group will generally reconstitute itself in his absence. What is so difficult, but so important, is for the members to stay in and live with this transitional relationship, which means to be part of the group and separate from it at the same time, member and individual.

Group Development and Political Theory

Group development occurs when members reclaim lost and alienated parts of themselves that they have previously devoted to the group. Through projective identification members take the best, and worst, parts of themselves, their competence as well as their rage and despair, locating them in the group. It is this that ties the individual to the group, preventing his genuine engagement with it. The consultant-leader fosters group development when he interprets the little dramas as expressions of the members' alienation from themselves. This is what the little dramas are: members cooperating with each other to alienate large parts of themselves in the group. An example may help to clarify the importance of leadership in this regard. In one small group the consultant-leader pointed out that the members' perceptions of her seemed quite fragmented: one saw her as a kind old lady, another as a vicious bitch, still another as senile, yet another as experienced and helpful. In fact, she suggested, each member probably thought all these things about her and more; the group had just distributed around the group the labor of thinking such troubling and confusing thoughts all at once.

The group members did not have much to say in response, but shortly after began to criticize each other in a more productive manner than before, which means in a way more in touch with the actual strengths and weaknesses of each member. Later the consultant-leader pointed out that this development seemed to be a direct reaction to her intervention. As members came to recognize the complex ambivalence of their perceptions of the consultant-leader, not relying quite so much upon the group drama to hold these perceptions for them, they could begin to recognize the reality of each other as well. This is group development qua individual development. It is fostered by the interpretation of those characteristic defenses (dramas) that get in the way of members' reclamation of lost and alienated parts of themselves. In the end this is the goal, which is not to say that the group exists to serve individual development, but that individual development without group development is almost impossible.

Interpretation fosters group development because it is, as Winnicott points out, a type of holding, in which the interpreter takes over for a moment the task the group is trying to perform for itself, containing its chaotic and fragmented emotional state in various dramas. This allows group members the opportunity to integrate some of their previously divided emotions rather than distributing them in group dramas. *Interpretation is not magic, and not especially powerful.* It is merely the most powerful strategy for group development that exists. The terrified group, confused and regressed, generally cannot hear an interpretation or use it. But not all interpretation is verbal. The more regressed the group, the more important is nonverbal interpretation. A consultant-leader who sits quietly when attacked, neither raging nor falling apart nor appeasing the group, is making an interpretation: that the group's rage is not all-powerful and hence perhaps not so terrifying. Interpretation is the key to political leadership. Churchill's greatness, according to Franz Neumann in *The Democratic and the Authoritarian State,* stemmed from his ability to transform an unknown danger "into a danger known in kind and extent. He fulfilled those functions of leadership that can be compared to those fulfilled in the life of the individual by the organization of the ego."[16] I would not put it in terms of ego psychology as Neumann does, but my conclusion is similar. Leadership is about interpreting anxiety, not making it disappear but giving it a more realistic focus, allowing members or citizens to put together the parts of themselves they keep separate so as not to know what they fear to know. In the previous example the consultant told the members that she thought each feared that she was senile and incompetent and so cooperated to idealize her wisdom to protect themselves from their own fearsome insight. Her interpretation allowed

16. Franz Neumann, *The Democratic and the Authoritarian State* (New York: Free Press of Glencoe, 1957), pp. 406–407.

each member to bring his hopes and fears into contact with one another and so assess her and the other members more accurately.

Simple interpretations work in the small group because members are generally not particularly disturbed. Members may be terrified and forlorn, but they are terrified and forlorn adults, often able to take an interpretation and use it, as their tendency toward the schizoid compromise is balanced by integrative potentials within each member. It is to this potential that interpretation is aimed. Interpretation works no miracles. It can deal with only one issue at a time, and group development requires that thousands of issues be addressed. But it helps—though not always. One or two disturbed adults in a group, a particularly traumatic experience, or an incompetent consultant-leader can cause so much anxiety that the adult in each member is unavailable to hear and use the interpretation. Leadership then becomes impossible. Thucydides writes in his *History of the Peloponnesian War* that Pericles understood that responsible leadership is impossible when the polis becomes terrified of itself, of its own terror. Then demagogues must take over (*History,* II. 56–65).

Here is the difference between England during World War II and former Yugoslavia today. In England an intact society and culture helped to contain the terror sufficiently that responsible leadership was possible (not guaranteed: whether a responsible leader emerges depends on other factors, including luck). This is not the case in what was Yugoslavia, where responsible leaders cannot be heard. Because leadership is crucial but fragile, there is a tendency either to overestimate or underestimate its importance, to make it everything or nothing. It's neither. Leadership as interpretation is crucial but fragile, dependent for its effectiveness upon members' and citizens' ability to hear and understand. This depends in good measure upon the culture and institutions of a society, a topic discussed below, and throughout the book.

No Solution

There is, it must be recognized, no solution to the problem of individual and group. Nothing I have learned from my experiences with small groups is more important than this. Group members never solve the problem of coming to terms with the leader while finding a place for themselves as individuals and members. The tendency is always to oscillate, idealizing the leader as the source of wisdom and security one moment, devaluing him as less knowledgeable than the least member the next. Similarly, members oscillate between isolation and total belonging, a tendency made easier by the schizoid compromise, which allows members to do both at once, albeit at a price. But if there is no solution, there are ways to reduce the oscillation, to modify the swings. This is what group development is, group members spending more time in the middle: neither idealizing nor devaluing the leader, neither isolating themselves from the group nor submerging themselves in it. It is not merely the extremes but the movement from one to the other that makes the group so unstable.

A diagram, which I shall refer to from time to time as the cross diagram, may help to explain this. The vertical axis represents the group's relationship to its leader. The horizontal axis represents each member's relationship to the group, whether he is isolated or submerged. The goal of group development is to keep the group within the square in the middle, which means to minimize its oscillations. Oscillation increases when the leader is seen in a split fashion, idealized, deeply feared, and devalued all at the same time. This split, I have argued, gets carried over into the member's relationship to the group, so that the member splits himself, the schizoid compromise. Thus, each member takes up all four positions on the cross at once, as groupie and isolate, idolater and despoiler of the leader.

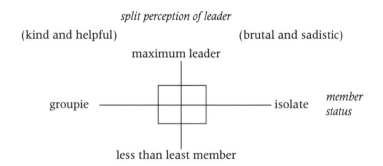

Though oscillations may be reduced by several factors, the single most important one is leadership, particularly in the small group. Can the leader identify and interpret the group members' split perceptions of himself? If so, then the members will find it easier to remain centered on *both* the vertical and horizontal axes. They go together: excessive oscillation on one produces excessive oscillation on the other, for all the reasons mentioned in this chapter. While groups are sometimes able to reduce oscillation on the horizontal axis themselves, if there is good leadership among members, it is generally the case that such oscillation is reduced only as a consequence of a reduction on the vertical axis, the result of the leader's ability to interpret the members' split perceptions of him. In larger grouplike entities, institutions and practices become more important in dampening the oscillations.

My theory of the group is inductively derived, so to speak. It stems from my experience with small groups, not an *idea* of what group relations should be or must be, such as communitarian, liberal, tolerant, authoritarian, and so forth. This approach is intimately related to my conclusion: that there is no solution to group life—or, as a group member once put it, the only solution is the final solution: obliteration of otherness. While there are no solutions, some resolutions avoid catastrophe, catastrophe that stems from the tendency of the group to oscillate between extremes. An idealized leader coupled with a unitary group is a familiar recipe for catastrophe, but there are others.

In response, it might be argued that even if I have interpreted the lessons of the small group correctly, its relevance for political theory must be minimal. Not just because political theory is about ideas, but because it is about institutions, and the small group has no institutions. About this last statement I disagree. The small group's dramas and rituals *are* a type of institution. Nevertheless, it is surely the case that the small group exhibits none of the institutions generally associated with political democracy, such as regular elections, constitutional guarantees, formal legal procedures, and all the rest. Such institutions, especially when they become part of the political culture, may act to buffer the oscillations of the grouplike entity we call the nation-state. Regular elections, constitutional protection of individual rights, congressional oversight and appropriation, a supreme court: all these and more may act to deidealize the leader, while protecting the individual from the regressive pull of the deindividuating group. So may the existence of a civil society. In chapter 1 I argued that constitutional liberalism plus strong (interpretive) leadership is the political implication of group psychology. This is the constitutional liberalism part: institutions and practices that dampen the group's oscillations along both axes, protecting individuals and limiting leaders.

Institutions and practices are, however, no alternative to leadership. Instead, they make leadership by interpretation possible, holding the group, containing its members' terror so that it can hear its leaders' interpretations. Coherent institutions, culture, and society allow the group to listen to a Pericles or a Churchill rather than just to demagogues like Milosevic. Institutions, culture, and society are a type of interpretation and hence a type of holding. For example, the Bill of Rights says that individuals count; the group is not everything. But institutions, particularly, are not a dynamic interpretation. They do not interpret what is going on at a particular moment: the drama that is being acted out, the roles being played, the fears being defended against. They are a type of constant background interpretation and in this sense help to keep the group within the central square, so that it can hear the dynamic (that is, about group process) interpretations of leaders. One may think of the central square as the arena in which interpretations can be heard and used. Whether the institutions that help keep the group within this square need be democratic ones is unclear to me. Probably not. But they must (almost by definition I would say) respect and protect individuals, not just the group, while setting limits on leaders. This is the point of the central square and the point of democracy as well.

While institutions are important, I have chosen not to emphasize them in the chapters that follow, and an explanation is in order. The tradition of state-of-nature–social-contract theorizing in which I am writing is not about institutions. It is about defining the needs and relationships of those who will subsequently establish institutions. This tradition is, in other words, a founding exercise, an outline of what the necessary institutions are to do, given humans as they are, not an outline of the institutions themselves. The social contract, as Gordon Schochet points out, was always more concerned with how people enter into relationships than an institutional characterization of the relationships themselves.[17] How people enter into these relationships will, of course, depend upon their needs and desires, including those they may be quite unaware of. I seek to characterize these needs and desires, so as to characterize the task of political institutions more clearly, as well as to set their limits. Concluding with a further discussion of constitutional liberalism plus strong leadership, chapter 6 returns to the institutional implications of group psychology. Institutions can't be ignored, but they are not the sine qua non of the social-contract tradition in which I write. Group relations are.

Even in the unlikely event that the reader should agree with the above, he or she might still object that the lessons of the Tavistock group don't apply to political entities. Tavistock groups lack formal leadership, whereas political entities are virtually defined by elaborate hierarchies of leadership. Such an objection would not be valid. Tavistock groups are not really leaderless at all. They just have a style of leadership that shows how tough it is for people to get in touch with the reality of leaders, which means to replace fantastic relations with leaders by real ones. Things are no different in the world of politics, as studies of voters' attitudes toward the American presidency reveal. Consider, for example, political scientists' studies of "policy projection" (even political scientists sometimes get the *mot juste*), in which

17. Gordon Schochet, *Patriarchalism in Political Thought* (Oxford: Basil Blackwell, 1975), pp. 81–82.

voters attribute good policies to candidates with "high net affect" (ones they like), whether or not the candidate actually holds these policies.[18] Conversely, political leaders are frequently missing, just like that Tavistock group leader: unavailable at the time for the purposes of the group. Often this is because the group has unrealistic expectations. Particularly in the regressed group, a real leader may be ready and willing but unable to lead because the group cannot acknowledge his existence. In this case the leader is missing not because he is absent but because the group is too regressed to find him.

Frequently, however, leaders fail. They can't be found because they are not there. Leaders fail out of fear, boredom, and depressive anxiety, the fear that they are not good enough to do the job. So leaders run off to meetings, travel to other countries, make war, and all the rest, to avoid the work of the group. George Bush was accused of this more than once, particularly regarding his preference for foreign policy. Men of the year, *Time* magazine called Bush several years ago, capturing perfectly the nation's schizoid perception of its leader. That *Time*'s account of Bush's neglect of domestic policy in favor of foreign triumphs had a basis in reality does not make this perception less schizoid. It just makes it more poignant and difficult to integrate.

Like the former president, most leaders, from corporate executives to congressmen, are missing leaders at least part of the time, unwilling or unable to connect with the needs of their followers. The Tavistock group is not unique in this regard. It simply brings this absence from the background into the foreground, rendering it problematic, something to be discussed and learned from. Indeed, political theory is itself a type of missing leader. Unlike the Tavistock leader, however, political theory has been unwilling or unable to address the importance of leadership in political life, so the issue goes unremarked. If we acknowledge how much every group needs leaders, it is evidently feared, democratic self-government will be seen as a charade and fascism as a legitimate political expression. It's not true. On the contrary, it is by ignoring the importance of leadership that democracy is weakened and authoritarian politics made more likely. Not the leader, but the group, is the real enemy of the individual. This is most apparent in Rousseau's political theory, but it is true of much contemporary political theory as well.

18. D. R. Kinder and S. T. Fiske, "Presidents in the Public Mind," in *Political Psychology,* ed. M. Hermann (San Francisco: Jossey-Bass, 1986), 193–218, p. 210.

4 ❋ *Groups Are the State of Nature*

The thesis of this chapter is that Samuel Pufendorf, Thomas Hobbes, John Locke, and Jean-Jacques Rousseau, traditionally seen as theorists of the contracting individual, are group theorists manqué. The term "theorists of the contracting individual" refers to the individualism generally seen as central to state-of-nature theory. The state of nature is supposedly an account of the relationship of autonomous individuals, who may or may not be innately social, coming together to sign the social contract, so that they might live more commodiously than before. My argument is not that Pufendorf and the rest are not telling this story, for clearly they are. My argument is that it is fruitful to view the story that they tell as rhetoric, an attempt to persuade man (and perhaps the author himself) that he is not the group animal that he is.

This approach requires that I read between the lines, finding in what appear to be claims about individuals in the state of nature claims about the group. It also requires that attention be paid to tropes, even when the state-of-nature theorists do not always seem to understand their language as figurative, as with Hobbes's science of man and motion. Aggressive reinterpretation, reading against the grain, deconstructing the individualism of the state of nature: these descriptions might well be applied to my project. Yet mine is not such an aggressive reinterpretation as all that. Each theorist recognizes man's fundamentally social character, his propensity to live in groups—that he is a zoon politikon in Aristotle's famous phrase—even if each does not build this into his state of nature but rather into the account of civil society that follows. It will require work, but no great imaginative leaps, to find in each of these theorists an account of group psychology: of man as a group animal at war with his own groupishness.

All, with the exception of Rousseau, see man as being at war with his own group in the state of nature. Rather than attributing this to man's conflict over his own groupishness, as I do, each attributes it to his inadequate socialization. The social contract is the instrument of man's socialization to group life. I, on the other hand, stress the continuity between the state of nature and life under the social contract. The inspiration for my approach comes from David Johnston's *The Rhetoric of Leviathan*, which suggests that Hobbes never truly believed the improbable proposition that man was an organic machine who feared death most of all. Hobbes believed that if the recently literate bourgeois public could be convinced of this fact, they might be governed more easily, as they could be threatened with greater precision and effect.

Seen from this perspective, it is not the deductive integrity of Hobbes's science of man and motion that is so important, but the function of science as image, metaphor, and rhetoric.[1] To be sure, Johnston does not argue that Hobbes is really a group theorist seeking to convince members that they are individuals who fear their own deaths most of all. This is my version. The connection between Johnston's thesis and my own is looser, based on the insight that state-of-nature theory is best seen not merely as myth but as rhetoric. What I add is a thesis regarding the aim of state-of-nature rhetoric. That it is designed to convince those who read it of the incredible proposition that man is first of all a rational, self-interested, utility-maximizing individual, not the group animal that millennia of history have shown him to be: one ready to kill, and perhaps even more ready to die, for the honor and glory of his group, its leaders, ideals, and idols. Though each of the four theorists conceptualizes the state of nature differently, each seeks to convince the reader that he is the autonomous individual the theorist desperately wishes he were but fears that he is not. It would have been better had the state-of-nature theorists sought to design a social contract that would have helped citizens truly become more autonomous and free rather than convince them that they already are. It's this that makes the social contract ideology.

Pufendorf and the Cynicism of Political Theory

The frontispiece of the first German translation (1681) of Pufendorf's *De officio* depicts a ruler sitting on a throne. On his lap is a book titled *Jus Nat-*

---

1. David Johnston, *The Rhetoric of Leviathan: Thomas Hobbes and the Politics of Cultural Transformation* (Princeton, N.J.: Princeton University Press, 1986), pp. 12–13, 85, 89.

urale, while a man who seems to be the ruler's philosopher and servant points toward a picture of a naked man crawling in the grass eating fruit. Here is the real state of nature, that depicted in the entire frontispiece, not just the naked man in the grass but the hierarchy of ruler, philosopher-servant, and naked, vulnerable group member. Already the state of nature is a political institution and hence a hierarchical one. If this is so, what are we to make of the picture within a picture of the naked man eating fruit, an image that becomes more powerful still in *On the Natural State of Men,* in which Pufendorf writes of man's natural state as one of weakness and abandonment, without any human support. "If we picture," he says, natural man with "the weakness of newborn infants, it seems that the first humans must surely have perished miserably had not some brute animal miraculously offered them its breasts. . . . (This cohabitation with brute beasts would have given the nursling a considerable share of their wild disposition.)"[2]

Isolation, abandonment, weakness, rescue by some brute animal, but at the price of his brutalization—this is the fate of man in the state of nature. The milk of animal kindness becomes the source of animal-like conduct in man. Similarly, survival in the group takes its toll on the individual and his humanity. Man becomes the group animal he is even as nursling, in order to survive. Let us combine the image Pufendorf asks us to envisage with the picture on the frontispiece, a picture whose image recurs in *On the Natural State of Men* (pp. 113–117). In this combined image the newborn segues into the naked man. But don't forget, the picture of the naked man is a picture within a picture, which contains an image of a king holding the Jus Naturale. Natural law, this image suggests, has the task of rendering man's brutalization by the group (he imbibes its brutishness like mother's milk) as somehow fine and noble. This seems to be the teaching of the philosopher-servant, pointing to natural man and so mediating between leader and group, constructing an ideology that represents man's brutalization at the hands of the group as though it were the culmination of his individuality in society. This is what philosopher-servants do. Not only does this fit Pufendorf's project, it fits those of the other three state-of-nature theorists as well. Not only does each fail to acknowledge the implications of man's groupishness, but each mistakes a regressed expression of his groupishness, the schizoid compromise, for individuality.

2. Samuel Pufendorf, *Samuel Pufendorf's On the Natural State of Men,* trans. and intro. by Michael Seidler (Lewiston, N.Y.: Samuel Mellen Press, 1990), pp. 112–113. In this and subsequent chapters, the second and following page references to the primary work under discussion—in this case Pufendorf's *On the Natural State of Men*—will be given in parentheses in the text unless this might cause confusion.

Natural Law and the State of Nature

Imbecillitas and *indigentia* are the terms used by Hugo Grotius (1583–1645), the founder of modern natural law theory, to characterize human weakness and need. Since Pufendorf is so deeply influenced by Grotius, the first great secularizer of natural law, it will pay to consider briefly Grotius's account. Grotius's reliance on reason to know this law should not lead us to overlook what might be called the material sentiments, social realities humans must acknowledge if they are to live as decently as possible. Or, as Grotius puts it, "The law of nature . . . has the reinforcement of expediency; for the author of nature willed that as individuals we should be weak, and should lack many things needed in order to live properly, to the end that we might be more constrained and cultivate the social life."[3]

Pufendorf grants even more weight to expediency than Grotius, arguing that it is expedience alone that makes man social and civilized. For this reason it is even more important for Pufendorf than for Grotius that man be convinced of his imbecillitas and indigentia. Usually located between Hobbes, who it is said fails to recognize the social nature of man, and Grotius, who it is often said makes human nature too spontaneously social, Pufendorf seems to carve out a middle ground, founding society on the collective recognition of weakness and need as an alternative to submission to a leviathan. It doesn't work. Weakness and need begin in the family and in this regard are the foundation of society. But they are only the foundation. By themselves weakness and need provide no basis for a mature and creative group. This does not deny that group members are weak and needy, for they are. But a mature and creative group can only be built upon confrontation with weakness and need, not their exploitation for the purposes of making men and women sociable. Furthermore, this confrontation must include the recognition that individuals are not all weakness and need but possess strengths as well, which, if respected, may contribute to the life of the group. Otherwise these strengths will be split off and driven underground, unavailable to individual or group.

A true natural state never existed, says Pufendorf. While one can readily imagine the human race so dispersed that each is his own master, free from the authority of another, an act of imagination this must remain. In reality families came first, "wherein God has commanded the wife to be subject to her husband . . . their offspring were under the father's authority. And . . . those special bonds can never be removed from the human race as a

3. Hugo Grotius, *De jure belli,* par. 15; quoted in Seidler's introduction to Pufendorf's *On the Natural State of Men,* pp. 17–18.

whole." It is almost immediately after making this statement that Pufendorf goes on to write of the traditional state of nature in which "those living in it are subject to no one on this earth and acknowledge no ruler over themselves besides God Almighty" (pp. 118–119). In short, he drops his consideration of families and goes on to write of the state of nature in terms he previously suggested were unrealistic, as they fail to take the bonds of family into account. This move is not unique to Pufendorf. Hobbes, Locke, and Rousseau do the same. Which makes it even more important to figure out what is going on.

Pufendorf makes a distinction between three states of nature: (1) a pre-cultural state of absolute need (the abandoned infant nursed by beasts); (2) a pre-civil state of absolute freedom (the "subject to no one on this earth" version); (3) really existing natural states (a series of loosely linked patriarchal families).[4] True enough, but not only are these accounts incompatible, they form no plausible historical sequence: if families come first, as Pufendorf says they do, then states 1 and 2 never existed and never could exist. To this it might be replied that these states of nature are only a fiction, an act of imagination; it matters not whether they exist. True enough, but then one must at least ask what purpose these fictions serve, which is another way of asking what purpose the picture within a picture of the naked man crawling in the grass eating fruit serves. It serves to separate the reader from the rest of the scene, which already contains the ruler and his advisor and servant, which is just another way of saying that it already contains the family and the authority relationships embodied in it.

The state of nature as a state of autonomous individuality becomes strictly and merely an ideology, serving to deny that it is the small group, originally the family, and the authority relationships rooted in it, relationships of love, hate, and fear, that is the real state of nature. In other words, it makes "civic submission," as Pufendorf calls it, a rational choice, not an act of fear or desire. Not the Tavistock group but the family, in which every drama and dynamic observed in the Tavistock group are first played out, is the original state of nature. Pufendorf, like the other state-of-nature theorists, knows this. Though he never heard of Tavistock, he knows the fundamental truth it reveals: the origins of family relationships in the dependent love and fierce hate the child feels for its parents and the parents for the child. He knows this because he knows what happens in families. And like the other state-of-nature theorists, he organizes his account to deny it—or rather, to deny its relevance to politics. This is the norm among political theorists, then and now, connecting Pufendorf with Judith Shklar, whose similar attempt is considered in chapter 6.

4. Seidler, Introduction, p. 51; examples are my own.

Carving out a position between Grotius and Hobbes, Pufendorf argues that sociality is like language, a historical product of collective human development, arising out of individuals' self-interested dealings with others "in a context of relative scarcity, weakness, and consequent insecurity."[5] This position is reflected in Pufendorf's view of natural law, a position that owes much to Grotius, particularly its assumption that human self-interest, weakness, and sociality combine to yield the following supreme principle of natural law, as stated in *De jure naturae*: "Even man, so far as in him lies, should cultivate and preserve toward others a sociable attitude, which is peaceful and agreeable at all times to the nature and end of the human race" (II. 3. 15). From this principle of sociability all other human obligations and rights are derived, as Pufendorf goes on to derive from it family, civil, national, and international roles and responsibilities.

The principle of sociality embodied in natural law is, Pufendorf states, an alternative to civic submission, which is not to say that Pufendorf holds that civil society is unnecessary, but only that it is not so urgently required as to make any conceivable order superior to the state of nature. Superior is that civil order that promotes commercial relations, whose complexity makes man insufficient in the first place.[6] In this regard Pufendorf comes closer to Locke than to Hobbes. While all three are philosophers of the early bourgeois era, only Pufendorf and Locke see the mutual need and dependence inherent in complex economic relations as sufficient to hold society together in the absence of an absolute ruler. Nor is this simply a statement about the attractions of riches. It implies a genuine belief in the inherently sociable character of men and women.

The problem is that Pufendorf's sociability is not really an alternative to submission but a version of it. The sociability upon which Pufendorf draws emerges out of neither a genuine fondness for and interest in others nor a genuine pleasure in fostering their interests as they foster mine, the pleasure that stems from cooperating in a challenging activity. It does not emerge from a belief that the group to which I belong might recognize my individuality and enhance my creativity as I contribute to the life of the group. Rather, Pufendorf's sociability emerges from scarcity, weakness, and insecurity: the sense that I am powerless in the world, so it is best not to anger or estrange those who might help me in my desperate need.

In fact, the situation is really worse than this. Not merely the desperate need of the infant cast out to be suckled by beasts, but the fact that "there is in humans an innate wickedness that enjoys harming others as

5. Ibid., p. 50.
6. Ibid., pp. 50–51.

much as possible, and that can never be entirely extirpated," is the ground of insecurity and hence the impetus to sociability (p. 129). We should, in other words, be sociable to others lest they harm us, or we them. This is the "sociability" I practice when, driving in some drug-plagued areas of Washington, D.C., I refrain from honking at cars that block traffic for purposes of conducting a commercial transaction with someone on a street corner. I am sociable because I do not want to get shot by a drug dealer. It works, so far, but it is hardly an ideal solution, containing within it the seeds of its own destruction. Behind the submission of sociability lie fear and rage. It is this rage that is enacted in the little dramas of the group. Rage at other group members who demand so much self-sacrifice to belong, just to survive, redirected at the leader who fails to protect members from this bargain struck out of weakness. Here too is why members withhold the most real and creative parts of themselves from the group, so as to remain in an unconscious fantasy relationship of dependent love with the leader and so reduce their imbecillitas and indigentia in this fantastic way.

It is an unstable solution. Even were it stable, it would be undesirable, as it freezes the group members into roles and obligations that are developmentally immature, which means based upon splits in the self, splits that leave the best parts of the self outside the group. It should be the task of state-of-nature theory to recognize this reality, confront it, and so chart a course that begins but does not end here. It should not be the task of political theory to valorize developmental immaturity, transforming it into natural law. When it does so, political theory becomes enormously cynical, just what one sees in Pufendorf's account, even as he takes pains to put the best face on it.

A consideration of the natural state of individuals and its misery is very useful for making citizens love and devote themselves completely to the civil state's preservation. . . . Indeed, one who has reflected thoroughly upon this natural state will bear more patiently the unreasonable inconveniences that he sometimes experiences at the hands of rulers. . . . Moreover, a judicious citizen will by no means attribute these inconveniences to the character of the civil state . . . rather, he will acknowledge the general imperfection of human affairs. (Pp. 134–135)

Cynicism does not stem from harsh realities realistically confronted but from the failure to fully confront the implications of what one knows about reality. Pufendorf is cynical.

Not only that, but his solution doesn't work. A judicious citizen may well go along with the state, he may bear patiently its unreasonable inconveniences, he may even love and devote himself to the state, but only in the most superficial manner, holding back just those parts of himself that could contribute to the creativity, energy, and renewal of the state. Which is why, in the end, it matters not to Pufendorf how well or how poorly the state is governed, nor by whom. The character of the regime is unimportant, except that it not be totally corrupt. What matters is that neither single citizens nor groups of citizens become powerful enough to "become an enemy of the current order—one all the more dangerous because he has in a sense already been received within the walls" (p. 135). A more cynical conclusion is hard to imagine: the current order at almost any price.

It is important in reading political theory not to pass over such cynicism too quickly, simply because it is so familiar and so often mistaken for realism. In such familiar cynicism is reflected the deepest despair about group life, the hopelessness that stems from the belief that groups are incapable of development and growth. Cynicism holds that things can't get better. Realism stresses the hard work required to make things even a little bit better, but better they can be if we confront the reality of human nature in groups. Against the conclusion that Pufendorf is merely cynical it might be argued that he was born in the middle of the brutal Thirty Years' War (1618–1648), during which whole cities disappeared at the hands of mercenary soldiers. "Even the Second World War, in sheer depopulation, was not as devastating for Germany as was the Thirty Years' War."[7] In the face of this, almost any order at almost any price seems a good bargain. True enough, but this is not my point. My point is that Pufendorf, like the other state-of-nature theorists, comes at this problem, the problem of constructing a decent civilization, from the wrong direction. Man is not first of all an independent and autonomous creature who must be socialized so as not to ravish his fellows. He is first of all a group member, like a mercenary soldier, who must be taught to be an individual within the group, which means not to leave important parts of himself outside the group, including the part that accepts individual responsibility. Only then is there a chance that the group might come to act as humanely as its members are capable of acting at their best.

While some mercenaries are brutal toward wives, children, and fellows as well, it is not uncommon (it is almost a cliché) for the soldier to be kind, loving, and self-sacrificing toward some while brutal toward others. Robert Jay Lifton's *The Nazi Doctors* concerns an extreme version of this phenomenon, in which a doctor might be caring and loving to his family and patients while sadistically brutalizing Jews. Lifton uses the concept of doubling, a

7. R. R. Palmer and Joel Coulton, *A History of the Modern World,* 2d ed. (New York: Knopf, 1962), pp. 130–131, quoted by Seidler, Introduction, p. 4.

version of splitting, to explain this phenomenon.[8] I am making a similar argument. To the degree that individuals are encouraged, as part of a schizoid compromise, to leave large parts of themselves outside the group, groups will find it easier to commit evil, as the evil that is within us all is enacted in the group, one more little drama, uncontained by the "luggage" that is the self. A social order based upon imbecillitas and indigentia invites this, as it discourages the development of a self who might take responsibility for the role it is called upon to play in the group.

Hobbes and the Sacrificial Leader

It is unusual, but not unprecedented, to treat Hobbes as a group theorist. Generally he is regarded as the single most individualistic social theorist, one who reduces all social thought to the aims and motions of individual members. Gregory Kavka argues in *Hobbesian Moral and Political Theory* that Hobbes holds to the following six premises about individual human nature:

1. *Egoism*. Individuals are primarily concerned with their own well-being and act accordingly.

2. *Death aversion*. Individuals are strongly averse to their own death and act accordingly.

3. *Concern for reputation*. Individuals care about their reputations, about what others think of them, and act accordingly.

4. *Forward-lookingness*. Individuals care about their future, as well as present, well-being and act accordingly.

5. *Conflicting desires*. Satisfaction of one person's desires often interferes with or precludes satisfaction of another person's.

6. *Rough equality*. People are fairly equal in their intellectual and bodily powers. They are equal enough, in any case, that each is vulnerable to death at the hands of others.[9]

While it might be argued that the last two assumptions are social, rather than individual, Kavka views these assumptions in an individualistic fashion: as something individuals know about the world they live in that requires them to be more competitive, albeit more careful too. Kavka finds much to agree with in Hobbes's account. In *The Political Theory of Possessive Individualism*, C. B. Macpherson finds far less to agree with, arguing that

8. Robert Jay Lifton, *The Nazi Doctors: Medical Killing and the Psychology of Genocide* (New York: Basic Books, 1986), pp. 418–429.

9. Gregory S. Kavka, *Hobbesian Moral and Political Theory* (Princeton, N.J.: Princeton University Press, 1986), pp. 33–34.

Hobbes quite overlooks the socially cohesive forces of the market and social class. A leviathan was never necessary to contain the centrifugal forces released by the breakup of feudalism; the self-interest of property owners was enough.[10] Both, however, agree with Lawrence Berns that Hobbes is the theorist of liberal individualism par excellence.[11]

Not all see Hobbes in this fashion. In "Liberal Individualism Reconsidered," Deborah Baumgold argues that neither Hobbes's nominalism (only individual entities are real) nor his resolutive-compositive method, which takes everything apart into the motions of its individual parts, implies that Hobbes's unit of analysis is the abstract individual. I made a similar argument in chapter 1. Neither methodological individualism nor nominalism implies or requires that the individual in isolation be the unit of analysis. Methodological individualism and liberal individualism have nothing to do with each other. Baumgold goes on to argue that Hobbes is first of all a role theorist, treating the obligation to fight for one's country, for example, as an obligation adhering to a particular role, not an individual.[12] Such a focus on roles *is* group theory, the individual being understood in terms of his role in relationship to others in the group and the obligations that stem from it. Contrast Berns's observation that Hobbes is the first to define the state as an artificial man with Hobbes's characterization of man as a machine. "For what is the *Heart,* but a *Spring;* and the *Nerves,* but so many *Strings;* and the *Joynts,* but so many *Wheeles,* giving motion to the whole Body."[13] It is as though the state is more organic and more human than its members, which is why, perhaps, Hobbes writes of the sovereign as the soul of the state, while taking great pains to argue that the actual human soul is just one more body like any other, an ordinary corporal substance (pp. 81, 689). In fact, for every mechanical image of the parts of man, such as spring or string, Hobbes posits a corresponding human role in the state. The sovereign is the soul, "the *magistrates* and other *Officers* of Judicature and Execution, artificiall *Joynts,*" and so forth (pp. 81–82). It is as though the members (itself an organic trope: the term "group member" was originally a metaphor invoking the flesh of the body, from the Latin

10. C. B. Macpherson, *The Political Theory of Possessive Individualism: Hobbes to Locke* (Oxford: Oxford University Press, 1962), pp. 95–100.

11. Laurence Berns, "Thomas Hobbes," in *History of Political Philosophy,* 2d ed., ed. Leo Strauss and Joseph Cropsey (Chicago: Rand McNally, 1972), 370–395, p. 375.

12. Deborah Baumgold, "Liberal Individualism Reconsidered," in *Liberals on Liberalism,* ed. Alfonso J. Damico (Totowa, N.J.: Rowman and Littlefield, 1986), 151–166, pp. 152–154.

13. Thomas Hobbes, *Leviathan,* ed. C. B. Macpherson (Harmondsworth, England: Penguin Books, 1968), p. 81. Page references in the text are to this edition.

membrum[14]) of the commonwealth become real and human, not just machines, only in the performance of their civic roles and obligations, an observation that corresponds with Baumgold's argument that Hobbes is a theorist not of individuals but of social roles. Man in relation to others in the group is the fundamental unit of analysis, even when Hobbes seems to be writing about individual man as an object of scientific theory. Not only that, but man for Hobbes seems hardly human, the group seeming more organic and whole than its individual members, who are compared to things.

While it makes intuitive sense to call that portion of *Leviathan* that describes civil society under the sovereign a type of group theory, it might be asked how I can claim that Hobbes's state of nature is an account of the group. The simplest answer is also the best. Not only did Hobbes's state of nature never exist, but Hobbes never suggests it did. It is metaphor, or rhetoric, as Johnston points out, designed to convince a recently enlarged literate public of some basic principles of human nature: principles that, should the public come to believe them, would make social peace more probable, as they are principles that make men especially susceptible to coercion, ultimately the fear of their own violent death. In fact, these are most unlikely principles, as Johnston suggests. As if men had not willingly died by the millions throughout history for their leader, their group, or their ideology. Recognizing that the state of nature is a trope, it will be fruitful to reinterpret its figurative language. Though Hobbes inveighs against metaphor and "Poesy" throughout *Leviathan,* the book is filled with it. Even the title is metaphor, drawn from the book of Job (41:1).

The State of Nature is the Regressed Group

What Hobbes calls the state of nature is fruitfully seen as an account of the regressed group in the autistic-contiguous position, which can neither acknowledge nor confront its leader. Nor can the group acknowledge its own existence qua group. The group seems like a bunch of autonomous individuals, but only because the members are in such a state of dedifferentiation that all they can know of the other is that he is other, his otherness constituting the threat that dedifferentiation defends against. Not as autonomy but as isolation is how individuality is experienced in the regressed group, as members avoid knowing each other as individuals so as to more readily fuse with the group while denying that this is what they are doing.

14. According to the *Oxford English Dictionary,* the term was first used metaphorically in 1375 to refer to all those members of the Body of Christ. The term soon came to refer to the member of a jury or a community.

Whether the regressed group proves a productive interpretation of the state of nature will not, in the end, depend upon how close it comes to Hobbes's presumed intent but upon how well it reveals new and interesting aspects of life in the state of nature, aspects not revealed by other readings. One advantage of my approach is that it preserves and emphasizes the continuity between the state of nature and civil society that so many commentators have felt to be important. The principles that impel man in the state of nature, such as the six listed by Kavka, are exactly the same principles that are manipulated by the sovereign to achieve civil peace. Civil society under the sovereign moves the group from a regressed to an undeveloped stage, but in such a way as to guarantee that further development is impossible. In other words, state of nature and civil society remain too continuous, too similar, a result determined by the character of Hobbes's solution.

In the state of nature men seek ever more power, says Hobbes. "In the first place, I put for a generall inclination of all mankind, a perpetuall and restlesse desire of Power after power, that ceaseth only in Death" (p. 161). Not only this, but in the end everything is measured in terms of power: the worth of a man is measured by his power, as are his dignity and honor (pp. 150–160). These are, it should be noted, social statuses that make sense only within the group. Behind the quest for power, says Hobbes, lie three motives: competition, diffidence, and glory. The first leads men to make themselves masters over other persons; the second leads men to defend themselves against such intrusions; and the third leads men to do almost anything to protect their reputations (p. 185).

What might this look like in the small group? It looks like the fear of every member that the group will fail to recognize his or her individuality; that the group will require the member to abandon himself to the group in order to survive, a demand so terrifying because it appeals to an aspect of the member's psyche that wants to do just this. The restless search for ever more power that Hobbes rightly identifies is a search for protection from the group's assault on the member's individuality. Only power and more power can protect against the intrusive, leveling forces in the group and in the group member himself.

This interpretation is supported by three considerations. While Hobbes stresses the relative equality of all men in the state of nature that is the group, he does not mean that men actually are roughly equal in wit, wisdom, and the like. He means that out of envy and jealousy each underestimates the other, so that in the end all are reduced to the same low level. An active leveling process is at work, which is precisely what occurs in the group and is an important dimension of what it means for the group to deny the individuality of its members. Role suction, enforced by interpersonal pressure that recognizes only behavior in conformity with role and backed up by the ultimate sanction of sacrifice, is the mechanism the group employs in the service of deindividuation. Against these pressures more wit and wisdom will not suffice. Only power holds out the possibility of protecting the member's individuality, which is precisely what Hobbes says when he reduces almost every virtue, such as eloquence, dignity, judgment, wisdom, and wit to power: the power to persuade, to compel respect, to oblige others to "harken to a man's counsell," and the power to prevent others from sleeping or talking while one is speaking (pp. 150–153). Which is, of course, just how groups force members into roles, members becoming carelessly inattentive or overly talkative when an individual member fails to play his part. Against this power only more power suffices.

Second, it is widely recognized that the desire for power is at base a desire for recognition. This is the point of Hegel's dialectic of mutual recognition, in which power is sought not for its own sake but to compel recognition that would not otherwise be forthcoming. Leo Strauss argues that the political philosophy of Hobbes is the foundation of Hegel's dialectic, in which the struggle to be recognized as an individual gets played out as a life-and-death struggle within society, each member withholding recognition of the rest unless he himself is recognized, a contest in which all must lose in the end. Hans J. Morgenthau makes a related point in "Love and Power," arguing that the quest for power is at base a misguided quest to be loved, which means to be recognized and cherished for oneself.[15]

The third reason why this account of the state of nature as a primitive group is plausible is that while commentators on Hobbes generally emphasize the fear of violent death that motivates men, Hobbes fully appreciates the complexity of human motivation. Honor, glory, dignity, respect, and a good reputation get far more attention than the fear of death as prime motives of human action. Not only this, but in *Leviathan* and other works Hobbes grants envy and honor a status comparable with fear as motivators of human action. Thus, "many a man had rather die," says Hobbes, than let his humiliation at the hands of another go unavenged.[16] If we assume (and it is no great psychological leap) that at the core of the experience of humil-

15. Leo Strauss, *The Political Philosophy of Hobbes*, trans. Elsa Sinclair (Chicago: University of Chicago Press, Midway Reprint, 1984), p. 57. Hans J. Morgenthau, "Love and Power," in *The Restoration of American Politics* (Chicago: University of Chicago Press, 1962), pp. 7–14. Originally published in *Commentary*, March 1962.

16. Hobbes, Introduction to his translation of Thucydides' *History*, in *English Works of Thomas Hobbes*, ed. William Molesworth (London: Bohn, 1840), vol. 8, p. xxviii. Idem, *Leviathan*, p. 150.

iation is a sense that one's individuality is neither recognized nor respected, then it makes perfect sense to argue that the power sought in the group is the power to protect one's individuality, an individuality that has its basis in physical existence but is hardly reducible to mere life. Hobbes compares the individual who does not fit in with a building stone "that cannot be easily made plain, and thereby hindereth the building," so that "the builders cast [it] away as unprofitable" (p. 209). It is the power to remain in the group without being "made plain" that members most desire.

When every member of the group sees himself as involved in a virtual life-and-death struggle for his individuality, the group itself becomes a terribly dangerous place. Here is the origin of the fear that so dominates the group, the fear that is so palpable in the first minutes of the group but which never disappears, each member asking himself, "Can I survive this group whole, or will it demand my individuality as the price of membership and survival?" Against this interpretation it might be argued that while it describes the small Tavistock group, it does not describe Hobbes's state of nature, which is, after all, a state of individual conflict: the war of every individual against every other individual, not group warfare. Perhaps; but once again we must not be too quick to assume that the popular impression of Hobbes conveys the whole story. Hobbes actually pays considerable attention to the family, so much so that Gordon Schochet argues that it is a mistake to see the state of nature as a state of free individuals. Rather, it is "composed of familial social units," which remove the individual from the state of nature, placing him from the very beginning under patriarchal authority. Filmer, that great defender of patriarchal authority, did not hesitate to turn this aspect of Hobbes's system against Hobbes's own conclusions.[17] Not the war of every individual against every other but the war of every family against every other (that is, tribal warfare) is arguably Hobbes's original vision. As with Pufendorf and Locke, the state of nature is a way of denying the family, the original small group.

Carole Pateman agrees that Hobbes puts the family first, going on to assert that the way he does so makes him a matriarchalist, not a patriarchalist, as Hobbes makes the mother's right over the infant the original right. In the state of nature there are no laws of matrimony that would give the father dominion over his children. Which does not mean that the children are born free but that "every woman that bears children, becomes both a *mother* and a *lord*." At birth the infant is in the mother's absolute power. As a result, if she decides not to expose the infant, there is an implicit con-

17. Sir Robert Filmer, "Observations on Mr. Hobbes's *Leviathan:* or his Artificial Man—a Commonwealth" (1652), in *Patriarcha and Other Political Works,* ed. Peter Laslett (Oxford: Oxford University Press, 1949).

tract between them that "he become not her enemy."[18] This is, of course, just one more case where Hobbes identifies enforced submission with voluntary agreement, conquest with consent.

But is Hobbes really a matriarchalist? Perhaps no more than he is really a patriarchalist, but no less either. My point is not that he was either, but that his state of nature is filled with families. Which means filled with groups and their primitive bargains, such as don't expose me and I won't attack you, a bargain struck in more than one Tavistock group as well. Indeed, this is probably the fundamental bargain in groups, the way in which group members use the threat of sacrifice to contain their own aggression. The move out of the state of nature into civil society does not change the terms of this bargain. It simply rationalizes it, putting the power to sacrifice a member in the hands of the leader, the sovereign. Yet, there is an irony to this transfer of power. Through it Hobbes seems to be setting up the mighty sovereign to become the ultimate sacrificial leader.

The Designated Individual

How to get out of the state of nature, in which being an individual seems to require the destruction of every other individual in the group, by either absorption or obliteration? Hobbes's answer is to appoint a designated individual, so to speak: the sovereign, who will have all the attributes associated with individuality in the small group. In particular (for this is how individuality is defined in regressed and undeveloped groups), the sovereign has the power to force others to recognize and succumb to his will and so make their wills his own. "To the end he may use the strength and means of them all, as he shall think expedient" (p. 228). Against this interpretation it might be argued that I am confusing power with individuality, the latter a much more subtle concept than Hobbes intends. Perhaps, but it should be noted that Hobbes takes great pains to characterize the psychology behind the transfer of power to the sovereign as a transfer of individuality. The sovereign, he argues, is not really an alien power at all, but an extension of the selves of the subjects who grant him his power. "But by this institution of a Common-wealth, every particular man is Author of all the Soveraigne doth; and consequently he that complaineth of injury from his Soveraigne, complaineth of that whereof he himself is Author; and therefore ought not to accuse any man but himself; nor himselfe of injury; because to do injury to one's self, is impossible" (p. 232).

18. Hobbes, *Philosophical Rudiments Concerning Government and Society* (English version of *De Cive*), in *English Works of Thomas Hobbes,* ed. Molesworth, 2:116; quoted in Carole Pateman, *The Sexual Contract* (Stanford, Calif.: Stanford University Press, 1988), p. 44.

In order to share his power, the individual identifies totally with the leader, at least in one part of himself, the part that is so scared of the group that it becomes one with its leader. This is the schizoid compromise, for we shall shortly see that this identification with the leader does not translate into loyalty to him. Nevertheless, it represents a step forward in group development, from the regressed group, which can hardly acknowledge the idea of a leader (as to do so requires recognition that he is an individual separate from the group), to the undeveloped group, which grossly identifies with the leader, above all with his power, in little dramas. Unfortunately, the way in which Hobbes takes this step means that no more will be forthcoming.

Over and over Hobbes says that the subject should not complain about the acts of the sovereign, as the sovereign is an extension of the subject. Whatever the sovereign does is tantamount to the subject doing it to himself. "For seeing every Subject is Author of the actions of his Soveraigne; he punisheth another, for the actions committed by himself" (pp. 264–265). The only apparent exception—that if the sovereign orders you to kill yourself you may refuse—is no real exception at all. It is inserted not to protect a realm of individuality from the sovereign (the sovereign is within his rights to demand your death for whatever reason; you are just under no obligation to cooperate by killing yourself [p. 269]) but to preserve the logical structure of the argument: that fear of violent death is the leading motive for choosing a sovereign. Were the citizen required or expected to cooperate in his own violent death, it would make logical mincemeat of Hobbes's science, in which fear of violent death is the first postulate.

By encouraging citizens to identify with the sovereign, so that his will and power become extensions of their own, Hobbes would grant citizens a vicarious individuality, the only type of individuality safe for society, he seems to believe. This requires that citizens be reminded of their subordinate status. It is not enough for the sovereign to be powerful; those around him must be weak and know it. "As in the presence of the Master, the Servants are equall, and without any honour at all; So are the Subjects, in the presence of the Soveraign. And though they shine some more, some less, when they are out of his sight; yet in his presence, they shine no more than the Starres in presence of the Sun" (p. 238). Sheldon Wolin argues that Hobbes encourages the mentality of Fallada's *kleiner Mann*, "the little man who rejoiced when the proud and mighty were humbled . . . who watched without complaint the growing distance between subject and sovereign, resentful only when the sovereign failed to maintain the equality between citizens, and who soothed his own political impotency," by identifying with the power of his leader.[19] Hobbes recognizes that the citizen cannot be persuaded to give up all hope of recapturing his individuality from the group. He can perhaps be persuaded that it is best and safest to experience it vicariously, via identification with the power of the sovereign—if, that is, other individuals are not there to remind him by their very existence of his cynical and desperate bargain.

Here is Hobbes's social contract. Life in groups is a constant and unremitting struggle for individual recognition, which only makes the group more insecure, while doing nothing to foster genuine individuality. There is, Hobbes apparently believes, no solution. Peace, however, can be achieved if everyone agrees to give up his individuality to the group, as long as others do likewise. "I Authorise and give up my Right of Governing my selfe . . . that thou give up thy Right" (p. 227). While Hobbes does not use terms like "individuality," the "Right of Governing my selfe" seems to cover much the same territory, especially since he includes under self-governance freedom of expression, mobility, and intercourse, as well as freedom from humiliating intrusions into one's private life (pp. 262–271). In return for giving up his individuality to the group, the group designates an individual whom it calls sovereign. Members are encouraged to identify with him and so gain some recompense for their lost individuality without disrupting the life of the group with invidious displays of individuality manqué, such as fighting each other for honor and glory or breaking up into tribes of warring individuals (itself an oxymoron) so that the members can at least know who they aren't.

Most of the themes that characterize the Tavistock group are apparent in Hobbes's account. This is not surprising when one considers that the Tavistock approach succeeds not so much in making new discoveries about groups as in elaborating what astute observers of groups have always known. Particularly apparent is the way in which Hobbes's solution encourages—indeed is—the schizoid compromise. The individual is encouraged to abandon himself to the group by offering as reward the opportunity to identify with the power of the leader. The trouble with this compromise is that it guarantees that the individual will withhold the best and most creative parts of himself. This is just what one sees in Hobbes.

Beginning with Hobbes's contemporary James Harrington, a number of commentators have observed that the sovereign is no mighty leviathan but a "mere spitfrog." He is a spitfrog because the power to act creatively as a leader of a group demands not merely that the members stand aside, all

19. Sheldon Wolin, *Politics and Vision: Continuity and Innovation in Western Political Thought* (Boston: Little, Brown, 1960), p. 280.

that Hobbes requires, but that they actively identify with and support the goals of the group, contributing their individuality and creativity to it. As Wolin says, "If sovereign power were effective because it induced withdrawal, how could the sovereign ever hope to join his subjects' wills to his in the pursuit of a common endeavor?"[20] Identifying with the sovereign in one part of themselves, citizens withdraw into themselves and their private lives in another, something Hobbes seems to recognize when he writes about the "silence of the Law," assuming that the sovereign will not wish to rule every aspect of his subjects' lives (p. 271). Such split selves may be tractable and peaceable, but they will contribute little to the group, as members' individuality will itself be divided into pieces and devoted (if it is not destroyed) to private life. Creative individuality and all that goes with it do not stem from passive identification with the power of another but only from active identification with the goals of the group. Nor is it likely to stem from terror, as when Hobbes states that the sovereign "hath the use of so much power and strength conferred on him, that by terror thereof, he is enabled to form the wills of them all."

Terror may overawe the will, but it is unlikely to form it. Or rather, the form that terrified will takes is a split one, in which one part allows itself to be formed, while another withdraws into the formlessness of the self that refuses to recognize all power that stems from outside the self, legitimate and illegitimate alike. Which is why individuality in the group so often takes the form of pure negativity, the "no" of the two-year-old. Hobbes seeks to solve the first and fundamental problem faced by the regressed small group: how to keep the insecurity and rage of its members from destroying it. The way in which Hobbes solves this problem guarantees that the group will never move beyond the stage of schizoid compromise, in which members vicariously share in the individuality of the leader but only to protect a latent and split-off individuality that they dare not offer up to the group. This in turn guarantees that the group will make no further progress.

Yet, perhaps there is something else going on in Hobbes. Perhaps in the end the sovereign is intended by Hobbes to be little more than the sacrificial leader, a spitfrog, ordained to fail because he lacks the active and creative support of the group. Hobbes's assertion that the obligation of the subjects to the sovereign "is understood to last as long, and no longer, than the power lasteth, by which he is able to protect them," supports this interpretation (p. 272). By reducing the question of obligation to the sovereign to pure power and then depriving the sovereign of this power, he seems des-

20. James Harrington, *The Oceana and Other Works of James Harrington*, ed. John Toland, p. 41, quoted in Wolin, *Politics and Vision*, p. 285.

tined to fail. Could this have been the point all along? To save the group from itself by appointing someone who only appears to be an all-powerful leader but is in reality a sacrificial leader, the scapegoat, whom the group allows to fail in order to save itself from civil war? Perhaps; but Hobbes, like the other state-of-nature theorists, fails to address what comes next. At best this is only the beginning of group development, and then only if it is subject to interpretation.

Locke and Leadership

Locke's *First Treatise of Government* (written shortly before 1683 and published in 1698 according to Laslett's dating), his refutation of the Sir Robert Filmer's defense of patriarchy, is not much read anymore. Critical consensus seems to be that Filmer's *Patriarcha* is so flawed and Locke's treatise so devoted to it that the *First Treatise* cannot have lasting value. Such a view is mistaken. Locke's *First Treatise* comes closer to the truth than his *Second*, which posits that men are born free and equal in the state of nature. Locke's *First Treatise* comes closer to the truth because it wrestles with the thesis that government is rooted in the patriarchal family. To be sure, Locke never denies that this is historically the case. His thesis of the state of nature is justification, not history. Nevertheless, there are important truths that Locke might have learned from Filmer: not merely about the historical origins of government but about its psychological origins as well. The family is the original small group, one reason why political life can be explained in terms of the small group. The family is the middle term in the equation, connecting the small group with the politics of nations.

My position is not unique, Peter Laslett arguing that Locke did not learn enough from patriarchalism: "Not enough to understand such institutions as the family, the nation, the community of a neighbourhood, as we think they should be understood. . . . To him patriarchal societies were those 'the concord whereof dependeth on natural lust,' and that was all." In this regard Hobbes and Locke are on exactly the same side. Hobbes is not the opponent but one who shares Locke's goal of rationalizing government so as to release it from its historical roots. "A controversy between Locke and Hobbes would have been within one party only, and could never have given rise to the characteristic political attitude of the modern world."[21] The problem is that this characteristic political attitude of the modern world is too often rooted in denial, beginning with assumptions about individual autonomy in the state

21. Peter Laslett, Introduction to *Two Treatises of Government*, by John Locke (New York: New American Library, 1965), p. 83. Reference to both *Treatises* in the text is by paragraph.

of nature that are not merely historically false but deny the work and development required for individuals to emerge in the group. Individualism is not the beginning but the end of group development, but only rarely, when things go just right.

Puzzling about the *First Treatise* is Locke's engagement with Filmer's literalism. Why, for example, would Locke devote over a hundred pages to refuting Filmer's claim that kings and queens of the present era owe their title to descent from Adam or Noah? To be sure, Locke seems quite correct that even if the descendents of Adam are rightfully kings, how could we know who they are? (Or are we all descendents of Adam and Eve, every man a king?) But who cares? What's the point? The point, one might argue, is that Locke is pursuing a clever argumentative strategy, accepting the literal reading of the Bible practiced by his opponent while debating its implications. Perhaps; but even so the strategy has consequences, not allowing Locke to consider that Filmer's account, while literally false, may be psychologically true. That it is man's relationship to authority, the way in which he fears, hates, and loves it, that sets the stage for almost every aspect of group life, from family to nation. Instead, Locke matches Filmer's literalism, the result being an almost equally literal (and certainly far more misleading) counterclaim: that men are born free, equal, and independent.

In fact, Locke has a great deal to say about patriarchal authority in the *First Treatise,* seeming to regard it not merely as an imposition on freedom and equality but as a source of terror. For Locke, patriarchal authority knows no constraints, no limits, and no concern for its subject, being no more than an expression of "natural lust."[22] Locke criticizes paternal power on the grounds that it is so complete and perfect that it is likely to lead to the selling of children into slavery, the castration of male children, an attitude of ownership that will stop only at the enslavement of the whole world and the practice of fattening up one's children in order to eat them (pars. 217, 182, 205, 218). About this last practice, demonstrating *"Absolute Fatherly Power* in its heighth and perfection," Locke tells a story "so remarkable, that I cannot but set it down in the A——'s Words," going on to write of how the Incas of Peru sucked the blood from their dying children (pars. 56–59). Locke "cannot but set it down" because he is fascinated (that is, obsessed) with a marauding parental authority that will stop at nothing until it has devoured its own children.

Since it is the same A——'s account of the Incas of Peru that in Locke's *Second Treatise* serves as an actual historical example of the state of nature

22. Laslett, Introduction, p. 83.

(par. 14), it seems fair to conclude that Locke is not really writing about two distinct states at all: the state of patriarchy and the state of nature. The state of nature is not so much the transcendence of patriarchal authority as its denial. Denial of an authority so terrifying that it would not hesitate to drink the blood of its own children. In the state of nature there are no fathers or mothers: men are autonomous and free. In historical reality, fathers stand ready to castrate and devour their children, who stand defenseless against them. What Locke might have done is seek to carve out a position between these two, between no fathers and cannibalistic, castrating ones. This, though, would have required that he confront the reality of parental authority and hence authority generally, particularly the way in which subjects cleave to authority as a defense against it.

Filmer does a better job of this than Locke, recognizing that it is the desire for the leader by the led that is the foundation of the group. To be sure, Filmer is quoting Scripture when he states that "thy desire shall be to thy Husband, and he shall rule over thee" (Genesis 3:16). Nevertheless, Filmer understands that this principle is not only the foundation of the original small group, so to speak, but "the Original Grant of Government" as well (*Second Treatise,* pars. 44–47). What Locke might have done is argue that while government begins in the desire of citizens to be led and so protected from their own fear and destructiveness, it is the task of social theory to clarify this. Citizens might then come to know the strength of their own desires, including their desire to possess and consume the leader. While there are good reasons to fear patriarchs, the intensity of the fear in Locke's account suggests a paranoid element: that the devouring leader is a projection of citizens' own desires to consume the leader, as in the group drama of the sacrificial leader. Rather than interpreting it, which is what leadership in political theory is about, Locke turns this drama into political theory.

The State of Nature

Consider the state of nature according to Locke in the *Second Treatise* (also written shortly before 1688, according to Laslett), in which all men possess perfect freedom to order their actions and dispose of their possessions as they see fit, "without asking leave, or depending upon the Will of any other Man." It is a state of equality, in which none has more power or jurisdiction than another. While it is a state of liberty, it is not a state of license. God has given man reason so that he can know God's law, "that being all equal and independent, no one ought to harm another in his Life, Health, Liberty or Possessions." But knowledge of the law of nature is not enough. In the state of nature every man possesses "the Executive Power of the Law of Nature," as Locke calls it, which means that every one has the right not merely to defend himself against transgressors but to punish any transgressor and so "be Executioner of the Law of Nature." Even the law of nature is vain if there is no one to enforce it. In the state of nature all may enforce it, not only to punish a murderer with death but to "punish the lesser breaches of that Law" with a severity that fits the crime (pars. 6–13). Everyman his own judge, jury, and hangman: this is the state of nature. It is, of course, inconvenient, as even the best-intentioned men are likely to be biased in their own cases as well as in those of their friends. It is for this reason that government is established. Not, as with Hobbes, to create the conditions of a civilized society; but to make a basically civilized society better, which means more reliable and predictable.

Let me put it as simply as possible. Locke's state of nature is the organized denial (not ignorance, denial) of the psychology of groups, especially their complex and ambivalent relationship to leaders. For the key attribute of Locke's state of nature is not that every man is equal or rational, or even that there are no leaders, only members. It is that every man is the leader, what it means to say that "every one has the Executive Power of the Law of Nature" (par. 13). Not only is it unnecessary in Locke's state of nature to deal with the psychologically very difficult relationship of leader and led, a relationship involving desire, envy, hatred, fear, and all the rest. But the identity between every member and the leader, an identity that in the small group is based on a fantasized connection between the leader and the most powerful (or at least the most grandiose) parts of oneself, is realized in fact. In Locke's state of nature an unconscious fantasy of identification with the leader becomes reality. Everyone his own leader.

That this is what Locke has in mind is clear from his comment that actual leaders of today, such as "all *Princes* and Rulers of *Independent* Governments all through the World, are in a State of Nature," as are all governors of independent communities (par. 14). To be in the state of nature is, by definition, to be the leader, just as the father, leader of his household, remains in the state of nature vis-à-vis his children according to Locke (par. 105). In reality, Locke's state of nature is tantamount to the earliest stages of group development in which each member identifies so completely, albeit unconsciously, with the idealized leader that he or she cannot join the group as an individual member, which of course is the point. Identification with the leader is a defense against the regressive pull of the group.

One sees evidence of this in the quality of the members' relationships in the state of nature. They are strictly instrumental. No one gets into fights over love lost, honor impugned, or friendship betrayed. Only the possibility that men might be less than impartial judges in their own cases seems to disturb the state of nature: cases involving for the most part, it seems, the transfer of property, strictly a question of interest. As such, Locke's state of nature denies the single most obvious, important, and tangible aspect of group life: that it is the love, hate, and fear of the members for each other and their leader that makes the group go around. In fact, Locke's is more than an act of denial. It is an accurate characterization of the alienation that results when the reality of the emotional life of groups is suppressed within the group itself. Unconscious identification with the idealized leader is coupled with remarkably superficial and instrumental relationships among members, relations that deny a deeper deindividualization within the group. If others were truly recognized, the reasoning seems to go, then they would be so exposed to my rage and anger, and I to theirs, that we would destroy each other. Best to remain a formless mass, which quite ironically means to see each other as isolated individuals with no real emotional connections.

What is the evidence, it might be asked, for my claim that the apparently superficial and instrumental relations of the state of nature deny deeper and more troubling relations? The best evidence is the puzzling connection between the state of nature and the state of war in Locke's account. While the state of nature sounds like a pretty nice place, it may with devastating suddenness be transformed into a state of war. In this sense the state of nature is remarkably unstable, "the least difference . . . apt to end" in the state of war (*Second Treatise*, pars. 16–20). Not only this, but Locke later writes of the state of nature as "very unsafe, very unsecure," a place where the enjoyment of individual rights is "very uncertain, and constantly exposed to the Invasion of others," so that it is "full of fears and continual dangers." All this is because "the greater part [of mankind are] no strict Observers of Equity and Justice." It is not the depredations of a few but the inability of "the greater part" to govern itself by the law of nature that makes the state of nature such a tough place (par. 123).

What is it about the state of nature that makes it so unstable? Because, "all being Kings," each will be concerned neither with any other nor with any other's rights, but only with themselves (par. 123). It is not the disparity of the citizens but their similarity as kings that makes the state of nature so unstable, likely to suddenly devolve into a state of war. From the perspective of group theory this makes sense. A group in which each member has identified with the idealized leader so completely that he becomes one, a virtual king, is a regressed and frightened group. In such a group individuals check their selves at the door, bringing with them a superficial group self inadequate to contain the fear and rage they dump in the group. It is this fear and rage flying about the group, seeking scapegoats, that makes it so frightening and unstable, superficially pleasant one minute, a blood bath the next—just as the state of nature may revert to the state of war in the blink of an eye. If all are kings, not only are there no members, but there are no real individuals either. Kings demand recognition but rarely give it. When all are kings, no one remains to recognize anyone else. Nor are kings capable of being led by a real individual, a real leader. Only an idealized leader, so distant and abstract that he lends himself to easy and total identification, will do.

State of Nature, State of Denial

The state of nature is not Locke's only account of the origins of political society in the *Second Treatise*. This work also contains a historical account, as Locke calls it, of the origins of government in the rule of the father. Questionable as history, this account makes great political psychology. Puzzling is how the two accounts fit together. Locke's position seems to be that while the state of nature might have existed at various points throughout history, "if we look back as far as History will direct us, towards the Original of *Commonwealths, we shall generally find them under the Government and Administration of one Man. . . . The Government commonly began in the Father*" (par. 105). Not only this, but most found such an arrangement quite satisfactory, "even when they were Men, and out of their Pupilage." Paternal affection, coupled with paternal power and the "Custom of obeying him, in their Childhood, made it easier to submit to him, rather than to any other" (ibid.). The result was a *"Golden Age,"* in which the Father accustomed them to the *"Rule of one Man,* and taught them that where it was exercised with Care and Skill, with Affection and Love to those under it, it was sufficient to procure and preserve to Men all the Political Happiness they sought for, in Society" (par. 107).

What more could one ask from a leader than this, that he use his skill, care, and love to procure all the political happiness men seek? Perhaps this is the real state of nature, not the denial of leaders but their idealization as the source of all happiness. In fact, these two states of nature are one, two halves that don't make a whole—and won't until their status as reciprocals is grasped. What is needed, of course, is that this split be lessened so that real leaders may be confronted: real leaders with real limits, but real contributions as well. About this Locke has little to offer. Not only that, but his writings, which themselves might exert intellectual leadership, interpreting the split leader as the problem, not the solution, don't. They serve only denial.

We have moved about as far as it is possible to get from Locke's state of nature of free and equal men, each possessing the executive power of the law of nature. In so doing, we have come closer to the reality of life in groups. The family is the original small group, setting the tone for every group that follows, including the nation, a principle that Locke recognizes full well in taking on Filmer, who is almost as much the subject of the *Second Treatise* as the *First*. As Laslett states, "The central issue of *Two Treatises* . . . is primarily concerned with the structure of the family and its relevance to social and political authority."[23] From this perspective, Locke's state of nature is pure denial, denying not only what it takes to make society work in the first place, the love of leaders, but also the work that is required to transform this love from a dependent, authoritarian love to mature affection, so to speak, that knows the limits of leaders and hence the efforts required of citizens and members to make the group work. In defense of Locke it might be argued, much as Locke himself does, that the issue is not one of history or even political psychology but of legitimation and justification of government. Government, as Locke states, might have everywhere begun as patriarchy. Certainly children are almost everywhere brought up so as to be responsive to the combination of love and discipline, whether exerted by mother, father, or leader. This does not matter. The only justification for government is consent of the governed, the social contract. History and justification are two different things.

It's a familiar defense, but it doesn't work. History and justification are two different things, but they do not belong to separate universes. When justification denies history—the history of a species that lives in hierarchical groups, as well as the history of the individual who grows up in families—it becomes not justification but something else: rationalization and denial—that is, ideology. Freedom and equality are not a matter of right—or at least, not only a matter of right. They are a matter of work. Group development, upon which freedom and equality depend, is an achievement, not a given. To be sure, Locke sometimes writes as though the move from the patriarchal family to the state of nature is itself a developmental sequence (pars. 102–105). But since he never discusses in his political writings the work required to foster this development, which means how members and citizens might come to terms with their anger at, and dependency on, leaders, as well as their tendencies to act out this conflict in the life of the group, his is not truly a developmental account. Instead, it is a fantasy of instant development without work. One would not expect, of course, that Locke would address all this in the language of group psychology. The lan-

23. Ibid., p. 57.

guage of self-denial, self-esteem, and self-control, the language of *Thoughts Concerning Education* would suffice. In his diary Locke states that "credit and reputation . . . shame and disgrace [are] the principle spring from which the acting of men take their rise, the rule they conduct them by, and the end to which they direct them." *Thoughts* is concerned with employing credit and reputation, shame and disgrace, to raise children who might become free and independent citizens.[24] I disagree sharply with the strategy but not the insight behind it. Development, maturity, independence, and good citizenship don't just happen. It takes work—that is, group development, beginning in the first small group, the family. It is this that Locke's state of nature denies.

In fact, Locke's state of nature is in many respects an account of a group even less developed than the patriarchal family, which at least recognizes the reality of the father-ruler. In the state of nature the apparent absence of leaders serves as a cover for the fantasy that every man is leader, every man the father of his own tribe. In this sense the state of nature is a regressed group in the autistic-contiguous position, unable to confront the reality of leaders. Such denial has consequences for how Locke would solve the problem of leadership under the social contract.

Consider Locke's view of the leader standing in a trust relationship with the people, so that his power becomes a "Fiduciary Trust," held for the people strictly for purposes of their convenience. The people cannot encroach upon the prerogative of the leader, as the leader has no prerogative, being merely an agent of the people (*Second Treatise,* par. 163). Widely regarded as a noble ideal, the seminal moment in responsible government, Locke's view trivializes leadership, turning the leader into an old family retainer, the family lawyer who devises the trusts that protect the value of the estate and draws up the wills. In a word, it turns the leader into a high-class servant. Within a particular context Locke's position makes sense, one in which the relationship of leader and led is seen strictly in terms of penetration: who penetrates whom? The context, in other words, is one of leader as marauder who must be contained within fences. "The Doctrine of a Power of the People . . . is the best fence against their abuse by leaders" (par. 226). This is what members of the Tavistock group do; they construct fences made of legs, chairs, and studied ignorance of the consultant-leader, so that his

24. John Locke, "Some Thoughts concerning Education," in *The Educational Writings of John Locke,* ed. James Axtell (Cambridge: Cambridge University Press, 1968), 111–325. In the "Epistle Dedicatory" Locke states that "the Welfare and Prosperity of the Nation . . . much depends on" how children are bred. Locke understands that child-rearing is politics. So too does Nathan Tarcov in *Locke's Education for Liberty* (Chicago: University of Chicago Press, 1984). Axtell quotes from Locke's diary in his Introduction, p. 154.

actual presence will not intrude upon fantasies about him. Locke treats this early stage in the group's relationship to its leader as though it were the fullest development of the relationship between leader and people. Yet Locke's view of leadership is superior to that of Hobbes or Rousseau, which simply shows how inadequately traditional political theory has dealt with the issue. For Hobbes, the social contract is the schizoid compromise, in which citizens abandon themselves to the leader while withholding their energy and creativity from him. Rousseau simply transforms the group into the most tyrannical leader of all.

In his *Second Treatise* Locke moves from the state of nature, in which everyman is his own leader to the emasculated family retainer, who is no leader at all. In the background stands the castrating, marauding, devouring patriarch of the *First Treatise*. Missing, of course, is any real leader at all, and now we see why. Everyman his own leader and the emasculated fiduciary are both defenses against the patriarch—or rather, defenses against the desire to submit to him. In the face of this desire to submit, the alternative of a good leader, a real leader, is too threatening. Everyman as leader and the emasculated leader are the only acceptable alternatives. In fact, they are not so much alternatives as complements. The emasculated fiduciary exists only to regulate disputes among men who are all leaders. Locke has constructed a world in which there is no room for real leaders—which, I believe, is precisely his point.

Rousseau and the Denial of Interdependence

Rousseau begins his *Second Discourse,* "On the Origin and Foundations of Inequality among Men" (1754), with a piece of advice to all who write about the state of nature: "Let us therefore begin by setting all the facts aside, for they do not affect the question."[25] About this winsome prescription I have taken exception. Rousseau's is not the best way to proceed. While imagination and creativity count for much, it is important that the construct of a state of nature not fundamentally misrepresent social reality, that it be in accord with the basic principles that govern human existence. The appropriate standard is that of Plato, who has Socrates ask whether "our words are any the less well spoken if we find ourselves unable to prove that it is possible for a state to be governed in accordance with our words?" (*Republic*, 472e). A traditional answer, the answer implicit in Socrates' question, is

25. Rousseau, *First and Second Discourses*, p. 103. The full title of the *Second Discourse* is "Discourse on the Origin and Foundations of Inequality," cited by page number in the text.

that it depends upon whether this city in speech, impossible to realize in every detail, is nonetheless in accord with basic principles found in nature. If it is, details don't matter. While the details of Rousseau's account of natural man don't matter either, the basic principles are so out of accord with how humans really are that it can only be regarded as a defense against, and denial of, the truth: that man is a group animal at war with his own groupishness.

Interesting in this regard is Rousseau's insightful suggestion that Hobbes and Locke did not go back far enough. They "have carried over to the state of nature ideas they have acquired in society: they spoke about savage man and they described civil man" (p. 102). C. B. Macpherson makes a similar claim, arguing that Hobbes and Locke took man as they found him in nascent capitalist society, alone, scared, and greedy, and made this human nature per se. It is a powerful criticism, one that various critiques of the indeterminate subject have done much to make postmoderns aware of: the danger of reifying as human nature a particular historical expression of it. Nevertheless, it is equally important not to fall down dead before such criticism, which does not require the conclusion that there is no human nature (or that there is), but only that we must respect the subtlety with which it might manifest itself. Studying Tavistock groups is one way to capture this subtlety, one way to perform the thought experiment that Rousseau recommends, by which we bracket reason so as to know the true nature of man. It is still a thought experiment requiring imagination and creativity to interpret, but not such a radical one as Rousseau imagines is necessary (he delicately suggests that one might crossbreed an ape with a man [pp. 208–209]), as it does not assume that natural man is fundamentally different from man as he appears in every type of group. Not, however, because I project the current decadent state of civilization into the distant past, as Rousseau accuses Hobbes and Locke of doing, but because the past is alive in every group if one will but look.

Rousseau's State of Nature

Consider natural man in the state of nature according to Rousseau. He lives alone, coming across others in his wanderings whom he does not know as individuals, as there is nothing to distinguish one from another. He would not recognize another individual were he to meet him again (p. 137). Natural man possesses no language and no way to express his needs. This is hardly a handicap, however, as he has no needs that require the cooperation of others, with the exception of brief sexual encounters. He is tough, stoical, and without fear of death, apparently because he lacks the concept of an individual who must die his own death. There are, of course, no families, children staying with their mothers only as long as is absolutely necessary for survival, which is not very long, as natural man develops much more quickly than his pampered civilized descendents.[26] Above all, natural man is independent of others, needing nothing from them, having nothing that another might take, possessing no property and no abode. Consequently, there is no jealousy and no need for the cooperation of others, not even to receive their good opinion. "The savage lives within himself; the sociable man, always outside of himself, knows how to live only in the opinion of others; and it is, so to speak, from their judgment alone that he draws the sentiment of his own existence" (p. 179).

Rousseau's account of natural man is a catalog of denial of man's groupishness, which includes his dependence upon others to realize himself. Certainly almost every aspect of natural man serves to demonstrate his independence of others. The best experimental verification of Rousseau's theory, so to speak, is found in autistic adults, who like Rousseau's natural man live entirely within themselves. Object relations theory has shown that far from being narcissistically self-absorbed, normal humans are from birth deeply engaged with others. If, however, one takes this claim, the foundation of psychoanalytic group psychology, seriously, then it is pointless to search for contemporary analogs. There are none, except perhaps among the insane. Or rather, there are no *individual* analogs. There is, however, a group one. Rousseau's natural man is best seen as a characterization of the regressed small group. "Never even recognizing anyone individually," says Rousseau about natural man (p. 137). This is the prime characteristic of the regressed small group.

Rousseau's point is that natural man is free, freedom being defined as the sheer absence of constraint, so that any relationship with another is bound to be an insult to freedom. As Robert Nisbet points out, the chains that Rousseau refers to in his famous statement that "Man is born free, and everywhere he is in chains," are not just the chains of tyrants.[27] They are the chains implicit in any human connection, including those with family, friends, and community. Or as Rousseau puts it, the trouble with relation-

26. *Second Discourse*, p. 218. Rousseau contradicts himself in par. 7 of *Social Contract*, ed. and trans. Charles M. Sherover (New York: New American Library, 1974), where he states that "the earliest of all societies, and the only natural one, is the family." It is a contradiction not because Rousseau states that the family is the earliest of all societies (this is compatible with the *Second Discourse*) but because he states that it is the only natural one. None of the state-of-nature theorists know quite what to do with the family, as it is so obviously the real state of nature.

27. Robert Nisbet, "Rousseau and Equality," in *Rousseau's Political Writings*, ed. Alan Ritter and Julia C. Bondanella (New York: W. W. Norton, 1988), 244–260, p. 256.

ships between humans is that "by dint of seeing one another, they can no longer do without seeing one another again" (p. 149). Fortunately, this does not occur in the state of nature, where no one remembers any other individual anyway. Jean Starobinski, psychiatrist and author of *Jean-Jacques Rousseau: Transparency and Obstruction,* argues that Rousseau defines freedom "essentially as freedom from difference or otherness."[28] The regressed small group also defines freedom as freedom from difference or otherness, and it is this that connects natural man with the small group. Or rather, it is this that shows that natural man, far from being truly autonomous and free, is actually a typical member of the regressed small group. In writing about the freedom of natural man, Rousseau is actually writing about a fantasy of absolute freedom from otherness common to members of the regressed group. One way to be free of otherness is, of course, to become just like everyone else. The other way is to obliterate or ignore all others. The schizoid compromise is about doing both at once.

Rousseau's state of nature is only apparently about isolation, autonomy, and utter freedom. It is actually one in which individuals are bound so closely to each other in the group that they are unaware of their differences, which is why its members cannot recognize each other. Recognition requires difference and distance, distant nearness. Yet, if this is so, how to explain the insistence on autonomy that one finds in the regressed small group, as when members say things, as they so often do, like, "Whether I get anything from this group will depend entirely on me." Or, "Learning is such a personal matter that I will learn what I want from this group, no matter what happens." When an individual asserts that he needs nothing from the group, that the group can offer him nothing he cannot do for himself, teach him nothing he cannot learn for himself, it is a good bet that he is defending against an unconscious experience of desire of being fused with the group in some way. A genuine expression of individuality would recognize that while the individual does depend upon others for his experiences, he may within limits actively interpret them and so take responsibility for his own learning.

Stupid expressions of individuality, on the other hand, in which members assert in various ways that they need nothing from each other, are a cover for and defense against the experience of a desire to lose one's individuality to the group, "ihnen zu Liebe," as Freud puts it—that is, out of the desire to be in tune with the group, as the lover desires to be one with his beloved. This desire to lose oneself to the group may itself be a defense

28. Jean Starobinski, *Jean-Jacques Rousseau: Transparency and Obstruction,* trans. Arthur Goldhammer, intro. by Robert Morrissey (Chicago: University of Chicago Press, 1988), pp. xxii–xxiii.

against not being recognized, a type of anticipatory protective coloration, blending with the group so as not to take the chance of not being recognized. But it is still the desire to merge, denied by its converse, idealized assertions of absolute autonomy. Not merely those group members who state that they have nothing to learn from each other, but also natural man, so independent of others that he does not even recognize them, is in this sense a stupid individual: willfully ignorant of his desire to be one with others. There are, after all, two ways in which one may be ignorant of another's individuality. One may not know him at all, or one may, in a sense, know him too well, be fused, so that difference and otherness are obliterated. Claiming the first for natural man, Rousseau is actually writing about the second, so that freedom becomes merely the obliteration of difference and otherness.

The Social Contract

Much of the scholarship on Rousseau is concerned with reconciling the individualistic and communitarian moments in his work—in particular, with how to reconcile the *Discourse on Inequality* , with its emphasis on the autarky of natural man, with the *Social Contract* (1762), in which man can be forced to be free. Each of the four positions that can be taken has supporters. Some, such as Emile Faguet, argue that Rousseau is essentially an individualist. "All of Rousseau can be found in the [*Discourse on Inequality*]," he says. Others, such as Ernest Barker, hold that Rousseau is essentially a collectivist, even a totalitarian, albeit a democratic one. Still others hold that Rousseau is simply confused, whereas C. E. Vaughan argues that Rousseau's work must be seen in terms of a journey from individualism to collectivism.[29] My position is that Rousseau is writing from such a primitive level of experience, that of the regressed small group, that the distinction between individual and collective becomes meaningless. Otherwise expressed, the schizoid compromise thinks that it can have complete individuality and total collectivism together at once; compromise is unnecessary. It can't, for the schizoid compromise is in the end an illusion, but it is Rousseau's clever fostering of this illusion that accounts, I believe, for his continuing popularity, especially among liberal individualists, who feel sad about the implications of their beliefs for human community.

How to explain Rousseau's claim that while the freedom of natural man is irrecoverable, life under the social contract, in which every individual sub-

29. Emile Faguet, *Dix-huitième siècle,* 43d ed. (Paris: Société française d'imprimerie et de librairie, n.d.), p. 345. Ernest Barker, Introduction to *The Social Contract,* by Rousseau (New York: Oxford University Press, 1948), p. xxxviii. C. E. Vaughan, *The Political Writings of Jean-Jacques Rousseau,* 2 vols. (Oxford: Basil Blackwell, 1977), 1:80–81.

mits all that he is to the group, can restore and perfect this freedom? To understand this is to understand Rousseau. It is not an easy question, for the social contract is not some democratic compromise but the total surrender of the individual to the group. The goal, says Rousseau, is to "find a form of association . . . by means of which each, coalescing with all, may nevertheless obey only himself, and remain as free as before" (par. 40). The answer is "the total alienation to the whole community of each associate with all his rights. . . . Since each gives himself up entirely, the condition is equal for all" (par. 43). "Each giving himself to all, gives himself up to nobody. . . . In return we receive in a body every member as an indivisible part of the whole. . . . This act of association produces a moral and collective body . . . which receives from this same act its unity, its common self (*moi*), its life, and its will" (pars. 44–46). Rousseau summarizes the thinking behind his legislation this way:

In a word, it is necessary to deprive man of his native powers in order to endow him with some which are alien to him, and of which he cannot make use without the aid of others. The more thoroughly those natural powers are deadened and destroyed, the greater and more durable are the acquired powers, the more solid and perfect also are the institutions; so that if each Citizen is nothing, and can be nothing, except in combination with all the rest . . . we may say that legislation is at the highest point of perfection which it can attain. (Par. 108)

Recall that the question is not simply how does Rousseau create community, but how does this community restore and perfect the freedom of natural man? One might, as critics have, debate the meaning of freedom. Is freedom simply release from external constraint, or does it also involve the freedom to develop one's capacities to the fullest? If the latter, then it is not automatically self-contradictory to write, as Rousseau does, "that whoever refuses to obey the general will shall be constrained to do so by the whole body; which means nothing else than that he shall be forced to be free" (par. 54). If one could assume that the general will, like the ideal leader, always knows what is in the long-term developmental interests of the citizen, then the phrase "forced to be free" need not be strictly the province of Jacobins. Nevertheless, the phrase (or rather, the thinking behind it) is extremely troubling and, from the perspective of psychoanalytic group psychology, most revealing.

Rousseau's *Social Contract* is simply the second half of the schizoid compromise. In the first, represented by the *Second Discourse*, the individual seeks autarky. In the second, represented by the *Social Contract*, the individual desires to be nothing "except in combination with all the rest." The *Second*

Discourse and *The Social Contract* are two halves that don't make a whole. But they don't contradict each other either, because they don't confront each other. They never even touch. Or as Rousseau puts it, when an "opinion opposed to my own prevails, that simply shows that I was mistaken, and that what I considered to be the general will was not so. Had my private opinion prevailed, I should have done something other than I wished; and in that case I should not have been free" (par. 329). There is an element of what George Orwell calls doublespeak in Rousseau's account, a term whose evocation of splitting should not be overlooked. Both doublespeak and splitting try to have it both ways at once. All animals are equal, but some animals are more equal than others.

Not all of the *Social Contract* is doublespeak. Rousseau's redefinition of sovereignty from power to legitimate consent is a major contribution to democratic theory, as I have argued elsewhere. Nevertheless, Rousseau does not so much reconcile individual and community as pretend they need not conflict. In the end this is the failure of his project. It is superficial, because Rousseau fails to confront the possibility that the individual and group must always be at odds, if for no other reason (and there are others) than that man's individuality and groupishness are at war within himself. Writing of the relationship of individual and group in such a way as to suggest that the work of group development is unnecessary, the *Social Contract* portrays a regressive solution to the tension between individual and group as though it were the epitome of individual and group development. It is as though man is so greedy, needy, envious, and vainglorious that the work cannot be even begun, lest he be forced to recognize that these attributes must destroy any group that tries to find a place for individuals in it.

It is ironic. Rousseau, who intuitively grasps the dilemmas of group life more deeply than do Pufendorf, Hobbes, or Locke, devises a social contract more regressive than theirs. They move the group from the stage of a regressed group in the state of nature to that of an undeveloped group in civil society. Or rather, the state of nature in their accounts is the regressed group, as civil society is the undeveloped group. Unfortunately, they foster group development in ways that guarantee that it will remain frozen at the stage of the undeveloped group. Rousseau, on the other hand, simply moves from one side of the schizoid compromise to the other, from the utter autonomy of the state of nature to the "common self" of the *Social Contract*. There is no development here at all, only movement within a position. The reason, I believe, has to do with the fact that Rousseau does not value individuality and the difference it represents—at least, not in others. He is always asserting his own individuality, or at least, his own uniqueness. His *Confessions* opens this way: "I am made unlike any one I have ever met; I will even venture to say that I am like no one in the whole world. I may be no better, but at least I am different."[30] But perhaps this is the problem. For Rousseau, individuality is simply difference. A sacred word these days, at least when written in French (*différance*), it may be that difference is a poor substitute for genuine individuality, the cheapest and least substantial way in which individuality can be expressed. Just be different. In fact, Rousseau grasps this point well, perhaps too well. He simply has no idea what to do with it, as he lacks a more substantial concept of individuality. It will pay to consider this point further.

Individuality and Leadership

Rousseau has what is in many ways the darkest view of the individual of any state-of-nature theorist. This statement may surprise and certainly runs counter to romantic interpretations of Rousseau's natural man as a noble savage, but it is readily demonstrated once it is recognized that Rousseau regards almost all distinctions among men as invidious. The *Second Discourse* is not just about natural man. It also concerns what happens to man after he steps out of the state of nature, which means when he steps into the society of others. What happens is that he tries to distinguish himself and in so doing becomes bad. Each wanted to be looked at and admired by others, so each developed a talent: some wore attractive clothes, others sang and danced, still others cultivated their beauty. Some practiced rhetoric, while others became skilled craftsmen. More troubling still to Rousseau, ideas of merit and beauty developed, so that some people and their talents came to be preferred over others (pp. 148–149). The result was jealousy, vanity, and corruption, exacerbated by the division of labor, as each came to depend upon the skills of others for his existence.[31]

Individuality is no value to Rousseau, because the only things that distinguish men from each other are invidious and trivial distinctions. That individuality might be a source of creativity and spontaneity, a font of stimulating difference, finds no place in his account. That individual difference might enrich the group never occurs to Rousseau, which is why there is no coming together to debate and discuss the general will. The general will is decided upon by each member in isolation. It is no accident that Rousseau held that the remote Swiss mountain cantons were especially well-suited to

30. Rousseau, *The Confessions,* trans. J. M. Cohen (Harmondsworth, England: Penguin Books, 1953), p. 17.

31. The *First Discourse* ("On the Sciences and Arts") goes further. Progress in science and the arts is bad because the resulting knowledge and skill only accentuate natural inequalities and so feed pride and vanity. See esp. p. 48.

democracy, their citizens kept indoors and apart by the weather for almost half the year. This does not conform with the ideal, promoted by Rousseau himself, of "peasants regulating the affairs of the State under an oak," but it is what he says (pars. 315–322). The general will is to be determined not by discussion and debate but by each individual in the privacy of his heart. Society is made up of individuals, but since all that distinguish one from the other are pride and vanity, individuality is not a value to be protected or shared with others. What must be protected is not individuality but the vulnerability of men to narcissistic injury: humiliation when faced with the superiority or just the otherness of the other. It is this that leads to envy, jealousy, competitiveness, and all the evils of society. *The Social Contract* is this protection, in which individuals are shielded from narcissistic injury by being kept from the experience of individuality in themselves or others.

What of the leader in Rousseau's account? All along I have stressed the centrality of the leader, in whose individuality the members vicariously participate and so ease the pain of their own loss of individuality to the group. Is the leader truly absent in Rousseau's account, and if so, is this good? The simple answer is that Rousseau is writing about a regressed group that has, in fantasy, so incorporated its leader that nothing of him remains outside the group. He has been swallowed whole. This can be seen in Rousseau's definition of the term "sovereign," generally seen as his great achievement. Traditionally defined as *summum imperium*, supreme power, sovereignty is redefined by Rousseau as the people as a collective body (par. 46). Progressive insofar as it has the effect of making consent central to the concept, Rousseau's redefinition has the effect of denying the existence of legitimate leaders. In fact, the sovereign people is a terrifying leader, subject to no limits, indivisible, omnipresent, and omnipotent, with the authority, for example, to condemn to death citizens who disrespect religious dogma. Not, however, because religious dogma is important in itself, but because adherence to it is evidence of "sentiments of sociability, without which it is impossible to be a good Citizen or a faithful subject" (pars. 49–54, 440). *The Social Contract* is an account of a group so regressed that it can make no contact at all with its leader, acting out within itself its most fearsome fantasies about him, all the while pretending that he does not exist.

In fact, the real leader does not entirely disappear in Rousseau's account. Instead, he is unintegrated in it, important but possessing an ambiguous role, successively philosopher-king and functionary. This too is characteristic of the way the small group thinks about leaders, as Führer or lackey, a schizoid view central to Locke's account as well. Elsewhere in *The*

Social Contract Rousseau discusses the virtues of aristocracy: "In a word, it is the best and most natural order of things that the wisest should govern the multitude, when we are sure that they will govern it for its advantage and not for their own" (par. 204).

Many have tried to reconcile statements like this, of which there are many in *The Social Contract*, with the ideal of the general will. The usual strategy is to distinguish basic constitutional legislation, province of the general will, from government and administration, the realm of the aristocracy (par. 284). This, though, lends more coherence to the distinction than is warranted by Rousseau's discussion. Consider, for example, Rousseau's praise of the government of Geneva as exemplifying his principles, when in fact this government was an oligarchy. While Rousseau is frequently excused this excess on the grounds that his motives were political, the number of excuses necessary to account for similar discrepancies adds up, as when Rousseau grants the prince the power of life and death over the citizens: "And when the Prince has said to him: 'it is expedient for the State that you should die,' he ought to die, since it is only on this condition that he has lived in security up to that time, his life being no longer merely a gift of nature, but a conditional gift of the state" (par. 90). Charles Sherover says that neither monarchy nor even aristocracy is necessarily implied by "prince," a term also used at this time to refer to the administrative officers of government.[32] What a relief! No wonder the group members are terrified, caught between a sovereign people who would kill them for lacking the proper social sentiments and a prince or apparatchik who would kill them for the sake of expedience. Is it any surprise that they cleave to the group, so as to gain some control over their terror by participating in its administration?

Conclusion: What's Wrong with All This?

Liberal individualists are often surprisingly taken with Rousseau, holding that he captures needs and experiences not well represented in liberal theory, such as the need to belong to a community of others, participate in its affairs, and so become more moral by taking others into account in the determination of one's own welfare. Rousseau's attempt to reconcile individual freedom with the needs of the group serves, for many liberals, to assuage some of their concerns about forcing men to be free. In fact, this reading misunderstands both individualism and community, a misunderstanding that is most intense with Rousseau, but which is shared by all the state-of-nature theorists. Rousseau, like the others, gets it backward. The

32. Sherover, Introduction to *The Social Contract*, by Rousseau, p. 54.

real work necessary is not to socialize individual men but to individualize social men, to create individuals out of groupies.

In fact, it is a little more complex than this. While I have reversed the causal arrow to stress the difference between my account and those of the state-of-nature theorists, the way it really works is that groups develop only in interaction with the individuation of their members. Both must take place at once, an example being that members can come to terms with the reality of the leader, what he can and can't realistically contribute to group development, only when they become convinced of their own reality as individuals. Similarly, the group can contribute to the development of its members only when it can respect and draw upon their creative individuality while harnessing it to group purposes. This is a terribly difficult task, and most groups never get it right. Most don't even come close. But it doesn't matter. The task of political theory is to confront the work necessary to achieve it, indicating the steps necessary to come to terms with Bion's insight that man is a group animal at war with his own groupishness.

My argument concerns not what political theorists should conclude about man's groupishness but that they confront it. All the state-of-nature theorists considered in this chapter, but Rousseau most of all, fail in this regard, writing as if man was already an individual who needs only to be convinced of the virtues of association. Or at least, this is their rhetorical aim. Yet, in some ways it is Rousseau's failure that is most disturbing, as he comes closest to the truth, only to deny it the most completely. The truth is that man is profoundly uncomfortable with his tendency to live for, in, and through the group, yet generally is in a position to do nothing about it. Nothing, that is, except rage at the group and so make it an even more threatening entity. And a less supportive one as well. The ironic reality is that even (or especially) individuation requires the support of the group.

Rousseau's novel, *La Nouvelle Héloïse,* concerns the sufferings of Julie, whose father refuses to allow her to marry the man she passionately loves, insisting instead on her marriage to a man old enough to be her father. Rather than criticizing the harshness and possessiveness of patriarchal authority (the first authority that most groups know), Rousseau sentimentalizes Julie's suffering as the epitome of virtue. This is the pattern in all Rousseau's works. He feels the inhumanity of groups, the way in which they force the individual to live "always outside himself, knowing how to live only in the opinion of others . . . [from whom] he draws the sentiment of his own existence" (p. 179). However, rather than confront this inhumanity, the pain and rage it causes and the unceasing hard work necessary for individuals and group to reach a humane *modus vivendi,* Rousseau denies it, looking for neat, transcendent answers that deny the tragedy of human life in groups. He does this, I believe, because he does not really believe in individuals, that they possess within themselves the creative potential to transform the group, to make it live. How unexpected and how simple. To believe in group development, one must believe in the reality of individuals who make it possible.

5 ❋ Tocqueville and the Schizoid Compromise: A Reinterpretation of Contemporary Political Theory in Light of Group Theory

This chapter criticizes aspects of contemporary political theory in light of the group theory developed in chapters 2 and 3 and the critique of traditional social contract theory in chapter 4. The civil privatism of liberal individualism is interpreted as a version of the schizoid compromise, an insight that Tocqueville got just right 150 years ago. Epigoni of Tocqueville, the participationists argue that participation is the solution to the problem of civil privatism. The participationists include Benjamin Barber, author of *Strong Democracy*; Robert Bellah and colleagues, authors of *Habits of the Heart*; and Carole Pateman, author of *Participation and Democratic Theory*. Mistaken in important respects, they are not as subtle as Tocqueville. Political theorists influenced by postmodernism, such as William Connolly and Iris Young, reach a conclusion almost identical with mine regarding the tension between individual and group. Yet their approach remains self-enclosed, unable to generate a critique. Contemporary communitarian alternatives developed by John Rawls and Michael Sandel are next addressed. In approaching Rawls in this fashion, I am buying Sandel's argument that Rawls's *A Theory of Justice* is a communitarian theory in individualistic disguise, but I don't buy Sandel's conclusion that the explicitly communitarian version is good—on the contrary, it idealizes the regressed group.

Carole Pateman argues in *The Sexual Contract* that Rawls's abstract individualism is the epitome of male political theory. If Rawls is not seen as an individualist at all but as an abstract communitarian, then Pateman's argument in *The Sexual Contract* must be reconsidered, as it is in this chapter. Wrong in important respects, Pateman talks about sexual conflict, so important in group life and so ignored by most political theorists. After considering Pateman's argument I propose a contract that takes her insights and the insights of group theory generally into account. Such a contract concerns how social institutions might help individuals reclaim lost parts of themselves, parts previously devoted to the group.

Tocqueville's Account of Privatism Is the Schizoid Compromise

The key characteristic of regressed and undeveloped groups is that they are at once too unified and not unified enough. Members are so fearful and isolated that they give a part of themselves over utterly to the group. But only a part. Because the group does not recognize individuals, the members hold themselves back. They hold back the less attractive aspects that are nonetheless real and important parts of what it is to be human; they also hold back the best and most creative parts of themselves, lest these parts be crushed, rejected, or exploited. The result is that there is no real loyalty to the group and no real community either, as the group is made up not of whole human beings but only of partial ones. This is the schizoid compromise.

Tocqueville recognized it 150 years ago, though of course he did not call it that. But that is what he found, and it is an important part of my argument that Tocqueville's account of privatism in America is not somehow analogous to the schizoid compromise that characterizes the undeveloped small group. Nor is Tocqueville's account a metaphor or simile for the dynamics of the undeveloped group. Tocqueville is characterizing the quality of relationships within a civic culture, and the quality of these relationships partakes of the schizoid compromise just as surely as the quality of the relationships in the small group. Tocqueville's account of privatism in America *is* the schizoid compromise, understood as a characterization of the quality of the individual's relationships to himself and others. A grouplike entity, rather than a group, is the subject of Tocqueville's analysis, but this hardly matters. At issue is strictly the pattern of relations, which are identical in Tocqueville's America and the Tavistock group.

Tocqueville was fascinated by the way in which individualism and conformity, seemingly so antithetical, go together in American life. They go together because individualism isolates the individual within the solitude of his own heart, cutting him off from traditional sources of support. In his isolation, the individual is likely to turn to others for confirmation of his own judgment, not individual others, but the group.

When the inhabitant of a democratic country compares himself with all those about him, he feels with pride that he is the equal of anyone of them; but when he comes to survey the totality of his fellows, and to place himself in contrast with so huge a body, he is instantly overwhelmed by the sense of his own insignificance and weakness. *The same equality which renders him independent of each of his fellow-citizens taken severally, exposes him alone and unprotected to the influence of the greater number.* The public has therefore, among a democratic people, a singular power, which aristocratic nations cannot conceive of, for it does not persuade to certain opinions, but it enforces them, and infuses them into the intellect by a sort of enormous pressure of the minds of all upon the reason of each. . . .

I know of no country in which there is so little independence of mind and real freedom of discussion as in America. . . . The master no longer says "You shall think as I do, or you shall die"; but he says, "You are free to think differently from me, and to retain your life, your property, and all that you possess; but you are henceforth a stranger among your people. . . . Your fellow creatures will shun you like an impure being; and even those who believe in your innocence will abandon you, lest they should be shunned in their turn. Go in peace! I have given you your life, but it is an existence worse than death."[1]

The new master is, of course, the group, and the price of nonconformity is not merely isolation but alienation. Tocqueville's characterization fits the regressed small group almost perfectly, particularly the way in which individualism and conformity go together, the schizoid compromise. He also captures the source of this compromise in the individual's experience of how the group "exposes him alone and unprotected to the influence of the greater number." The individual is terrified of the group, of being absorbed by it and of standing out from it. It is a dilemma, one which individuals solve by saying to themselves, generally unconsciously, something like this: "If I just think the same thoughts as everybody else, then I won't be so isolated, alone, and vulnerable. But since I will think them to myself and for myself, not developing them in intercourse with others, they will be strictly my thoughts, all me." Conformity is absolute loyalty to the *idea* of the group, identifying with the ideas held by the group as though they were one's own, making no distinction between them. Conformity is not less powerful, but more, and certainly more insidious, when the group in question is really no group at all but millions of men and women who just happen to be citizens of the same republic. Isolated in the privacy of one's home, thinking the same thoughts becomes the only way to join this republic.

Often those who admire Tocqueville, such as William Sullivan in *Reconstructing Public Philosophy,* admire him for the wrong reasons, not fully appreciating Tocqueville's grasp of the connection between individualism, equality, and conformity. Sullivan argues that "Tocqueville confusingly conflated equality with self-interested individualism because the two seemed to

1. Alexis de Tocqueville, *Democracy in America,* ed. Richard D. Heffner (New York: New American Library, 1956), pp. 148, 117–118, emphasis added.

emerge together with the rise of liberal society" (p. 215). Sullivan seeks to show that the problem isn't equality at all, but the way in which self-interested individualism destroys the ties that bind, the living connections that hold a society together, including ties of equal respect and dignity. In fact, equality *is* a problem, as the group-theoretic perspective suggests. Individuals frightened of both individuality and the group seek a type of dedifferentiation within the group as defense. Anyone and everyone can be an individual as long as they are just like all the other individuals in the group. Isolation with others just like oneself is mistaken for individualism. But not for long, isolation being so painful that it leads to dedifferentiation, so as to merge back into the group, all the while denying what one is doing. Never having an original thought is one such strategy. Tocqueville captured this phenomenon perfectly, and it is not progress, but only denial, to suggest that he has conflated them. It is the undeveloped small group that conflates them. So too does liberal democracy—or at least, most recent political theories of liberal democracy.

Tocqueville suggests a subtle point grasped by few of his epigoni. That civil privatism, a life devoted to getting and spending, is actually quite compatible with—indeed invites—the invasion of the private by the public, so that the only thing really private that remains is private property, things that belong to one man rather than another. It is to this that Tocqueville refers when he states that "the aspect of society in the United States is at once excited and monotonous" (p. 254)—excited, because everyone is busy running around acquiring things, but monotonous, because everyone wants the same things in the same ways for the same reasons. Property is private, but individuals are not; they are identical frenetic monads. This too is dedifferentiation.

Barber, Bellah, Pateman, and Sullivan are aware of this aspect of Tocqueville's study. They do not draw upon it, however, to enrich their analyses of the relationship between individual and group so as to make it more subtle and sophisticated. This stems from the way in which they frame the problem of civil privatism as strictly one of excessive individualism, rather than the more complex one that I have called the schizoid compromise. Seen as a problem of excessive individualism, participation in group life becomes the solution to civil privatism. Seen from my perspective, the solution is more complex and subtle. These political theorists have accepted as truth the ideology of the social-contract theorists, that man really is first and foremost an individual. The social-contract theorists have done their rhetorical work too well.

Jürgen Habermas defines civil privatism as

an interest in the steering and maintenance performances of the administrative system but little participation in the legitimizing process. . . . Civil privatism thus corresponds to the structures of a depoliticized public realm. Familial-vocational privatism complements civil privatism. It consists in a family orientation with developed interests in consumption and leisure on the one hand, and in a career orientation suitable to status competition on the other.[2]

Expressed in less turgid prose, civil privatism means that citizens are concerned with getting, spending, and family life, regarding government as though it were little more than an administrative system whose purpose is to keep the economy running smoothly. Locke's view of government as fiduciary is exemplary.

In fact, the thesis of civil privatism has it backward. The problem is not too much privatism, but too little, especially in the late twentieth century. Even in the 1830s Tocqueville recognized that civil privatism was not so private at all. Bellah and his coauthors invert the truth when they argue that "separation and individuation" are too advanced in our culture. On the contrary, real separation and individuation are not advanced enough. Freedom within the walls of one's own house, as Bellah characterizes the American ideal of freedom (a schizoid image if ever there was one), is not a freedom opposed to the group but simply a way to be an isolated groupie, one who thinks like others without knowing them, probably the worst of both worlds.[3] My argument is not original. It is the thesis of the Frankfurt school of critical theory, developed most fully in their studies of the decline of the patriarchal bourgeois family.[4] Herbert Marcuse's *One-Dimensional Man* develops a similar argument. One-dimensionality means that mass society has so invaded every aspect of life that there are no longer any alternatives, any sources of opposition, not even deep within the psyche.

When individuals find their souls in the consumption of commodities, including mass entertainment, they are not living private lives at all. Nor are they living public ones. They are living lives in which what they will and want, as well as who they are, are defined by industry. Not the industry that produces coal and steel, but the culture industry, the entertainment industry, the advertising industry, even the educational industry, Clark Kerr's megaversity. This argument has been developed further and with greater

2. Jürgen Habermas, *Legitimation Crisis,* trans. Thomas McCarthy (Boston: Beacon Press, 1975), p. 75.

3. Robert Bellah, Richard Madsen, William Sullivan, Ann Swidler, and Steven Tipton, *Habits of the Heart: Individualism and Commitment in American Life* (Berkeley: University of California Press, 1985), pp. 275–276, 24.

4. Max Horkheimer, "Authority and the Family," in *Critical Theory,* trans. Matthew J. O'Connell et al. (New York: Seabury Press, 1972), 47–128.

insight by Christopher Lasch, who writes of families invaded by the values of commerce, industry, the "helping professions," and the mass media. Once, perhaps as late as the interwar years, the family was a "haven in a heartless world."[5] No longer, and not for some time. Today there is very little privatism to be civil about, as children are raised in preschools, by television, movies, and most of all by each other. The decline of the patriarchal bourgeois family has in some ways led to a more egalitarian family structure, but it has also led to a world in which society is the father, as well as the mother, to turn Alexander Mitscherlich's famous phrase around.

Why do Barber, Bellah, Pateman, and others get it so wrong? Their theories mislead them because they are too simple. Society is based upon either the individual or the group, or it falls somewhere between the two, as though the relationship between individual and group can always be characterized on a continuum. Not merely false, this formulation is insufficiently subtle to capture the complexity of the relationship between individual and group or the quality of the group itself, particularly whether it is regressed or developed. Recall the cross diagram in chapter 3, in which at least four positions may be taken up at once. Participation in the regressed group may only encourage individual regression, a possibility these theorists have no place for. Nor is the regressed group simply a bunch of Nazis screaming for Hitler. The frequently idealized New England town meeting may also be a regressed group.

Of all democratic participatory institutions, the most idealized is surely the New England town meeting. Barber praises these meetings as the foundation of democracy, a view held by Tocqueville, who states that "town meetings are to liberty what . . . schools are to science," as well as to most other participationists. To be sure, Barber recognizes that the studies of Jane Mansbridge and others have shown such meetings to be subject to social coercion.[6] This is hardly regarded by Barber as a fundamental criticism, however. Not cited by Barber is Judith Shklar's characterization of a New England town meeting:

New England town meetings in the eighteenth century were . . . meant to achieve consensus. Differences were generally called unhappy, and the primacy of peace rendered discord [and] argument . . . unacceptable. The meetings were not presented with a choice of competing interests or opinions. They met to reassert the unity of townsmen. . . . Neither the

5. Christopher Lasch, *Haven in a Heartless World* (New York: Basic Books, 1979).
6. Benjamin Barber, *Strong Democracy: Participatory Politics for a New Age* (Berkeley: University of California Press, 1984), pp. 234, 272–273. Jane Mansbridge, *Beyond Adversary Democracy* (New York: Basic Books, 1980).

defense of private interests nor the projection of personal ideas was welcome.[7]

A Tavistock group relations conference is not the only place to experience the regressed group.

This is not the place to argue about what town meetings in New England were really like, then and now. My point is simpler and more general than that. Participation is not a good in itself. Participation that is based upon and assumes the suppression of self (the suppression of "personal ideas"), individual desires, and interests can only reinforce the regressed group. Indeed, this is what the regressed group is, one in which unity is achieved only by deindividualizing and dedifferentiating the members. The result is a loyalty to the group that is a mile wide and an inch deep. The New England town meeting characterized by Shklar is a regressed group. Genuine group development is so difficult because it must be built upon individuals who do not melt into the group but stand out from it while still remaining members. Which is why participation that is merely the assertion of private interests doesn't foster group development either. Lobbyists don't belong to groups and don't contribute to group development; they belong to trade associations, sometimes (quite mistakenly) called "communities of interest." They are not communities of anything. *The only participation that matters, the only participation that fosters genuine group development, is participation that allows and encourages the individual members to reclaim lost and alienated parts of themselves.* This requires, at a minimum, that individual differences be valued but not idealized for their own sake. Not difference for the sake of difference but *individual* difference for the sake of individuals is what counts. Later, this chapter formulates a social contract with this principle in mind. It is the most important principle that group theory has to offer.

In "Democratic Theory and Self-Transformation," Mark Warren refers to "expansive democracy," as he calls it, whose theorists are among those I have labeled participationists. Warren is concerned that expansive democrats not be confused with communitarian critics of liberalism, such as Sandel and Sullivan. While expansive democrats share with communitarians an appreciation of how the desiring self is shaped by society, expansive democrats recognize that it is dangerous merely to stress the integration of individual and society. Political theory must always be concerned with power and dialogue, recognizing with William Connolly in *Identity\Difference: Demo-*

7. Judith N. Shklar, "Jean-Jacques Rousseau and Equality," in *Rousseau's Political Writings*, ed. Alan Ritter and Julia Bondanella (New York: W. W. Norton, 1988), 260–274, p. 270. Also her *Men and Citizens: A Study of Rousseau's Social Theory* (Cambridge: Cambridge University Press, 1969), pp. 12–32.

cratic Negotiations of Political Paradox that integration without democracy threatens to sacrifice self to community. The goal of expansive democracy is not to discover and formulate some sort of general will but to develop autonomy, without which self-governance is meaningless, as Habermas has emphasized. An interesting theoretical distinction between communitarians and expansive democrats, it does not hold up very well in practice, even though the expansive democrats have called attention to a significant issue.

An important reason why it does not hold up, as Warren points out, is that the lead thesis of the expansive democrats, that political participation fosters individuals who are both autonomous and socially connected, "is not sufficiently developed to support an alternative democratic theory." Warren characterizes the self idealized by the expansive democrats: "Such a self would be autonomous yet social, individuated yet defined by nonconflicting interests, rational but embodied in numerous different social relations, expressive of individuality yet public in orientation. . . . The problem is that there is as yet no account of the self that would support this image as it pertains to politics."[8] I'll say! To be sure, the ideal of the self that could do all these things is developed, hypertrophied one might say. But there exists no evidence and no experience to suggest that such selves exist or might exist, a conclusion Warren reaches after a review of the contemporary literature. Not only this, but there is almost no literature that even considers under what limited conditions—say in small voluntary associations—such selves might emerge. There is, however, a considerable literature and much experience with small voluntary associations in which such selves never emerge—the Tavistock groups I have written of.

Magical Words Avoid Tragic Conclusions

While there exist no studies of such selves, one would hardly know it from the participationist literature. On the contrary, what is so striking about this literature, and only infrequently remarked upon, is the magical quality of the language, in which opposition and tension are transcended in a surreal unification of opposites that would make Hegel proud. It is as if the theorist believes that if he could just get the words right, the adjectives strung together just so, then we could hold it and have it. This parade of adjectives is as characteristic of the best arguments, like Sullivan's, as of some not quite so good. It is why books on this topic tend to say the same thing over and over again, like a mantra, as though saying it just right would make it so.

8. Mark Warren, "Democratic Theory and Self-Transformation," *American Political Science Review* 86, no. 1 (Mar. 1992): 8–23, pp. 9, 13.

Consider, for example, Barber's statement in *Strong Democracy* that

citizenship is a dynamic relationship among strangers who are transformed into neighbors. . . . Because the sharp distinction that separates government and citizenry in representative systems is missing, the civic bond under strong democracy is neither vertical nor lateral but circular and dialectical. . . . It is neither in time nor in space but in the imagination that strong democratic citizens become "neighbors." Theirs is the neighborhood of creative consciousness . . . in which the necessity that outcomes be commonly conceived disciplines the adversary competition of the divided and plural present. (Pp. 223–224)

Such a statement abandons analysis for a magical web of words. That this statement, and many others like it, is from a highly regarded book in the field is a measure of the desperation involved. Bellah and his coauthors say it straight out. Americans need a new language and vocabulary to characterize the richness of their lives (pp. 20–21). What they really need is richer lives. The strategy is reminiscent of that of the original state-of-nature theorists, who sought to convince groupies that they were really autonomous individuals. As if saying it could make it so.

Why does saying it just right become so terribly important in participationist writings? Part of the reason is certainly that the participationist tradition has no institutional basis. The distance between the actual institutions of participation, such as jury duty and town meetings, and what participation is supposed to accomplish is measured in light-years. Another reason has to do with what Warren calls "the overly discursive self," the view that the self is constituted in and through language. Not just postmodernists, but theorists like Habermas hold that because the self's desires can be transformed into language, they may be generalized, shared in some way. "When Habermasian views of transformative potentials of language are combined with the view that the self is discursively constituted, then the conflation follows automatically," is how Warren puts it.[9] The conflation is between what language can say, virtually anything, and what people can actually do and share, far less.

This conflation is even stronger among those like Ernesto Laclau and Chantal Mouffe, who in *Hegemony and Socialist Strategy: Toward a Radical Democratic Politics* use postmodernist views of language to suggest that the self can be anything we want it to be—because in reality the self is nothing, like words in a text that can be rewritten at will.[10] Here, then, is an important

9. Ibid., p. 10.
10. Ernesto Laclau and Chantal Mouffe, *Hegemony and Socialist Strategy: Toward a Radical Democratic Politics* (London: Verso, 1985), esp. pp. 114–127. They state, e.g., that "whenever we use the category of 'subject' within the text, we will do so in the sense of 'subject positions' within a discursive structure" (p. 115).

reason why language becomes an almost mystical entity in the participationist tradition. If language can transform the self, then we can write about selves and individuals any way we want, and they will follow; they must follow, as we will constitute these individuals in language. And even if individuals don't, we won't be mistaken. The self *could* be the way we say it is, because it could be any way at all. Such a rhetorical strategy is not new, though the postmodern focus on the linguistic nature of the self has given it a new cachet. The traditional state-of-nature theorists pursued the same rhetorical strategy in reverse order, seeking to convince man that he was not a group animal but an individual, so that he might be more readily governed. *Plus ça change, plus c'est la même chose.*

The participationists, including those whom Warren calls expansive democrats, fail to confront the tragedy of human life in groups and all that goes into making up this tragedy. I use the term "tragedy" in the sense made famous by Hegel, in which the tragedy of *Antigone* resides in the confrontation of two principles, each of which is valid but cannot coexist.[11] In the case of the play by Sophocles, the tragedy is between the claims of the individual and the rights of the state. In the case of groups the tragedy is similar, only it is enacted not merely within the group but within every member, a conflict between the desire to be unique, autonomous, willful, and free and a desire to abandon oneself to the group, to become one with the group. Not just individuals, but groups enact this conflict within themselves; it is so much of what group life is about. While much of group life seems to be centered on the leader, it is actually this conflict that is being enacted in relationship to the leader, who represents at once both the unique, autonomous, willful individual (Freud's primal father) and the group. There is no resolution to this conflict. It will not be *aufgehoben*. But some ways of living with it are better than others. These better ways assume, and require, group development.

Barber's *Strong Democracy* lacks any hint of tragic spirit. It lacks any sense that one cannot have all of every good thing, that some goods conflict. Strong democracy becomes a list of all good things. Calling local institutions a "training ground for democracy," Barber goes on to argue that they must not become "privatistic, or parochial, or particularistic" (p. 235). As though this were possible. As though one could really have it all: local institutions with universal sentiments, total freedom and total belonging, privacy without loneliness, intimacy without constraint, love without heartache. In fact,

11. Hegel, *Aesthetik*, pt. III , ch. 3, iii.a. George Steiner, *Antigones: How the Antigone Legend Has Endured in Western Literature, Art, and Thought* (Oxford: Clarendon Press, 1986), pp. 39–42.

the only way to have it all (and then of course not really) is via the schizoid compromise, which is why Rousseau remains such a popular figure among participationists such as Barber and Carole Pateman.

In *Participation and Democratic Theory,* still the single most influential book on the topic, Pateman's leading example of the virtues of participation is workers' self-management in former Yugoslavia. Perhaps they just didn't try hard enough to overcome the "privatistic, or parochial, or particularistic" aspects of their society. Is this a cheap shot? I'm not sure. It is certainly not irrelevant that workers' participation has proved no barrier to the fractionating forces of ethnic nationalism. In any case, the same point can be made more fully using another of Pateman's examples, worker participation in the management of Glacier Metal Company in Britain. Pateman's objection, valid as far as it goes, is that Glacier Metal was insufficiently participatory, as the "highest level policy decisions do not come under the purview of" the workers' councils.[12] In fact, the problems at Glacier Metal were more subtle and more complex.

Glacier Metal is a fascinating example because it has been studied extensively by the Centre for Applied Social Research of the Tavistock Institute of Human Relations in London. Elliott Jaques's study of Glacier Metal remains the single most profound psychoanalytic study of an organized group. Pateman cites Jaques's study for Tavistock but not its conclusion, which is that Glacier Metal was subject to enormous inefficiencies because both workers and management took "those impulses and internal objects that would otherwise give rise to psychotic anxiety, and pool[ed] them in the life of the . . . [company]." This did not lead Jaques to conclude that Glacier Metal had become psychotic, whatever that would mean exactly. However, Jaques did find in the relations of the group manifestations of unreality, splitting, and paranoia, behavior that he regards as the social counterpart of psychotic symptoms in individuals "who have not developed the ability to use the mechanism of association in social groups to avoid psychotic anxiety."[13]

Jaques writes of what he calls the "phantasy social form and content of an institution," virtually a parallel organization in the minds of the members. Depending upon its content, this fantasy institution may further the aims of the group or sabotage it. In the case of Glacier Metal, this fantasy focused on a subcommittee of representatives from workers and manage-

12. Carole Pateman, *Participation and Democratic Theory* (Cambridge: Cambridge University Press, 1970), p. 76.
13. Elliott Jaques, "Social Systems as Defence Against Persecutory and Depressive Anxiety," in *New Directions in Psycho-Analysis,* ed. Melanie Klein, Paula Heimann, and R. E. Money-Kyrle (London: Tavistock, 1955), 478–498, p. 479.

ment. The semi-secret nature of this committee may have made fantasizing about it easier, and Jaques believes that its members were unconsciously quite aware that they were the objects of a good deal of fantasizing. When the committee had little of importance to do, this arrangement was actually quite functional, as the committee became the repository of all the fears and hopes of management and labor, allowing their day-to-day relations to be conducted on a more realistic basis. After the reorganization, however, the management–labor committee was given some difficult and important tasks, failing utterly to accomplish them. The reason, concludes Jaques, is that committee members were so busy acting out the unconscious fantasies of the group that they could not free themselves to perform real work.

It is not important here whether Jaques got Glacier Metal just right, just as it is not important whether Shklar got eighteenth-century New England town meetings just right. The point is that Jaques's study reveals a level of complexity in groups that is not merely ignored in most works on participation but is magically swept away by a language that assumes that such conflicts can be transcended if the words can be put together just right. Or assumes that participation itself works its effects as if by magic. "Participation fosters and develops the very qualities needed for it" is how Pateman puts it.[14] Sometimes it does, and sometimes it doesn't. It is necessary to analyze how participation might help members reclaim parts of themselves previously devoted to the group. The theory of participation must analyze at a deep enough level to understand what it would take to liberate the management–labor committee from its imprisonment in the fantasies of the group. The first step would be to confront them, which would require that the parallel organization in the mind be recognized and its assumptions explored.

The place to do this is not here. Jaques's work is a case study, not a piece of political theory, and it is about political theory that I am writing. Nevertheless, this should not become an excuse to ignore the issues raised by Jaques. If Jaques has captured basic principles of group relations, as I believe he has, then these should be neither disregarded nor contradicted by political theory. Above all, political theory is about groups. My group-theoretical account of the state of nature, drawing upon my experiences with small groups, is an attempt to generalize about group experiences such as those studied by Jaques so as to make them accessible to political theory. Without this experiential basis—without, in other words, a consideration of the state of nature—political theory risks becoming not merely empty words but magical ones, sweeping away all contradictions with its enchanted concepts.

14. Pateman, *Participation and Democratic Theory,* pp. 42–43.

Not only is this dangerously surrealistic, but it makes social life much less interesting as well. The tragic conflicts of group life may not be nice or pleasant, but they do show it to be deeply meaningful, as meaningful as human life itself in all its tensions and contradictions.

Postmodernism or Tragedy without Tears?

With Connolly's conclusions in *Identity\Difference* regarding the relationship between individual and group I am in agreement. Why, then, do I believe that his postmodern approach to this topic is all wrong? First, the points of agreement. Connolly coins the term "civic liberalism" to characterize those liberals who appreciate that individualism takes community for its realization. "The complementarity of perfected differences," as one civic liberal not mentioned by Connolly puts it, requires the "harmonization of diversity." Always a delicate balancing act, this harmonization should not be confused with Rousseau's "reconstitution of individuals as identical instances of the general will," says David Norton in *Democracy and Moral Development* (pp. 140–141). Rather, it finds a place for the creative individual in the group. Connolly argues that this conclusion fails to take the paradox of politics seriously. While we need the common good to enable and support an identity, this common good must always subordinate or crush identity in some way. "Any set of enabling commonalities is likely to contain corollary injuries, cruelties, subjugations, concealments, and restrictions."[15]

Everything I have written about groups supports this conclusion. The tension between individual and group will never be harmonized, and many who write of things like the "harmonization of diversity" presuppose "standards of unity and harmony [that] seem closer to death than to life," as Connolly puts it (p. 172). Connolly takes this tension seriously, so where does he go wrong? By adopting an approach that abandons explanation and theory for characterization. Consider, for example, Connolly's leading question: "Suppose internal and external nature contains, because it is neither designed by a god nor neatly susceptible to organization by human design, elements of stubborn opacity to human knowledge, recalcitrance to human projects, resistance to any model of normal individuality and harmonious community?" (p. 31). I agree, but what we should want to know is why. How is it that the world is so recalcitrant? Why are some aspects more resistant to human knowledge and will than others? It may be that this knowledge, that

15. William E. Connolly, *Identity\Difference: Democratic Negotiations of Political Paradox* (Ithaca, N.Y.: Cornell University Press, 1991), p. 93. All page references to Connolly in the text are to this work.

of how and why, must also remain stubbornly opaque to human knowledge. But is this really a good assumption with which to begin? And end? Doesn't it abandon explanation before we know whether it's impossible?

Connolly goes on to list factors, such as drug tests, credit checks, and home detention of convicted felons, that presumably affect identity (pp. 84, 148–149). He also employs a number of social-psychological hypotheses, such as: "If one holds that heterosexuality is the true sexual identity, then homosexuality must be bad, whether labeled as sin or disease. This is because identity claims work by exclusion" (p. 160). This is not wrong, but it doesn't really advance our understanding much either, not even when transformed into a political-psychological thesis: "Electoral politics contains powerful pressures to become a closed circuit for the dogmatism of identity through the translation of difference into threat and threat into energy for the dogmatization of identity" (pp. 209–210).

What is wanted is not a restatement of a familiar observation in a new postmodern language but a new *explanation* of the familiar observation. This is what I have tried to do with group theory. Why does identity work by exclusion? What exactly are the mechanisms and processes involved? Are there factors, such as good leadership, that might mitigate against this tendency? Are there exceptions that we might learn from? I don't know that my answers are always right. Certainly it is a big jump from the Tavistock group to civil society. But Connolly fails to address these issues, any of them, which means that he doesn't explain the problem. He restates it in a new language, one remarkable for its abstraction. This is not due to Connolly's neglect. It reflects the postmodern belief that the world can no longer be explained, as every explanation is an assertion of power that must distort the identity of the phenomena studied. Of course it must. But consider the alternative, in which social theory becomes the conjunction of excessively concrete lists with extravagantly abstract language.

In fact, one cannot write about society without doing group psychology. One sees this in Iris Marion Young's "The Ideal of Community and the Politics of Difference," which, like *Identity\Difference*, sees the issue in terms of the "metaphysics of presence," as she calls it. "This metaphysics consists in a desire to think things together in a unity, to formulate a representation of a whole, a totality."[16] The phenomenon she deplores is itself an expression of group-think, a manifestation of regression in groups, so that one understands it best by looking at the phenomenon's source in groups, rather

16. Iris Marion Young, "The Ideal of Community and the Politics of Difference," in *Feminism/Postmodernism*, ed. Linda J. Nicholson (New York: Routledge, 1990), 300–323, p. 303.

than its expression in language. My view reflects the group-psychological materialism discussed in chapter 1, in which ideas are the embodiment of social relations, not vice versa.

To demonstrate this, I shall interpret several of Young's philosophical claims about the metaphysics of presence in terms of group theory, showing not only how group theory allows us to see the problem more clearly, but also how the abstract philosophical idea embodies a belief about relationships in groups. The reader should be aware that Young is not doing transcendental philosophy, at least not for its own sake. She is criticizing a number of communitarians, particularly feminists, who seek to overcome "otherness" by relating to others internally rather than externally, as Carol Gould puts it. Among the works Young criticizes in this regard are Gould's *Marx's Social Ontology,* Isaac Balbus's *Marxism and Domination,* Roberto Unger's *Knowledge and Politics,* and Michael Sandel's *Liberalism and the Limits of Justice.* As with Connolly, I agree with the point she is trying to make. Why, I wonder, does she criticize theorists of community in such a remarkably abstract fashion, and what is the cost?

Consider the following three claims by Young.

(1) The move to create totality, as the logic of hierarchical opposition shows, creates not one, but two: inside and outside. The identity or essence sought receives its meaning and purity only by relation to its outside (p. 304).

Chapter 2 analyzed this phenomenon in terms of the way in which groups deny the individuality of their members. The advantage of this perspective is that it captures the conflict *within* each member between his desire to be part of the unity and his desire to be outside. Young doesn't capture this tension, humanity's war with its own groupishness. It becomes a war between polarized concepts, far removed from the individuals who hold them and the groups that realize them. Humanity's war with its own groupishness becomes truly Hegelian, the world as conflict of ideas.

(2) The metaphysics of presence represses or denies difference. . . . As I understand it, difference means the irreducible particularity of entities, which makes it impossible to reduce them to commonness or bring them into unity without remainder. Such particularity derives from the contextuality of existence (p. 304).

Groups deny difference constantly. Still, it is useful to recall that the "entities" to which Young refers are people and that the way in which difference is denied is subtle and complex. Particularly important is the way in which leadership may assist group development, so that differences can be appreciated and the group enriched by them. Young, on the other hand, turns to the diversity of the unoppressive city as an alternative, which is "defined as openness to unassimilated otherness" (p. 319). She frames the issue as otherness versus difference, an abstract formulation that actually *reproduces* the group's difficulty in coming to terms with difference and sameness (it must be one or the other) rather than explaining it or even characterizing it in more precise terms. Difference in respect to what? Same in respect to what? Drawing distinctions like this is what the group members must learn to do, so that they can move beyond the categories of just alike or completely different. Recall the difficulty one group had in conceptualizing a woman Jewish Zen master or a man who was of both Black and Hispanic heritage. The abstract approaches of Young and Connolly reproduce this group phenomenon instead of explaining it.

This is the fundamental problem with their approaches, which transform the problem of groups into philosophy. In losing its connection to actual relationships in groups, such philosophy *reproduces* the problem it is trying to solve by glossing the details. Yet, it is ultimately only these details that will allow the members to construct a modus vivendi between individual and group. "She is a woman, culturally Jewish, a Zen master, and a member of this group," for example. The problem of identity and otherness is insoluble as an abstraction. The problem of individual and group is virtually insoluble, as it too is so abstract. But *actual* individuals and groups can sometimes work out a compromise, a modus vivendi that preserves individual and group. Couples, husbands and wives, friends and lovers, do this all the time. Groups and individuals do it occasionally. To see this, however, we must look at actual individuals and groups.

Chapter 2 argued that the Tavistock group-as-a-whole perspective, in which the consultant speaks to the group as though it were a single entity, may foster and create the regression and deindividuation it discovers. The hyper-abstract approach of the postmoderns may do something similar, disappearing individuals in a veil of abstraction and so fostering the deindividuation and polarization it decries. Arthur Bentley, quoted in chapter 1, argues that groups and their relations are more real than ideas about them. Not only that, but the most repressive group is more humane than the most abstract concept. The repressive group is at least related to the individual, if only to suppress him, whereas the most abstract concept will have nothing at all to do with individuals, disappearing them into the ether of abstraction.

(3) The communitarian ideal participates in the metaphysics of presence because it conceives that subjects no longer need be exterior to one another (p. 308).

In reality, individuals in groups are neither interior nor exterior to each other, but both at once, in different parts of themselves, in different ways at different times. The schizoid compromise is about this. Once again the problem cannot be adequately formulated, much less characterized or explained, at this level of abstraction. Not merely because it is abstract, but because the abstraction forces the issue into polarities, such as that the subjects are interior to each other or that they are exterior to each other. They are both, at once, at the same time, in different parts of themselves.

Texts are not the same thing as world. Texts about individuals are not the same thing as the individuals they are about. But some texts are more distant than others. Young's and Connolly's texts are more distant than need be. The result is not merely the reproduction of the problem faced by the small group, in which identity/difference is an all-or-nothing affair, but a disconnection of text from life that renders the text sterile and dead. The cleverness of expression, including the jump from great abstraction to lists of things, covers a certain deadness in the text, a deadness that stems from the author's having given up the task of understanding or explaining the world. This is seen best in the way in which paradox and play are employed to deny the tragedy of human life in groups. Paradox becomes an alternative to tragedy, or rather its dissociation, in which the tragic conclusion is retained but not the feelings that must go with it if we are to take reality seriously. Light tragedy this might be called, following Stephen White's use of the term light care to characterize the approach of postmodernism.

The profile of this lighter care would, as I have suggested, share the mood and measure of more intense care; but its distinctness and palpability would not be directly anchored in the needs and motivations of intimate relations, but rather in the needs and motivations that are forming in the context of our frustrations and dissatisfactions with modernity.[17]

"This laughter and this dance," the phrase that Jacques Derrida uses to characterize this approach, is exemplified in Connolly's *Identity\Difference.*

My friends and I will sometimes have to contest elements in your identity, first, because the insistence that it is grounded in truth makes you appear too aggressive and destructive to us, even though you look beautiful and principled to yourself. You are too hellbent on conquest or conversion for our

17. Stephen K. White, *Political Theory and Postmodernism* (Cambridge: Cambridge University Press, 1991), p. 105.

taste. . . . Our affirmation of the irony in these stances will contain an invitation to you to affirm corollary ironies in your own. Let us laugh together, on principle. (P. 120)

In fact, rarely have people laughed together when elements of their identity are contested. They have generally suppressed each other or killed each other. One might consider a light, paradoxical, riddling approach superior, but it hardly matters. This is not how disputes about identity are resolved. What begs to be explained, the most obvious fact of all, is that for thousands of years millions—no, billions—of people have been killed while contesting elements of each other's identity. Not *because* they thought their identity was grounded in truth. Rather, some thought it grounded in truth because it is so terribly important, the way individuals survive in groups without going crazy. To see the issues as one of truth, as a problem of philosophical fundamental grounding versus laughter and dance, is to get it backward, to confuse philosophy with the human relationships that threaten or affirm identity. That it is postmodern philosophy makes no difference. It still confuses the idea with the relationship, which means that laughing about it won't make any difference. In other words, postmodern political theory uses words as magically as do the participationists.

People aggressively assert the truth and rightness of their identities because of the threats posed to their identity by the group. Not just the other group, but their own. Changing how we think about truth will change nothing. What needs to be changed is the actual relationships in groups and grouplike entities, and to do this one must understand how they work. Then truth will follow willingly, one might say. Finally, it is worth noting that Connolly does not say that "I" will have to contest elements in your identity. Rather, he says "My friends and I" will have to contest elements in your (singular) identity (p. 120). It's already a group fight. Not one group versus another, but a fight within one group, in which Connolly and his friends will sacrifice an individual who insists upon his identity. It will, apparently, be a lite sacrifice, but a sacrifice nonetheless.

The Political Implication of Postmodernism Is Liberal Pluralism

Toward the conclusion of "The Ideal of Community and the Politics of Difference," Young states that "our political ideal is the unoppressive city . . . defined as openness to unassimilated otherness" (pp. 317–319). By "city" she refers not so much to the size of the grouplike entity but to the quality of relationships in it. She goes on to characterize these relationships in terms of the "being together" of strangers, related not internally but externally (p. 318). City dwellers "witness one another's cultures and function in . . . public interactions, without adopting them as their own" (p. 319). As is so often the case among political theorists, she writes as if saying it would make it so: as if the projective identifications that lead to "internal" rather than "external" relationships could be turned off by a theoretical switch.

Striking is what Young does not write about: politics. Not one word about how resources might be distributed, disputes settled, legitimate claims to authority determined, and collective amenities, such as hospitals, schools, parks, and roads, funded and organized. Not one word about power and authority. Not one word about leadership. Not one. In part this is because an abstract, metaphysical approach to political theory (even in the guise of the anti-metaphysics of postmodernism) leaves no room for such details. There is, I believe, another reason. The ideal of the unoppressive city reflects a familiar group fantasy: not only are leaders unnecessary, but collective decisions need not be made if everyone just respects everyone else. The fantasy, in other words, is of autarky: that issues of power, authority, control, and resources need not be confronted, as each member is completely autonomous, in need of nothing and no one. Young extends this fantasy to groups of individuals—what I have called "tribes."

Young is aware that failure to address these questions risks liberal pluralism. "Many questions arise in proposing a politics of difference. . . . How does one provide representation to group interests that avoids the mere pluralism of liberal interest groups? . . . . These questions, as well as many others, confront the ideal of the unoppressive city" (p. 320). I would put it more strongly. Failure to address these questions *is* liberal pluralism, no matter what it is called. Not because Young and Connolly write about groups, but because in their writings about groups they fail to confront questions of legitimacy, value, authority, and decision. The failure to confront these issues, the assumption (often tacit) that they need not be addressed, *is* liberal pluralism, even if the metaphysical basis of postmodernism is different. Not the metaphysics, but the consequences for social relationships—that is, politics—is my concern.

In *The End of Liberalism,* Theodore Lowi defines liberal pluralism as holding that because there are so many groups, often with cross-cutting membership, no single group or group of groups will be able to dominate. One organized group can generally be found checking some other organized group, the assumption of countervailing power. The role of government is one of insuring access and ratifying agreements and compromises worked out among the competing groups. "This last assumption is supposed to be a statement of how a democracy works and how it ought to work. Taken together, these assumptions amount to little more than the appropriation of the Adam Smith 'hidden hand' model for politics, where the group is the entrepreneur and the equilibrium is not lowest price but the public interest."[18]

The result is a politics based on fantasy: that leadership and responsibility are unnecessary, as leaders are only for the dependent and easily led, and responsibility only for those whose acts affect others. Behind this fantasy stands another, an articulating fantasy, so to speak, one that makes plausible the fantasy that leadership and responsibility are unnecessary. This fantasy is that most familiar one in small groups, that everyone in the group is really just like everyone else—Rousseau's fantasy. Or if they are not, then the differences are unimportant, purely arbitrary, nothing to distinguish individuals. If they weren't, then there would be terrible conflicts over power, and the group would fly apart. Though Young and Connolly defend and idealize difference, both trivialize it by treating all differences as equal and so refusing to confront the necessity of choice, including moral choice among competing claims. If all differences are equal, then they are equally insignificant.

In response it might be argued that liberal pluralism is not based on fantasy. It is simply untrue. Some groups are more powerful than others, managing to capture institutions of government so as to achieve virtually monopoly status. I agree. Not the untruth of the theory, but why such an obviously untrue theory would exert such sway, albeit sometimes cleverly disguised, is my concern. My answer is not unlike Lowi's. Liberal pluralism exerts such sway because it reflects a powerful underlying fantasy: not merely that differences need not be confronted, but that "if sovereignty is parceled out among groups, then who is out anything?" (p. 55). This is the fantasy of acting out the missing leader in the group, patriarchy without the father. Only rather than worrying about how to hold the sovereign pieces together without obliterating their individuality, liberal pluralism holds to the fantastic proposition that the pieces can work together harmoniously if only we let them alone. Why? Because one piece is really no different from any other. They are all just interchangeable, undifferentiated parts, which is why liberal pluralism is not interested in making any judgments as to the relative importance of interests or the validity of members' claims. This is, of course, the world view of the undeveloped group; or rather, the group that stands on the cusp between regression and undevelopment. Differences among members exist, but these differences are basically differences among interchangeable member-parts.

Such a fantasy is tantamount to corruption, as citizens take no respon-

18. Theodore J. Lowi, *The End of Liberalism: The Second Republic of the United States,* 2d ed. (New York: W. W. Norton, 1979), p. 51.

sibility for their acts, as though no one was really affected by anyone anyway. As though moral choices and ethical decisions weren't being made. American political science, says Lowi, is similarly irresponsible and hence corrupt. Rather than analyze and interpret the way in which interest-group liberalism avoids the responsibility of action, decision, and choice, political science transforms this fantasy into a method. So does political theory when it refuses to even consider what happens when differences confront each other, which means when politics can no longer be avoided by ratcheting up the level of abstraction. There is, I have repeatedly argued, no solution to the problem of individual and group and hence no solution to the problem of groups in conflict, as men and women fight out their own groupishness in conflicts with other groups. For all its love of paradox and play, postmodern political theory is one more attempt to discover a solution. The irony, of course, is that this solution claims that no solution is necessary in the unoppressive city. Not only is this false, not only is it based on fantasy, but it devalues real differences and the individuality they may represent by failing to judge among them.

The Abstract Individual Is Always a Groupie: Rawls and Sandel

Rawls, like the other social-contract theorists who are part of the tradition in which he writes, is actually a group theorist. But Rawls's group is far more regressed than the groups written about by Hobbes and Locke. I shall support this claim in a simple, straightforward fashion, arguing in favor of Michael Sandel's position in *Liberalism and the Limits of Justice* that Rawls is no individualist but a communitarian in disguise. Sandel gets Rawls spot on. Where I disagree is over the question of whether such a community is desirable, for I do not believe that it is. It is an extremely regressed group, with no space and no appreciation for individual differentiation — indeed, no space for individuals. The abstract individualism of Rawls and the communitarianism of Sandel turn out to be the two halves of the same schizoid compromise. I assume that the reader is familiar with Rawls's *A Theory of Justice*.

At the heart of Rawls's theory is the "difference principle," which states that social inequalities are permitted only to the degree that they benefit the least advantaged man, and that they concern offices and positions that are open to all.[19] A seemingly simple and straightforward statement, its implications are startling. We see then, says Rawls,

19. John Rawls, *A Theory of Justice* (Cambridge, Mass.: Harvard University Press, Belknap Press, 1971), p. 83. All page references to Rawls in the text are to this work.

that the difference principle represents, in effect, an agreement to reward the distribution of natural talents as a common asset and to share in the benefits of this distribution. . . . Those who have been favored by nature, whoever they are, may gain from their good fortune only on terms that improve the situation of those who have lost out. . . . No one deserves his greater natural capacity nor merits a more favorable starting place in society. . . . In justice as fairness men agree to share one another's fate. (Pp. 101–102)

Rawls is a state-of-nature–social-contract theorist in the tradition, he says, of Locke, Rousseau, and Kant. What Rawls calls the original position is akin to the state of nature (p. 11). In the original position, free and rational persons would agree, in effect, that there are to be no individuals in the group. My talents, my abilities, my hard work, even my good will and my good character—none of these belong to me in Rawls's scheme. "The assertion that a man deserves the superior character that enables him to make the effort to cultivate his abilities is equally problematic," says Rawls (p. 104). Everything that I am, all that I have become, even my good character, is regarded solely and strictly as a group resource, to be cultivated only to the degree and extent that it serves the group.

This is the mentality of the regressed group. A still more regressed group is imaginable, one in which differences are simply denied, so that not even a "difference principle" is imaginable, but only a sameness principle. Rawls's group is slightly more advanced. Differences are acknowledged but quickly and completely severed from real individuals who possess them, as though the existence of embodied individuals with different talents, skills, and personalities is too painful to contemplate. The denial of competence is, I have argued, characteristic of most small groups, the presence of individuals with abilities that might serve the group being conspicuously ignored by all, including those who possess them. Rawls develops a marvelous group-sanctioned defense to deal with this fear. Keep the competence, but surgically separate it from competent individuals. Only the group is allowed to be competent.

You are taking this all too seriously, too literally, it might be argued in response. The difference principle was developed by Rawls to fit his game-theoretic approach to justice, its big advantage being that it generates a determinate solution, the maximin solution to the problem of social justice (p. 152). In another book I have argued that there is a deeply fearful—indeed, paranoid—quality to Rawls's theory, insofar as the strongest argument on its behalf is that it is the theory one would choose if one knew that one's place in society would be selected by one's worst enemy. Here I shall simply note that it is a mark of respect to take Rawls seriously and literally, that others such as Sandel have done so with fruitful consequences, and that Rawls himself takes great pains to demonstrate that the difference principle represents a social ideal, not just a game-theoretic piece of cleverness. The difference principle reflects Rawls's utopian vision of the good society.

What kind of society? Here Sandel's insight into Rawls's communitarianism is supported by a group-theoretic perspective. Rawls's ideal is the total community, the total group. "Only in the social union is the individual complete," says Rawls. In such a social union, "each person can participate in the total sum of the realized natural assets of the others" and so "cooperate in realizing their common nature" (pp. 523, 527). "The self is realized in the activities of many selves," he continues, and through participation in the many selves of the group we "attain the excellences that we [as individuals] must leave aside, or lack altogether." The result is that "we cease to be mere fragments," as we share in the wholeness of the group (pp. 565, 529).

It is difficult to know exactly how to interpret Rawls's assertions. Were it not for the difference principle, one might suppose that he is making an argument akin to civic republicanism, in which I can achieve my full development as a person only in a community of others. The human excellences are social excellences, such as generosity and courage. As such, they require a life intimately involved with others in order that they may be expressed and developed. But the difference principle puts an end to this interpretation of Rawls. In Rawls's view individuals are fragments, bits and pieces, becoming whole only to the degree that they partake of the group. Rawls's argument that in the group we "attain the excellences that we [as individuals] must leave aside, or lack altogether" does not mean that in the group we develop ourselves as individuals. That would mean that in the group members cooperate to reclaim lost and abandoned parts of themselves, parts that they have projectively identified with others, as when men attribute their own longing and subjectivity to women, as Pateman argues that they do in *The Sexual Contract*.

Such an interpretation of Rawls cannot be right, for it would be completely incompatible with the difference principle, which requires that every part of the individual, every talent, every competence, every asset, must remain forever alienated, always strictly a group asset. Rawls's argument can only mean that in the group we attain the excellences that we lack as individuals, because only in the group are we whole, fusing with it and so becoming more than the broken, fragmented selves that we are otherwise destined to be. Not only is this a recipe for the totalitarian group, it is a recipe for the failed group, one that cannot mobilize the talents and energies of its individual members as there are not any individual members left. Group development is individual development and vice versa. This does not mean that there is no tension between them; there is, and it is constant and unremitting. It means that groups that exploit the assets of their members, discouraging their members from appropriating their own talents, are bound to become stultified, reified, and deadened. Man, says Marx in the *Grundrisse*, is "an animal that can individuate itself only in the midst of society." Just right, individuation being a matter of reappropriating aspects of oneself projected into the group, understanding that while these aspects belong to me, their expression needs a community of others with whom to share them.

The reason why there are no individuals in Rawls's utopia is that there are no individuals in his state of nature either—what he calls the original position. Though Rawls takes great pains to argue that his is a social-contract theory, there are really no individuals anywhere who might debate, discuss, disagree, bargain, and make a contract. My evidence? Individual differences are unknown in the state of nature, behind the veil of ignorance as it is called. Indeed, individuals are so alike that "each is convinced by the same arguments." "If anyone after due reflection prefers a conception of justice to another, then they all do, and a unanimous agreement can be reached" (p. 139). It is as though in the state of nature there is just one big rational organism. The result is that there is no bargaining or negotiation behind the veil of ignorance, a point Rawls takes pains to emphasize (pp. 139–140). There exist no individuals to bargain. Again, one might argue that Rawls looks at the situation this way simply in order to arrive at a determinate solution to a bargaining game. "Without these limitations . . . the bargaining problem of the original position would be hopelessly complicated," he says (p. 140). It is the strength of Sandel's *Liberalism and the Limits of Justice* to take Rawls more seriously than this, demonstrating that these "limitations," as Rawls calls them, make perfect sense once one understands that Rawls is not really writing about individuals at all. He is writing about the total group, the total community, in which there is so little differentiation among individuals that each is convinced by exactly the same arguments. In Rawls's ideal world, there can be no horse races, or at least no betting on them.

Pateman argues in *The Sexual Contract* that in Rawls's version of the state of nature "there is only one individual, duplicated endlessly. How the duplication takes place is a mystery."[20] Sandel solves the mystery. The duplication takes place in the total community, the total group, that tolerates no indi-

20. Pateman, *Sexual Contract*, p. 223.

vidual variation. There is really no difference between the state of nature and civil society in Rawls's scheme. The social contract simply clarifies and justifies what was always the case: that regressed groups hate individuals, regarding them at best as food for the group. While Sandel solves the mystery, he doesn't correct its author, arguing only that Rawls was really talking about the community that constitutes the self all along. And that's just fine with Sandel. At no point does Sandel set any limits on this community, display any qualms about its totality, or make any effort to reclaim the individual from it. His theoretical comments about the "radically situated subject" hardly count in this regard, being made *en passant*.[21] For the totally abstract individual Sandel substitutes the totally abstract community—one in which the individual remains totally abstract, of course, for there remains no differentiation between individual and group. Sandel's program is truth in advertising, making explicit what is only implicit in Rawls: the individual stripped of all his assets, who exists only to improve the lot of others, is really no individual at all, but a mere reflection of the group. Once it is spelled out, Sandel has no difficulty with this message. I do.

Sandel concludes that the "constitutive conception of community" that he champions is no more "metaphysically problematic" than the totally abstract individual constituted by a concept of justice that Rawls defends.[22] True enough, for the problem is not metaphysical at all. It is real, down to earth, and highlights the great virtue of the traditional state-of-nature theorists, Pufendorf, Hobbes, Locke, and Rousseau. For all their limits, which are considerable, each employed the state of nature as a fictional way to talk about human nature—especially, I have argued, human nature in groups, which is what politics is about. Much contemporary political theory, especially that pursued by Rawls and Sandel, is a regression behind this achievement, substituting metaphysical individuals and metaphysical groups for real ones in order to tell more pleasant stories. There is no more troublesome trend in political theory today, its escape from the real problem of how individuals might live with each other in groups into the metaphysics of abstract individualism or community or the magical language of participation in search of the perfect parade of adjectives. Not merely postmoderns, but most contemporary political theorists, take refuge in abstraction.

In the end, of course, there is no difference at all between the abstract individual of Rawls and the abstract community of Sandel. Both obliterate the individual in the name of a group that doesn't really exist, as it has no

21. Michael Sandel, *Liberalism and the Limits of Justice* (Cambridge: Cambridge University Press, 1982), p. 21.
22. Ibid., p. 174.

real members. Groups do this too, of course, with equally unfortunate results. It is a mark of the regressed group to treat its members as stereotypical abstractions, such as rational older man, angry young student, frustrated menopausal woman, and so forth (to mention the categories in which some of the members of a recent group that I participated in were placed). This is important. The categories that regressed groups use to characterize their members are not concrete at all, but remarkably abstract, so general as to fit no one. The fact that these categories are generally clichés should not cause us to overlook this. The political theory of Rawls and Sandel mirrors what regressed groups do, turning their members into abstractions. There is no difference between them in this regard, no difference at all. Both are theorists of the regressed group, mimicking unawares what real regressed groups do. In this sense, at least, their theories are not abstract enough, reproducing the problem rather than stating the solution, group development.

Rawls's *A Theory of Justice* is not really a theory of justice at all. It is a codification of what regressed groups do anyway all the time, how they regard their members as manna for the group. This is, of course, a terrifying experience, to be regarded as little more than food for the group, which is why individuals hide themselves in regressed groups. This is why there is no real difference between the state of nature and civil society in Rawls's account. The latter is simply a restatement of what regressed groups do in the state of nature. Rather than being concerned with how individuals might reappropriate aspects of themselves lost to the group, what the social contract should be concerned with, Rawls's social contract takes this loss and calls it justice.

What about Sex?

So far not a word about sex. This can't be right, as group theory shows how terribly central sexual desire and conflict are to the group. In *The Sexual Contract* Carole Pateman makes some progress on this issue but stops far short. From a group-theoretical perspective, Pateman is quite correct to disagree with Gayle Rubin and others who argue that patriarchy is no longer a relevant political category.[23] Patriarchy remains relevant because it is not just about paternal right, the power of the father. Nor does it apply only to "societies of 'Old Testament-type pastoral nomads,'" but to the power of the man over the woman, a power expressed in the marriage contract (pp. 27–28).

23. Pateman, *Sexual Contract*, pp. 22, 30–31. All page references to Pateman in this section are to this work, unless otherwise noted.

Certainly men are constantly asserting power over women in the small groups that I have studied, just as certainly as women assert that the price of intimacy with men in the group seems to be violation and subordination. These small groups are, of course, deeply embedded in the culture, so that I have no way of knowing if this competition is natural, whatever that would mean exactly. But it is certainly central to almost every aspect of group life, as I have argued. The real question is why would political theory ignore what is perhaps the fundamental conflict in group life?

Pateman's answer is that political theory has not really ignored sexual conflict at all. It has fought to win and almost succeeded. The abstract individual so central to social-contract theory from Pufendorf to Rawls *is* male, in the sense that this individual is an abstract, disembodied reasoner, a maximizer of expected utilities, a follower of universal principles (pp. 223–225). This may not be what men are really like (I don't believe that it is), but it is nonetheless a masculine cultural ideal, as authors from Carol Gilligan to Sigmund Freud have recognized. Because girls do not fear castration as boys do, says Freud, girls never internalize father's authority in the form of general principles of morality, the origin of the superego. Consequently, women never learn to govern their actions by principles and rules to the same degree as men. They remain enemies of civilization, guiding their conduct by particular attachments, rather than universal ideals.[24]

If being a man is a matter of using one's reason to follow universal principles (be they the maximization of expected utility or Kant's categorical imperative), free of particularistic attachments, then almost all political theory has been about men and for men. If women are not explicitly excluded, then they are included only to the degree that they become like men, disembodied reasoners. Arlene Saxonhouse makes this argument about Plato's philosopher-queens, but it fits Rawls just as well, and most philosophers in between. Women are admitted as (almost) equal partners to men only to the degree that they abandon everything embodied and female about themselves.[25] It is to this that Pateman objects, and she is quite right. It is incredible, for example, that in all Barber's concern to bring politics down to earth and back to reality—the "real present" he calls it— he has not one word to say about women, or even women and men. It is as if everyone who participates is of the same sex. One can, of course, say precisely the same thing about Pateman's own earlier work on *Participation and Democratic Theory.*

24. Freud, *Civilization and its Discontents,* pp. 51–56.
25. Arlene Saxonhouse, *Women in the History of Political Thought: Ancient Greece to Machiavelli* (New York: Praeger, 1985), pp. 39–52.

The homogenization of men and women is characteristic of the earliest stages of group development. In a small group in which I recently participated, increasing sexual desire and conflict within the group led one participant after another, male and female, to extol the virtues of androgyny, as though the group could become one warm, fuzzy, sexless entity, androgyny as defense. Political theory has done something similar, even if its abstract entities are not quite so warm and fuzzy, but coldly abstract. Conversely, Pateman has it just right when she states: "To take embodied identity seriously demands the abandonment of the masculine, unitary individual to open up space for two figures; one masculine, one feminine" (p. 224). Only this is where Pateman stops, whereas I would add that to take embodied identity seriously means to open up space first for two figures . . . then three, then four, and then as many figures as there are group members.

Sexual differentiation, sexual embodiment, is an important dimension, probably the single most important dimension, in individual differentiation. But it is—or should be—individual differentiation that counts. The goal should be individual differentiation that takes sexual embodiment seriously but does not stop there. A group of men and women who take each other's sexuality seriously and so begin to see each other as individuals in a new way is the goal. Sexual embodiment is not the sine qua non of individuality but its threshold. Pateman, on the other hand, would halt group development when it reaches the stage of the tribe of men versus the tribe of women. She does not say this explicitly. But what she does not say, particularly what she says about what she does not say, shows this to be so.

Pateman titles her last chapter "The End of the Story?", apparently because she knows that it is not. She concludes her story this way: "I have completed what I have to say about the sexual contract, but the story is far from finished. The political fiction is still showing vital signs and political theory is insufficient to undermine the life supports" (p. 234). What would it take to finish the story? Only, I believe, a political theory that *begins* with the differences between men and women but does not end there, instead using these differences to construct an account of what it is to be an individual in the group and why this is so terribly difficult. Pateman's account stops short because her theory stops short. It is vital to recognize that the members of groups are embodied, sexual individuals. Without this insight, no further progress in group development is possible. But this insight is not the end, as it is in Pateman's book, but only the beginning.

The beginning of what? Of a political theory that takes group development seriously, organizing its basic principles so as to take these findings into account. Pateman complains that "classical patriarchalism took infantile dependence as a basic political fact" (pp. 91–92). So it should. Patriarchalism recognizes truths about human life in groups, particularly the hunger for leadership, the desire to be led and cared for, that are never outgrown but may nonetheless be expressed differently by adults than by children. Conversely, much of Locke's theory is a defense against the insights of patriarchalism into the origins of groups and politics in the dependency of children in families. Pateman recognizes this in principle. It is what much of *The Sexual Contract* is about. But this recognition does not translate into a developmental theory, an account of politics that recognizes its origins in childish dependence, working to move beyond these origins without seeking vainly to escape them. Instead, Pateman simply concludes that "there is good reason to confine the term 'political' to relationships among adults" (p. 91). Once again the risk is the magical use of words, as though confining the term could somehow confine the reality.

Group theory stresses leadership, and it might be argued in response that leadership is itself a patriarchal category connoting hierarchy and control (chapter 6 argues that it is more about interpretation than control). A perspective that takes the experience of women seriously would stress more cooperative, egalitarian relationships. *In A Different Voice* by Carol Gilligan discloses a way of thinking about ethical problems that depends less upon subsumption of cases under universal principles and more on feelings for the relationships involved. Not exclusively the province of one sex, this way of thinking is, at least in our culture, more closely associated with women. Perhaps there is a women's voice regarding issues of leadership that remains unspoken. I do not believe that this is the case, but it is a possibility that cannot be dismissed. What can be dismissed is the attempt by Pateman, so characteristic of contemporary political theory, to solve with words and definitions ("There is good reason to confine the term 'political'") what can only be settled empirically. That even an empirical study such as Gilligan's only leads to more questions is no argument against an empirical approach, only against a naïve view of empiricism.

Political theory, and not just Pateman's, is terribly afraid of the idea of *development*, that a group or society might begin in a childish relationship to leaders but grow into a more developed one, perhaps with the help of leaders themselves. Social-contract theory posits a one-stage model of development, then and now, the state of nature and life under the social contract. Most contemporary works on participation, on the other hand, argue in effect that development is complete when we get the adjectives strung together just right. In fact, the fear of development (that it takes work, time, courage, and is never complete) is itself a primary characteristic of the undeveloped group. Groups fear development because their members fear they lack the strength, courage, and goodness to do the work. So they tell themselves that they are just fine, or would be if they could only be rid of the enemy, be it Communists, the cultural elite, or the metaphysics of presence. Finding and fighting enemies is always a good diversion, but groups are remarkably inventive in redefining the task—anything but the work of development. Political theory, I have suggested, is similar in this regard, even Pateman's, which finds in men the perfect enemy. Enemies may be real and still serve this diversionary function.

What would the work of development look like from a perspective that takes Pateman's thesis in *The Sexual Contract* as its starting point? It would look like what the work of group development always looks like: members taking back into themselves parts of themselves that they have disowned and projectively identified with other group members. This is how the social contract should be reinterpreted. In the case of men and women, group development would look like men coming to understand that the embodied, desiring, connected self that men (and women) so often attribute to women is a disowned part of themselves. Conversely, women would come to understand that the rational, instrumental self, so often attributed to men, is an attribute of any woman who wishes to get on and make a difference in the world, to make history. This is not to say that the sexes are the same, for they are not. It is to say that there is frequently massive collusion between the sexes, aimed at persuading the other sex to "hold" disturbing, frightening parts of one's own. Not necessarily just bad parts, but often good ones as well. It is this collusion we should focus on, the shared responsibility in creating and maintaining sexual stereotypes.

In *The Mermaid and the Minotaur* Dorothy Dinnerstein writes of the "socially sanctioned existential cowardice" that has often led women to dare less than they might have to be what they could be. What they could be, says Dinnerstein, is history-makers.

In [Simone] de Beauvoir's view, the central bribe to which woman succumbs is the privilege of enjoying man's achievements and triumphs vicariously, honored and treasured by him as arbiter, witness, nurturant servant-goddess, while enjoying immunity from the risks he must take. He too, de Beauvoir points out, would like to have this immunity—all fear the freedom and responsibility that we must, as a species, accept—but life does not offer him this option: the option is hers, in return for acting as supportive "other" to him while he makes the human world for both of them.[26]

26. Dorothy Dinnerstein, *The Mermaid and the Minotaur: Sexual Arrangements and the Human Malaise* (New York: Harper Colophon Books, 1976), p. 211.

Dinnerstein develops de Beauvoir's argument, pointing out how this arrangement has so often seemed to serve the interests of both sexes that both have become adept at perpetuating it—collusion. Man needs woman as mirror, because he is so busy history-making that he forgets who he is, his inner world at risk of impoverishment. Woman acts as mirror for all the reasons mentioned. It is the collusion that is central, and a perspective that takes group development seriously is the only one that addresses it. For that is precisely what we are talking about here. How the group that is composed of men and women might help each other reclaim lost parts of themselves, the history-making potential of women, the inwardness of men.

Neither sex is innocent in this collusion. "What do women want?" asks Freud. They want, says Dinnerstein, to stop serving as scapegoats for human resentment of the human condition, especially human dependence, vulnerability, and mortality (p. 234). True enough, but not always, for often the scapegoat colludes, as both Dinnerstein and de Beauvoir recognize. Pateman doesn't. Nor does most political theory, which is afraid of developmental issues and developmental perspectives, perhaps because such a perspective takes infantile dependence seriously. As Dinnerstein recognizes, it is infantile dependence that leads men frantically to remake the world, to show how strong they are, and women to share vicariously in men's achievements, rather than make their own history. Fortunately, this has begun to change in some societies, a change that may do much to release the developmental potentials of both men and women.

But it has not changed in political theory. Or the change is glacial. Even glaciers move, however, and one finds an awareness of this principle, often only in passing, in surprising places. Consider, for example, the following comment by Joyce Appleby in *Liberalism and Republicanism in the Historical Imagination:*

Obviously the liberal hero was male. Less obviously liberalism relied on gender differences to preserve the purity of its ideal type. Dependency, lack of ambition, attachment to place and person—these qualities were stripped from the masculine carrier of inalienable rights and conferred upon women. . . . This allowed the unsentimental, self-improving, restlessly ambiguous, free, and independent man to hold sway as a universal hero. *Without women to accept what was denied in men, the assertion of a uniform human nature could not have been maintained.* Nor could society have been analyzed in the social scientific mode without scattering to the periphery the poetic, the sensuous, the indeterminant—in short, the experiential burden carried by women. (Pp. 29–30, my emphasis)

In talking about sex, we are not *just* talking about sex. We are talking about the way one group gets another, usually through a combination of force and collusion, to hold its bad stuff—even if this supposedly bad stuff is good, but scary, a mark of vulnerability and hence humanity. To ignore sexual conflict, then, is to ignore not just sex but the most fundamental pattern by which group members make each other less whole. This has ramifications for every aspect of political theory and has for millennia.

While there are bright spots on the horizon, such as Appleby's comments, political theory generally ignores sexual conflict, substituting the abstract individual for the sexually embodied one. Or political theory states the legitimate complaints of women in such a way as to ignore the collusion between the sexes, as Pateman does. I say this not just as a man, though I know this deeply influences my reading of the issues. I say it as one who believes he understands what group development requires: understanding the way men and women use each other in groups to disown threatened and threatening parts of themselves. Men and women still need each other to be whole. Previously, albeit with many exceptions, men and women completed each other by acting as each other's complement. Together they might make a whole, as when spouses of my parents' generation introduced each other as "my better half." Another possibility exists, that men and women might help each other reclaim lost parts of themselves, so that each might become whole. This, though, takes work, the work of group development. In doing this work, men and women are rewriting not merely *The Sexual Contract* but the social contract as well. There are lots of issues about which the social contract needs to be rewritten. None is more fundamental than the relationship between men and women, because there is more socially sanctioned disowning of self between the sexes than in just about any other area of life.

The Social Contract

What if these considerations, generalized from the tribes of men and women to group relations among individuals, became the basis of the social contract? If the group is the state of nature, as I have argued, then its key characteristic is that members project so much of themselves into the group that there is not enough left over with which to make individuals. The social contract I propose would be concerned with reappropriating these too widely distributed parts. In approaching the social contract in this fashion, it is useful to keep in mind Gordon Schochet's comments on the idea of contract in seventeenth-century England: "Contract seems to have been used more as a formal explanation of how people entered relationships than as a definition of the nature and content of those stations." Gordon Wood differs from Schochet somewhat, arguing that prior to the eighteenth century the social contract referred not to rights and duties but to relationships. "Such contracts defined relationships between people rather than specific promises of action."[27] The social contract as an account of the requirements of a relationship or the social contract as an account of the relationship? It would be a mistake to equate these two views. Yet they share much, particularly the insight that the social contract is not a formal instrument, or even a set of promises, but a way of characterizing the almost intangible qualities of social relationships: what it takes to enter a relationship and to maintain it. It is in this older sense that I propose to think about the social contract.

The social contract I propose is straightforward: that the relationships it describes and the institutions upon which these relationships are based *not primarily serve to allow one or more parties to locate disowned parts of themselves in others*. The social contract as a series of institutions, arrangements, and practices by which citizens come to reclaim lost parts of themselves is the alternative I am opposing to the traditional social contract.

Pateman argues in *The Sexual Contract* that the marriage contract violates this social contract, encouraging men to locate disowned parts of themselves in women. Appleby recognizes the implications of this violation for liberalism. Hegel's dialectic of master and slave, discussed previously, also violates this social contract. Or at least the relationship it characterizes does, as Ego and Alter locate large parts of themselves in the other. Marx argues in the *Grundrisse* that the so-called free labor contract violates this social contract, in effect locating the creative labor power of the worker in the owner and his dead capital.[28] All four theorists stress the inequality in power that leads to this result. I am not sure that any of these theorists gets it just right. My point is that the principle of the social contract I am proposing should be familiar, even if the language and concepts that I employ are unfamiliar, drawn from the language of group psychology, a language less familiar to political theorists. The advantage of my perspective is that it puts the social contract in the service of group development, something that political theory has traditionally not done very well. The social contract becomes the threshold of group development, not its epitome.

Traditional political theory has been little concerned with group development. On the contrary, the implicit contract is an agreement to alienate

27. Schochet, *Patriarchalism in Political Thought*, pp. 81–82. Wood, *Radicalism of the American Revolution*, p. 162.

28. Karl Marx, *Grundrisse: Foundations of the Critique of Political Economy*, trans. Martin Nichols, in *The Marx–Engels Reader*, 2d ed., ed. Robert Tucker (New York: W. W. Norton, 1978), pp. 252–278.

parts of oneself. From Hobbes to Rousseau, each citizen gives up virtually all his rights, to either the sovereign or the entire community. The "total alienation to the whole community of each associate with all his rights. . . . The alienation being made without reserve, the union is as perfect as it can be," is how Rousseau puts it in his *Social Contract* (pars. 42–43). Though Locke's tone is different, the way in which government serves to secure property makes the outcome much the same, property becoming the entity in which man alienates himself through labor. Though Locke writes about how man's labor appropriates nature as property, it would be much more accurate to read the argument the other way round, property coming to contain the alienated powers of man, as though they were almost magically present in things but not in man himself. Marx had a thing or two to say about this. In his labor theory of value, which so intriguingly anticipates that of Marx, Locke writes exactly as if it is the thing, such as tobacco or sugar, that absorbs man's labor, taking from man what is human in him and reifying it in the value of the thing itself, a thing that has value only to the extent that it has absorbed human powers (*Second Treatise*, par. 40).

Locke's emphasis on property is widely criticized, though the characterization of him as a theorist of possessive individualism is not quite right. Locke is a theorist of possessed individualism, the individual being possessed by the things that own his powers, like the devil who owns his soul. But if Locke is a theorist of possessed individualism, so too are most other political theorists. Only, rather than making man the possession of his things, most make him the possession of the group, in whom man projectively identifies the most precious parts of himself. Or rather, most contemporary political theorists make man the possession of an *idea*, an idea, I have argued, that reflects group relationships.

Man as the entity who delights in unassimilated difference is the idea with which the postmoderns would possess man. Man as one who reconciles his contradictions through political participation is the controlling idea of the participationists. Man as one who realizes his self by participating in the selves of others is the idea with which Sandel and Rawls would possess man. In fact, men and women are all this and more. They are each of these things at war with each of these other things. Like the small group, each of these approaches to political theory takes an incredibly complex series of relationships and on the basis of very limited knowledge of the participants (intentionally limited: more knowledge would make it more difficult to do this) grossly oversimplifies the relationships, so reducing them to a single dimension. This is particularly ironic in the case of postmodernists, who delight in difference but proceed at such a high level of abstraction as to obliterate the details upon which difference depends. But this obliteration of detail is characteristic of almost every approach.

I too have obliterated detail and could not do otherwise. The difference is that my group-theoretic approach recognizes that the suppression of detail reproduces the problem it is intended to solve, the suppression of the individual by the singular and oversimplified idea of the group held by its members. In other words, the group-theoretic approach has the virtue of not confusing the problem with the solution. Not only that, but the suppression of detail on behalf of the idea of the group is not an all-or-nothing affair, but more or less. The group-theoretic approach does it less and does it more self-consciously. That is the best that anyone, any group member or any political theorist, can do.

I propose the social contract in the spirit of utopia, the spirit in which I write about the transformation of the Wolini into New Ones in the Epilogue. This story illustrates many principles of the social contract in a fictional way, much as the traditional state-of-nature theorists told a story about the state of nature to explore the social contract. My social contract does not idealize regression or confuse individuation with isolation and withdrawal. Occasionally it is realized, at least in part. Institutions and practices that encourage individuals to refrain from alienating the most troublesome and scary parts of themselves in others are not impossible. As noted at the conclusion of chapter 3 regarding the cross diagram, political institutions such as constitutional limits on authority, regular elections, and judicial review can mitigate the tendency of grouplike entities to oscillate between the idealization and devaluation of leaders. This may make it easier for the members of the grouplike entity to position themselves between isolate and groupie. Even when the social contract is not realized, which is most of the time, it may help us to understand better what the good is and so avoid confusing the good with the real. The nowhere of utopia can help us understand the somewhere we are now. This will not always draw us closer to utopia, but it may prevent us from confusing progress and regression.

I have argued that a group-psychological perspective is tragic, revealing the way in which men and women destroy the integrity of the one entity that could recognize their individuality, the developed group. There is no opposition between tragedy and utopia if we understand that the lesson of utopia is as much about why we can't avoid tragedy as why we should. In fact, the opposition between tragedy and utopia need not be this stark. Sound political leadership can help a regressed and undeveloped grouplike entity become a developed grouplike entity. *In other words, sound political lead-*

ership can help realize aspects of the social contract, which I understand to be a characterization of relationships in the developed group. Unlike traditional accounts of the social contract, mine is not so much about the authorization and legitimation of leaders as about a mature relationship to them. This takes leadership. In other words, a mature relationship to leaders assumes an immature relationship to them, an immature relationship that may be outgrown. This requires group development, and group development requires leaders. Both topics are anathema in political theory. The next chapter seeks to lift the curse.

6 ✻ *Leadership*

Unlike traditional social-contract theory, the contract I propose does not merely legitimate leaders. It depends on them. It is not just concerned with security and commodious living, but with improving the souls of citizens, a classical ideal. From a group-theoretical perspective, leadership and followership are the most important things about groups. Nothing happens in groups that is not about the leader and his relationship to his followers. Perhaps the leader is dead or missing in some way. It doesn't matter. The group will organize itself around the missing leader. In fact, groups often prefer it this way, as it is not necessary to confront the reality of an actual leader. To say that the group is always organized around its leader means that it is always organized around its *idea* of the leader, which may or may not have anything to do with the actual leader, if any.

For Freud, the love of the leader unites the group. The group is but a mass of individuals, each involved in a love affair (frequently imaginary, often unconscious) with the leader, one by one. What holds the group together is that the followers all have something in common: they love the same leader and so are alike in this way. They love each other strictly and only insofar they are identical in their choice of a love object—narcissistic love, Freud called it.[1] They hate each other for the same reason, each wanting to possess the leader for himself. Rather than arguing in terms of the libidinal constitution of groups, I have written of the leader as holding the idea of the group and so representing in one body the bodies of all its members. The famous frontispiece of the 1651 edition of *Leviathan*, in which the sovereign's giant body is composed of the tiny bodies of citizens, captures

---

1. Freud, *Group Psychology and the Analysis of the Ego*, pp. 43–48.

this idea, even if Hobbes draws the wrong conclusions. These explanations are not incompatible, even if they are incommensurable: Freud's about libido theory, mine about how the leader helps to contain the threat to the member's identity generated by his conflict over his own groupishness. What connects my explanation with Freud's is the insight that while love of the leader is not the ideal way to bind the group, groups bind themselves even more regressively in the absence of a leader. Freud calls this the psychological poverty of groups, arguing that

> this danger is most threatening where the bonds of a society are chiefly constituted by the identification of its members with one another, while individuals of the leader type do not acquire the importance that should fall to them in the formation of a group. The present cultural state of America would give us a good opportunity for studying the damage to civilization which is thus to be feared.[2]

The emergence of leader types in Europe in the years following the 1929 publication of *Civilization and its Discontents* lends more than a touch of pathos to Freud's remarks about America. What Freud fails to do, of course, is distinguish between bad leaders and good leaders. So does political theory, the result being even more tragic. In recognizing the importance of leaders, Freud opens the door (even if he does not step in) to a discussion of good and bad leadership. When leadership is ignored or devalued, the distinction is not even on the agenda. Why has political theory been willing to confront Hobbes's proposition that man is a predator who preys on his fellow humans but unable to confront man's deep need and desire for leadership? Hobbes sees strong leadership as an expedient to overcome man's wolfish nature. Is it really worse that leadership is something that man might desperately want and need to overcome his fear and loneliness and to realize his individuality?

Apparently the need for leadership and the desire to be led are experienced as degrading, shameful, and humiliating, a reminder of how much even adults depend on others. We all feel how deeply we want to be led and are embarrassed by our own need. Better (that is, more protective of an ideal of humans as autonomous and free) to see humans as needing a leader to keep them from killing each other than to see them as needing a leader to contain their anxiety, assuage their loneliness, and develop their potential, as well as the potential of the group to which they belong. This, at least, is how the small group thinks about leadership. Too often political theory seems to think about leaders in a similar way.

2. Freud, *Civilization and its Discontents*, p. 70.

Leaders are needed for so many things. Groups cannot lead themselves. Leaders motivate, inspire, educate, direct, guide. Leaders hold the frightened, constrain the bold and greedy, and stimulate the lazy. Leaders mobilize opinion. Leaders settle disputes, mediate among warring factions, and give comfort to the oppressed. Leaders keep hope alive. Leaders fuse with the groups they lead and so obtain narcissistic satisfaction from the success of their group. Followers can share in this satisfaction. Leaders get sick, and groups can care for them. In both senses of the term: take care of and, in larger groups especially, care about what happens to them and so gain confidence in their own reparative powers. Leaders die, and groups can mourn them and so better come to terms with their own ambivalence toward leaders. And, of course, leaders can make groups crazy, leading the group to its own destruction. Most of the things that leaders do can be explained in terms of the leader holding the idea of the group. Mothers and fathers are the first leaders, holding the idea of the child in their minds before the child has an idea of himself. Without a leader the group huddles together ever more tightly to keep from flying apart, crushing individuality worse than any leader.

Not only do leaders do lots of things, but the things they do can be seen from at least two perspectives. From an institutional perspective, leaders are executives and policymakers, establishing goals and policies, mediating disputes among warring factions, hiring good people, and arm twisting: In *Leadership,* James MacGregor Burns considers these functions under the rubric of transactional leadership, initiating the exchange of one valued thing for another. "Transformational leadership," as Burns calls it, is different, more like teaching, so that followers are led "to higher levels of motivation and morality," possibly carrying their leaders along with them.[3] What I shall call "interpretive leadership," or leadership by interpretation, is similar to what Burns calls "transformational leadership," but with a distinctive difference.

With the term "higher levels of motivation and morality," Burns is referring to the developmental models of Abraham Maslow, Erik Erikson, and Lawrence Kohlberg. Cautious and thoughtful, Burns assumes that development is best characterized as moving from a concern with means to a focus on ends and from situational to culturally universal values (pp. 428–432). My group-psychological perspective sees it differently. Leadership is about fostering group development, as only group development allows individual growth. While group development has substantive content, such as a reduction in scapegoating and an increase in responsibility, its elaboration will

3. James MacGregor Burns, *Leadership* (New York: Harper and Row, 1978), pp. 19–20. All page references in the text are to this edition.

vary enormously and in ways not necessarily best characterized as a movement toward universalism. This is, I believe, ethically desirable, compatible with the arguments of Carol Gilligan and the postmoderns, as well as empirically more accurate. Interpretive leadership is not about making people better according to the leader's criteria of better. It is about elucidating and interpreting conflicts, so that followers will know what they themselves feel and hence make more responsible choices. This, as Burns, quoting Suzanne Langer, points out, fosters morality. "'Values exist only when there is consciousness . . . Where nothing is felt, nothing matters.' The leader's fundamental act is to induce people to be aware or conscious of what they feel—to feel their true needs so strongly, to define their values so meaningfully, that they can be moved to purposeful action" (p. 44). It is this, and only this, that allows groups to act responsibly on the basis of what they value, not just on the basis of fear and convention, the emotions that bind the regressed group.

Although political scientists and historians such as Burns have devoted considerable attention to leadership, political theorists have not. But while political theorists may ignore the problem of leadership, the problem of leadership doesn't ignore political theory, coming back to haunt it. Just as in the Tavistock group the relationship to the missing leader is acted out in the group, so in the texts of political theory the missing leader is present in the structure of the theory itself, in what it says and what it doesn't. This is not because the world is a text, but because it is not. It is because our ideas about the world represent what we feel, often unconsciously, about our relationships in it. When the political theorist addresses these relationships so as not to talk about leadership and followership, leaders and followers don't disappear. They reemerge in the political relationships themselves and in the texts about them, just as the Tavistock group acts out in the group its fears and desires regarding the missing leader. For the same reason. Because leadership is a relationship and, like all relationships, readily displaced, so that repressed and denied in one place, it emerges in another: in groups, in texts, in life; in texts about life in groups, the subject of this book. As in the small group, the best way to study leadership is to study where it isn't: that is, to study how an entity, be it group or text, organizes itself to perform the functions of leadership in the absence of a leader.

Leadership is not merely neglected in political theory. It is devalued, treated as something dangerous and repellent. There is, for example, no entry on leadership in *The Blackwell Encyclopaedia of Political Thought,* edited by David Miller, Janet Coleman, William Connolly, and Alan Ryan, four of the leading scholars in the field. There are, to be sure, several index references to leadership, but all concern its dangers: Thomas Carlyle's idea of the heroic leader and whether it is a precursor of twentieth-century fascism; the Führer under fascism; Robert Michels's iron law of oligarchy as a theory of leadership; and Max Weber on the attractions of the charismatic leader. That leadership might help citizens reclaim parts of themselves alienated in the group and so foster individual and group development, the proper subject of the social contract, finds no place in the traditional account.

Classical political thought is an exception to this conclusion. Indeed, one might well argue that leadership is the central category of classical thought. Classical writers, such as Plato, Aristotle, and Xenophon, elevate leadership (*hegeisthai*), it is sometimes argued, because they are primarily concerned with what leadership does for the leader. It ennobles him, granting everlasting fame and glory to the ambitious. Political education is a matter of teaching leaders to seek fame for the right things, noble and good purposes, not power and glory for its own sake. Then all will benefit. True enough, but this is not the whole story, even for the classics. Good leaders also ennoble those who follow if followers pride themselves on choosing and demanding good leaders. For a number of years the Athenians under Themistocles and Pericles did so, according to Thucydides, turning to demagogues only when they became demoralized and discouraged. Good leadership, the classics teach us, promotes good followership, a category that is also ennobling if approached properly, the topic of this chapter.

One might expect that communitarians and participationists would find scant place for leaders, as is the case. But leadership is notably missing in other modern accounts as well. Marxist Leninism is the great exception to this generalization, and a troubling one insofar as it seems to suggest that an emphasis on leadership and totalitarianism go together (actually, Marxist Leninism is also based on a fantasy: that leaders are necessary only for the trip to utopia, after which they can be dispensed with, to be replaced by the administration of things). On the contrary, I have argued that good leadership may help overcome the totalitarianism of the group and so enhance individual freedom. For this reason it is especially troubling that classical liberals have so ignored and devalued leadership. In this vein I shall consider the political theory of Michael Oakeshott, whose group-theoretical materialism nonetheless fails to lead him to the proper conclusion. Considered next is Machiavelli, frequently considered a theorist of leadership although he is not. Following this I tell three stories about leadership, each of which says something about the proper role of leaders and followers. The conclusion returns to a consideration of why political theory devalues leadership.

Oakeshott: Rationalization in Politics

In "The Masses in Representative Democracy," Oakeshott argues that human individuality is not given. It stems from the collapse of a closely integrated manner of living, such as medieval feudalism. First in Italy at the close of the thirteenth century, the *uomo singolare* emerges, whose conduct is largely self-determined and whose activities express personal preference. "And together with him appeared, not only the *libertine* and the *dilettante*, but also the *uomo unico*, the man who, in the mastery of his circumstances, stood alone and was a law to himself."[4] Over the course of several hundred years, the individual spread throughout Europe. So too, says Oakeshott, did the individual manqué, one who feared his freedom and sought to return to the comfort and order of communal life. But the community no longer existed, so that by the beginning of the sixteenth century the individual manqué sought in government the security, order, and direction he once found in community.

> We need not speculate upon what combination of debility, ignorance, timidity, poverty or mischance operated in particular cases to provoke this character. . . . He sought a protector who would recognize his predicament, and he found what he sought, in some measure, in 'the government' (p. 371).

Striking is the hostility Oakeshott displays toward the individual manqué, who becomes in his account the "militant 'anti-individual.'" Not only is Oakeshott uninterested in whether the fears of such individuals might have a realistic and understandable basis that might be addressed, which is why he declines to speculate about its source, he also makes every effort to separate the real individual from the anti-individual, suggesting that they have nothing in common, like inhabitants of different worlds. Oakeshott constructs this split—for that is what it is—not only with his terms—individual and "anti-individual," individual and "individual manqué"—but by idealizing the individual and devaluing the anti-individual. This is how all splits are constructed. The individual is one who has the "propensity to make [his] own choices, and finds happiness in doing it" (pp. 426–427). The anti-individual, on the other hand, seeks to obliterate not merely his own individuality but that of those around him, so that he will not feel envy. The anti-individual wants not only to abandon his freedom to leaders and so escape the burden of choice, he demands that government impose its will on all.

4. Oakeshott, *Rationalism in Politics,* pp. 364–365. All page references in the text are to this edition.

The right he claimed, the right appropriate to his character, was the right to live in a social protectorate which relieved him from the burden of "self-determination." But this condition of human circumstances was seen to be impossible unless it were imposed on all alike. So long as "others" were permitted to make choices for themselves . . . his anxiety at not being able to do so himself [would] remain to convict him of his inadequacy and threaten his emotional security. (P. 378)

Only once does Oakeshott suggest that the individual and the anti-individual might be the same individual at war with himself (p. 381). But it is an insight neither pursued nor developed. Instead, terms like parasite on the individual or the shadow of the individual's substance serve to complete the demonization of the anti-individual. In fact, the individual and the anti-individual are one. That is the whole lesson of a group-theoretical perspective. The battle between the individual and the anti-individual is fought out not merely in the group but within each individual in the group, which is what makes group life so torturous. The anti-individual exists, of course, but because he exists within the individual, the possibility exists that good leadership could draw him out, so that he might lead himself one day. But leadership of any kind is anathema to Oakeshott, and now we see why: because it reminds the individual of the anti-individual within himself, the one who wants to be led.

Just as Oakeshott splits the individual and the anti-individual, so he splits rulers and leaders, the terms he employs. Individuals need and want only rulers, understood as neutral referees who will make fair decisions when the interests of individuals collide. Locke's fiduciary is exemplary. "The image of the ruler is the umpire whose business is to administer the rules of the game . . . but does not himself participate in it" (p. 427). Anti-individuals, on the other hand, want to be told what to think and so need leaders who will do this (p. 373). Leadership of such individuals is nothing less, Oakeshott states in "On Being Conservative," than the monomaniacal imposition of the dreams of one indignant half-crippled individual on anti-individuals—those who long to be told not merely what to do or think but what to dream (pp. 427–428). Oakeshott is not talking about a particular leader; he is characterizing leadership per se.

It is no accident that this terribly split account of rulers and leaders is joined to a split account of individuals and anti-individuals. They go together, the point of the cross diagram in chapter 3. By splitting the leader into savior and Satan, the group member maintains the schizoid compromise. If, however, the leader can interpret this split, then members may reappropriate parts of themselves previously devoted to the group. Group members may become individual members, finding some way of balancing membership and individuality within the group. In "Talking Politics," Oakeshott tells a story, attributed to Schopenhauer, that captures the ideal balance between individual and group. There was once, he says, a colony of porcupines. To shield themselves from the freezing weather, they huddled closely together. But while the communal warmth was satisfying, they kept pricking each other with their quills and so backing away, exposing each individually to the freezing weather.

> Thus they remained, distracted between two misfortunes, able neither to tolerate nor to do without one another, until they discovered that when they stood at a certain distance from one another they could both delight in one another's individuality and enjoy one another's company. They did not attribute any metaphysical significance to this distance, nor did they imagine it to be an independent source of happiness, like finding a friend. . . . Unknown to themselves they had invented civil association. (Pp. 460–461)

Harsh critic of the utopian pretensions of rationalists in politics, as he calls them, Oakeshott turns out to be as utopian as any he criticizes. Not because a politics of peaceable porcupines is impossible (though it is well to remember that some porcupines have longer quills than others and so prick others without being pricked themselves), but because it takes so much work, which means group development, and that requires leadership. Oakeshott, on the other hand, writes as though if we just don't expect too much from government and civil association, regarding government as referee and civil association as a conversation for its own sake, not for the sake of our needs and desires, then everything will be fine. This is absurd. The standard objection to Oakeshott's vision of politics is that he would transform politics into aesthetics, a poetic conversation that ignores the rough, coercive, violent, and threatening character of real politics.[5] I would put it somewhat differently. Oakeshott writes as though if we ignore the craziness of politics, the violent intensity of felt needs and desires, then they will go away. They don't, of course, and Oakeshott knows this, which is why he must split the individual at war with his groupishness into individual and anti-individual and leaders into rulers and monomaniacal tyrants. Only then can politics—or rather, an ideal of politics as conversation, purified of need and desire—be preserved from the reality of life in "hereditary, co-operative groups," which is how he defines the state.

The only conservative considered in this book, Oakeshott turns out to be just as utopian, just as in thrall to the magic of words and ideas, as any other. Which is a shame, since he knows the truth of group-theoretical

5. Timothy Fuller, Foreword to *Rationalism in Politics,* by Oakeshott, p. xix.

materialism: that abstract political ideas are but glosses on the real relationships embodied in traditions, the thesis of his most famous essay, "Rationalism in Politics." Yet, it is this very insight that leads him astray, as he tries to
get from tradition, understood as conversation conducted over time and generations, what it cannot provide: an alternative to leadership. In fact, only
political leadership stands a chance of interpreting and integrating the fears,
needs, and desires that always threaten rationalization in politics, by which
I mean the attempt to purify politics by splitting it from "felt need," that term
of desire for which Oakeshott has so much contempt (p. 27).

Machiavelli and the Appearance of Leadership

What about Machiavelli, it might be asked? Isn't he concerned with
leadership, even if his is a leadership style (that dreadful contemporary
expression) that must grate on those with democratic sentiments? Isn't that
what *The Prince* is all about, advice to leaders? *The Prince* may contain advice
to leaders, but it's not about leadership. It's about the appearance of leadership, quite a different matter, as Machiavelli recognizes. Machiavelli splits
leadership in two: the heroic founding leader and the appearance *Meister,* as
he might be called, leaving no room for a real leader. In this regard he is not
unlike Oakeshott. Why isn't the founding ruler a real leader? Primarily
because he is a fantasy figure, creating something out of nothing for his citizens and designing it so well that they cannot break it, no matter how hard
they try. In this fantasy followers don't work with leaders to build anything.
Nor do followers exercise judgment. All is given to them in final form, like
the Constitution of the Spartans or the laws of Moses. Consider Machiavelli's examples: Lycurgus, Romulus, Theseus, and Moses. These are not merely
figures elevated to mythic status, like George Washington, but actual mythical figures (about Lycurgus, the *Oxford Companion to Classical Literature* says
nothing is known, not even if he lived). Mythical figures for a mythical
enchanted world, in which followers are given all that is good for them
without asking, without work, and without effort. This is, of course, a leading fantasy of the small group.

Of all the attributes of the good prince described by Machiavelli, none
is about good leadership. All are about the appearance of leadership, aimed
at maintaining the support of the common people, so that they will be a
resource against enemies.[6] The strategy is simple. The clever leader keeps
the support of the people by *feeding their fantasies about princely power,* which

6. *The Portable Machiavelli,* ed. and trans. Peter Bondanella and Mark Musa (New York:
Viking Penguin, 1979), pp. 127–138. All page references in the text are to this edition.

is why it is so important not to appear "frivolous, effeminate, cowardly," as these are the appearances most despised by the people. Real leadership, I have suggested, is not about feeding people's fantasies about leaders but interpreting these fantasies so that people may come to reclaim some of their own projections about leaders. Only then can they come to act responsibly as individual members, which includes having realistic expectations of leaders. Machiavelli, on the other hand, writes as though Plato's Adeimantus were advising the prince. Adeimantus advised Socrates that it is better to *appear* just than to *be* just (*Republic* 361d–367e). Likewise Machiavelli advised the prince that it is better to appear to be a good leader than to be one.

There is, however, one example of genuinely good leadership in *The Prince,* the only example I have been able to find in either *The Prince* or *The Discourses.* It is a story about Philopoemen, Prince of the Achaeans, who went for rides in the country with his friends "and reasoned with them," asking them what they would do if the enemy were suddenly to appear here, or there. "And he proposed to them, as they rode along, all the contingencies that can occur in an army; he heard their opinions, expressed his own, and backed it up with arguments; so that, because of these continuous deliberations, when leading his troops no unforeseen incident could arise for which he did not have the remedy" (*Prince,* p. 125). Machiavelli does not elaborate on this story or draw out its lessons, so we must. The key point is that Philopoemen leads by participating in a dialectical, teaching relationship with his followers, in which together they construct a meaningful shared world. The prince of the Achaeans is no founder-ruler but a teacher, not about the appearances of things but their reality, a reality that is mutually constructed and hence the responsibility of all its makers. Not an ultimate reality, but one under construction. It is unfortunate that Machiavelli does not develop this way of thinking about leadership further. I shall try to do so shortly.

No more than *The Prince* are *The Discourses* about real leadership. Rather, they contain dozens of handy hints for leaders concerned with staying in power and not one word about what they might use this power for—except, of course, to gain still more. Yet it would be a mistake to conclude that these works are only about appearances. In both *The Prince* and *The Discourses* Machiavelli confronts a harsh reality head on: that virtuous intentions often lead to catastrophic results. Piero Soderini, gonfalonier of Florence, was a good and gentle man, forced to choose between destroying his enemies and observing the law. Being a good man, he chose the law, allowing his enemies to destroy him and inflict far more suffering on his country than if he had struck first.[7] There is for Machiavelli a deeply tragic quality to this reality, one which seems to mock men's intentions, which is how we ought to interpret his famous statement *"si guarda al fine."* Not "the ends justify the means," but that one must always consider the final result (*Prince*, p. 135). It is entirely appropriate that Machiavelli would sign one of his letters "Niccolò Machiavelli, *istorico, comico e tragico."*[8]

It is a puzzle. Machiavelli sees deeply into reality, not allowing superficial pieties to obscure the tragic situation in which men find themselves in this world. So why would he write about leadership in such a superficial way, as though it were about magical foundings or mastering the appearances? Because for Machiavelli the world is too fearsome and fearful to allow anything else. The result is that leadership becomes not merely the mastery of appearances but the externalization of psychic reality, what Sheldon Wolin means when he says that for Machiavelli "politics has become external to its participants." Wolin is contrasting Machiavelli's approach to politics with that of Plato and Aristotle, for whom "statecraft is soulcraft," a matter of improving the souls of citizens.[9] The Greek term that we generally translate as "soul" is *psyche.* I have interpreted this program of psychic improvement as helping citizens to reclaim lost parts of themselves, parts so bound to citizens' fears and desires that they cannot be reclaimed without confronting these emotions. This is what the social contract is properly about, soulcraft. Machiavelli's leader, on the other hand, becomes merely the ringleader of these fears and desires, manipulating them so as to convince his followers that only he can save them. Leaders have done this for millennia. As I write, the 1992 Democratic and Republican conventions have recently concluded, and most of the speeches have been about this. A group-theoretical perspective reminds us of the costs. When the fears and capabilities of citizens are externalized, rather than reclaimed, they go somewhere. Into the group, which itself becomes an even more fearful place, leading to all the craziness of groups, which then try to inflict this craziness on others—sacrifices, scapegoats, and enemies.

Machiavelli is often admired for his willingness to confront the tragedy of how even good men must behave in a bad world in order to prevent a worse one. Wolin writes of Machiavelli as an economist of violence, concerned with how to get the most from the least violence. There is an element of the classical concept of virtue remaining in this perspective, but not much. When even good men see the world as so fearful and fearsome that

7. Here I closely follow Wolin, *Politics and Vision*, p. 207.
8. Ibid., p. 208.
9. Ibid., p. 236.

leaders can survive only by mastering the appearances, they may prevent worse evils in the short run, but they pay a price higher than Machiavelli appreciates. Such leaders make the world even more scary than it is and citizens even more incompetent to deal with this reality or their own fears. This is, of course, the opposite of how the social contract should work.

Machiavelli writes of the good leader as fox and lion: "It is therefore necessary to be a fox in order to recognize the traps and a lion in order to frighten the wolves. Those who play only the part of the lion do not understand matters. A wise ruler, therefore, cannot and should not keep his word when such an observance of faith would be to his disadvantage" (*Prince*, p. 134). While leaders must on occasion lie, it is easy to overlook the obvious. Machiavelli is writing not about leadership at all, but about protecting the power of leaders. These are not the same. Furthermore, since citizens and members of groups are generally remarkably confused about who the leader really is, such a strategy is likely to make the confusion worse. Genuine leadership helps citizens and members integrate their split perceptions of the leader. Only by putting the pieces of the all good/all bad leader together can citizens and group members integrate themselves. The wily leader, the lion and the fox, the appearance Meister, will only make this more difficult. Yet it will not do to criticize Machiavelli too harshly in this regard, for he unintentionally heightens a tragic irony: that *what it takes to remain a leader may make genuine leadership impossible*. This is the real tragedy of political life, one that neither Machiavelli nor most of his critics quite grasp, because they lack a conception of genuine leadership. Once again a utopian ideal, in this case of genuine leadership, helps us think more clearly about what the world is like in its absence.

If all this is so, then why have I stated that Machiavelli's story of Philopoemen, prince of the Achaeans, is an account of genuine leadership? Isn't Philopoemen heightening the paranoid anxiety of his followers, creating with them a world in which even the tranquil countryside is filled with dangers? Certainly he is not interpreting his friends' anxieties, helping them to reclaim lost parts of themselves. Or is he? The key point is that Philopoemen is involved in a relationship with his followers, in which together they create a world, a countryside filled with threats, but threats that have a name, location, and collective response attached to them. Recall Franz Neumann's praise of Churchill's leadership in just these terms (chapter 3). The translators of *The Portable Machiavelli* write of Machiavelli's "individualism" of leadership, "his reliance upon a single heroic individual" (pp. 23–24). The story of Philopoemen is different, about a leader who encourages his followers to construct a world with him. He "reasoned with them," says Machiavelli, which is why this is not just one more story about the mastery of appearances. The threats don't disappear, the world still retains a deeply paranoid cast, but this is held and contained within a relationship between leader and follower, in which together they create a story about the world that puts its terrors in their place—like a fairy tale or many myths.

This is the best that groups of people can do. Tell each other stories about their fears, so as to give voice to them, while at the same time containing them in the relationships of the story itself, as well as the real relationship between storyteller and listener. Or perhaps both relationships are equally real. The alternative, the only alternative, is little dramas, like those in the small group, in which fears are acted out rather than verbalized. Because they are acted out, generally unreflectively, little is learned from these dramas, which is why they are endlessly repeated. In addition, the acting out has the effect of making the world even more fearful, as uncontained anxiety and aggression are dumped into the group.

Three Narratives about Leadership

What does it mean for a leader to contain a threatening world within a relationship between leader and led, in which together they create a story about it? Václav Havel is no contemporary Philopoemen, but the former president of Czechoslovakia participated in a similar relationship with his people, as all good leaders do. This is my first narrative. The second returns to a classical account of leadership, that of Xenophon in the *Anabasis,* to consider the question of leadership from the opposite direction: why is good followership so difficult? The third narrative, about the apparent desire of the American public for inhuman leaders, will explore further why leaders are so feared and leadership such a threatening idea, for political theorists as well as citizens.

Havel's New Year Address of 1990

Since Václav Havel seems to be every academic's ideal leader, I shall not bore you with a recitation of his virtues. Instead, I shall interpret his "New Year's Address" of 1990, the first of his presidency, as exemplifying an ideal relationship between leader and led, one in which the leader tells a story that interprets his followers' anxieties so as to make it easier to reclaim them. In so doing, the leader realizes the social contract. Havel's address has been widely published, in the *New York Review of Books,* the *Spectator,* and elsewhere. Rather than summarizing it, I shall quote only brief passages to illustrate ten points. The interpretations are, of course, my own, from a group-theoretic perspective. Though Havel did not succeed in holding the federation together, its separation has been a velvet one—at least compared to the situation in former Yugoslavia—and not a little of the credit belongs to the former president.

1. "I assume you did not propose me for this office so that I, too, would lie to you."[10] Probably nothing is more important than this as far as good leadership is concerned, because it helps citizens and members integrate their split perceptions of the good and bad leader. They need not agree with the leader. They must know where he stands and have confidence that where he says he stands is where he actually stands. Havel's trustworthiness stems, of course, not just from his words, though they ring of truth, but from his life, his willingness to "live in truth," as he calls it, at great personal cost for many years.

2. "Our country is not flourishing." Contrast this statement with that of former President Bush in his 1992 acceptance speech at the Republican Convention, where he states that presidents (actually, presidential candidates) should not say bad things about their country—in this case, that the standard of living in the United States has fallen behind that of its economic competitors. Especially interesting is the "personal observation" that accompanies Havel's statement. He recently flew over Bratislava and was appalled at the ugliness and pollution. That is, he simply stood back and looked. "This view was enough for me to understand that for decades our statesmen and political leaders did not look or did not want to look out of the windows of their airplanes." No one does, and no one wants to, which is why leaders must.

3. "The worst thing is that we live in a contaminated moral environment. We fell mortally ill because we became used to saying something different from what we thought. We learned not to believe in anything." The illness stems from within, not without. We have ourselves to blame, the way we split ourselves off from reality. "We have to accept this legacy as a sin we committed against ourselves. If we accept it as such, we will understand that it is up to us all, and up to us only, to do something about it. We cannot blame the previous rulers for everything." Paranoid projection, scapegoating, the sacrifice of failed leaders, the discovery of new enemies: all this is contained, rather than encouraged, by Havel.

4. But if the responsibility stems from within, so too will the solution. "Freedom and democracy include participation and therefore responsibility from us all."

10. Václav Havel, "New Year's Address," in *Open Letters: Selected Writings, 1965–1990,* ed. Paul Wilson (New York: Vintage Books, 1992), pp. 390–396.

5. Only if we accept both truths—that the responsibility lies within, but so too does the solution—will "hope return to our hearts." Overcoming depressive anxiety that we are not strong enough or good enough to repair the damage we have done by our own greed and fear requires that we first confront our responsibility for making things the way they are. Only then is genuine hope, as opposed to manic denial, possible. Depressive anxiety is, I have argued, the source of corruption.

6. The source of hope also lies within, not in a great leader but in our own traditions. "The humanistic and democratic traditions, about which there [has] been so much idle talk, did after all slumber in the unconsciousness of our nations and ethnic minorities, and were inconspicuously passed from one generation to another."

7. But even this hope is not free. Gaining access to it requires that we confront our responsibility not only for the current environmental and moral pollution but also for the suffering of those who all along tried to speak the truth and were persecuted for it. "Many citizens perished in jails in the fifties, many were executed, thousands of human lives were destroyed. . . . We should not forget any of those who paid for our present freedom in one way or another." There was a part of our group that always spoke the truth and was sacrificed for it. We must not forget them, for they represent, or held, a part of ourselves that knew the truth but would not speak it. Only by reclaiming this part can we go on.

8. This requires a certain self-confidence, the confidence to know the truth about ourselves and to look out of the window, even when it is not pretty. If we can listen to this truth, then we will be prepared to go forward with the work of restoration. "Self-confidence is not pride. Just the contrary: only a person or a nation that is self-confident . . . is capable of listening to others, accepting them as equals, forgiving its enemies, and regretting its own guilt."

9. If the source of hope and restoration is within, so too is the enemy. "Our home-grown mafia . . . are no longer our main enemy. Even less so is our main enemy the international Mafia. Our main enemy today is our own bad traits: indifference to the common good; vanity; personal ambition; selfishness; and rivalry. The main struggle will have to be fought on this field." To this I would add that the main enemies are fear and despair, the depressive anxiety that we are not good enough or strong enough or adult enough to face reality and change it. It is in the face of this anxiety that corruption, of ourselves, our leaders, and our relationships, seems the only alternative.

10. Ours is not a direct democracy, but a representative one, a small nation, but no tiny community. Whether we shall continue to confront real-

ity and work to make it better will depend upon our leaders. "The important thing is that the winners will be the best of us. . . . The future policies and prestige of our state will depend on the personalities we select and later elect to our representative bodies." A large part of taking responsibility as a citizen is about being a mature follower, Havel might have added. This has a lot to do with demanding that leaders speak the truth and listening when they do. What this means exactly is explored in the next two stories.

In traditional thinking about the social contract, the contract establishes a relationship among citizens and then between citizens and leaders. In Hobbes these moments are virtually simultaneous: citizens establish a civilized relationship among themselves as each gives up his powers to the sovereign. In Locke these moments are separated, which is why political revolution need not dissolve civil society. Citizens have a prior pact among themselves. In Rousseau, these two moments are again one, as citizens give up their political rights to the sovereign group. In my account, on the other hand, the relationship between leader and led comes first, temporally and in importance. Not because without this relationship there can be no relationship among citizen-members. But because without a good leader citizens are unlikely to reclaim enough of themselves from the group to relate to each other as individual members. Good leadership is a condition of the social contract I propose, a measure of its ambitiousness. It is not just about survival and commodious living. Like the classics, it too sees statecraft as soulcraft, the cultivation of the psyches of citizens. Every step in Havel's story is about this, encouraging citizens to reclaim both their fears and their capacity to confront them. Every step rejects the collusion between leader and led, the charms of corruption.

How best to understand the charms of corruption? Freud writes that the leader represents the ego ideal, what he calls a "differentiating grade in the ego," by which he means that part of the ego, or self, that contains the image of what it desires to be: whole, complete, powerful, fulfilled, and free, while never isolated or alienated. In other works Freud would subsume the ego ideal to the superego, but it is worth distinguishing them, as I argue in *Narcissism*. One reason is that it helps us to see that Freud is the first object relations theorist, writing of how the ego "enters into the relation of an object to the ego ideal which has been developed out of it, and that all the interplay between an external object and the ego as a whole . . . may possibly be repeated upon this new scene of action within the ego."[11] The leader,

11. Freud, *Group Psychology and the Analysis of the Ego,* p. 62.

Freud goes on to say, represents the ego ideal in the group, so that the group comes to relate to the leader as though the leader were part of the members' psyches. This is just as true of good leaders as bad leaders, just as true of Havel as Hitler. It's what group psychology is about, members relating to the leader as though he were an ideal part of themselves.

What makes the difference between a good and a bad leader is not whether he represents the ego ideal and not whether the group seeks to unite with its ego ideal, as it always does. What makes the difference is whether the leader promotes unification (actually reunification, as the ego ideal stems from the experience of primary narcissism, of union with the all[12]) by raising the ego ideal, while encouraging and supporting the members in their efforts to live up to it. Or whether the leader promotes unification by lowering the ego ideal and so telling members in effect that they are already perfect, having no need to develop and grow up. The latter strategy is corruption, the paradigm of all corruption, in which the importance of work, effort, maturity, and time to the achievement of valued goals is denied. Groups are always trying to corrupt their leaders, which means trying to get their leaders to lower their standards, generally by drawing the leader into some sort of compromising bargain, such as "Don't expect us to act as competent adults, and we shall not expect you to live up to your promises." The demagogue appeals by telling members that they are already perfect, if only they knew it or if only some enemy did not stand in the way of reunification with perfection. Often this enemy is characterized as polluted, dirty, or in some way diseased, so that perfection becomes tantamount to cleansing.

There is no single test or standard by which to distinguish genuine leadership from its simulacrum. But one standard comes close. Does the leader lead by upholding high ideals while encouraging and supporting the group in its efforts to live up to them? That is, by helping citizens reclaim both their fears and their capacity to confront them, the ideal of the social contract. Or does the leader lead by pandering to the desire for reunification by shortcut, lowering the ego ideal and so telling members who fear maturity and competence that they need not struggle with these issues, because they are already perfect. Václav Havel is a genuine leader by these standards. Most are not, as I argue in "Mastery and Retreat: Psychological Sources of the Appeal of Ronald Reagan." This is no surprise. What is surprising is that political theory has not held to this high standard of leadership. Leadership in political theory is so taboo that no distinctions are made. Which does not,

12. Alford, *Narcissism: Socrates, the Frankfurt School and Psychoanalytic Theory* (New Haven: Yale University Press, 1988), pp. 54–65.

of course, cause the problem of leadership to disappear, but only renders it more intractable.

The Anabasis

Machiavelli's story of Philopoemen is a story about a relationship between a leader and a few of his friends, not a leader and citizens or members. What would it look like to extend this relationship to larger grouplike entities? Another narrative about leadership will help answer this question. This story comes from a classical author often, and rightly, considered quite superficial, at least when compared with that other chronicler of the life of Socrates, Plato. Nevertheless, Xenophon can at times be remarkably insightful, his sound common sense attractive, especially on the qualities of good leadership and followership, practical issues with which he had experience as an army officer. Machiavelli admires Xenophon above all the classical writers for his practicality. But it is Xenophon's Cyrus who Machiavelli admires most, one who became a prince due to his cleverness at deception (*Prince*, pp. 93–94; *Discourses*, p. 315). Not only does Machiavelli ignore Xenophon's teachings about the proper relationship of leader and followers, but he neglects Xenophon's suggestion that Cyrus's failure to build an empire that would survive his death was due to his corruption (*Cyropaedia*, 7.574–76). Because he recognizes the distinction between just and unjust rule, Xenophon, unlike Machiavelli, understands that good leadership is more than just remaining in power.

In *The Anabasis*, or Retreat of the Ten Thousand, Xenophon tells the story of Cyrus, who in 401 B.C. hired 10,000 Greek mercenaries to help him enforce his claim to the Persian throne. Unfortunately for Cyrus, he was beheaded while fighting in Persia, his right hand cut off, his head mounted on a stake. The Greek army was isolated in Asia, without food or enough weapons—and, most important, without a task or a leader. The Persian king, Tissaphernes, invited the generals of the Ten Thousand to discuss their situation with him. The generals came calling and were similarly beheaded. Tissaphernes expected that, with their leaders gone, the demoralized Greeks would surrender themselves to almost certain death. Self-pity and envy overtook them, says Xenophon, one of the Ten Thousand. Self-pity for their horrible situation, stranded in a foreign land, and envy toward the enemy, in whose rich lands they were starving (3.1.19). Small groups express such sentiments all the time, one member saying, "I feel like a street person looking at the diners in a fancy restaurant. All this food, and I can't get any." On the verge of surrendering, the Greek army kept its head, electing new generals to lead them (3.1.32–47). It worked. Under the leadership of these new generals, including Xenophon, the Greek army fought its way out of Persia to the Black Sea, where in Xenophon's famous description they rejoiced *"thalassa, thalassa!"* The sea, the sea!"

The problem faced by Xenophon was not merely strategic, how to escape the king's realm. The problem was morale, the troops' conviction that the failure of the gods to support them was a sign that any action was futile. Xenophon's first task of leadership was to establish the possibility of human leadership in the face of the Greeks' submission to their fate. In part Xenophon does so by enumerating the horrible things that will happen to them if they surrender. But mostly he stresses that the Greeks are *worthy* of survival and nobility if they will work hard for it. That is, he addresses their depressive anxiety, so central to group life. Worthiness, Xenophon argues, stems not from divine or kingly grace but from within, from the nobility of each individual Greek (3.1.24). Victory is not guaranteed, he states, but it can be fought for. What is guaranteed to fail is the men's hope that if they are sufficiently pious their weakness will be transformed into god-given strength. Not cowardice but a feeling of being undeserving of the fruits of virtue and hard work is the biggest barrier to men's salvation (4.5.16). Bion would have readily recognized this fear of work and development. As Richard Ruderman puts it in a fine essay on the *Anabasis,* "Xenophon hides the Greeks' *need* to bear arms behind their worthiness to do so. . . . Xenophon here points out that the statesman is required as much to convince people that they are worthy of accomplishing what they can as to show them what is needed."[13]

Xenophon is an interpretive leader, recognizing that passivity, fatalism, and fear of being unworthy of the fruits of one's efforts are the most profound barriers to effective work. Such passivity is, Xenophon understands, a type of clinging to power, the power of gods and despots. Xenophon also seems to understand that it will do little good to state these things, if he even understands them quite this way (he may not; he is inspired to lead by an obscure dream of a great light from Zeus [3.1.11–12]). Instead, he does what countless leaders have done over two millennia: he reinterprets traditional piety to support worldly action. The gods help those who help themselves. Appealing "in the name of the gods" for the men to "rule themselves," he asks them to act nobly on their own behalf and in this way honor the gods who made them (3.1.24). This is interpretive leadership par excellence. The leader addresses the underlying anxiety ("We Greeks are not worthy of survival"), even if he does not speak of it, demanding excellence while

13. Richard Ruderman, "The Rule of a Philosopher-King: Xenophon's *Anabasis,*" in *Politikos II: Educating the Ambitious. Leadership and Political Rule in Greek Political Thought,* ed. Leslie Rubin (Pittsburgh: Duquesne University Press, 1992), 127–143, p. 133.

providing a reinterpretation of tradition that transforms the inchoate anxiety into a fear that can be addressed with excellence (Greeks are worthy to bear arms, and so they must if that's what it takes to survive), as Philopoemen did. There is nothing new in this vision of leadership. It's classic. What's tricky is distinguishing genuine interpretive leadership from its simulacrum, the demagogue who exploits anxiety to maintain power. I have suggested some guidelines.

The lessons for leadership implicit in Xenophon's story are not all quite so clear. Xenophon seems to say that in the absence of their official leaders, everyone of the Ten Thousand became a leader: "They think we are defeated because our officers are dead and our good old general Clearchus. But we will show them that they have turned us all into generals. Instead of one Clearchus they have ten thousand Clearchuses against them" (3.1.24–26). Similarly, Xenophon states when sending out a small force to find a pass through the mountains that "every one of you is the leader" (4.1.27–28). Yet it will not do to take this too literally, as Edith Hamilton does, arguing that it represents the pinnacle of Greek individualism. Xenophon's story captures the ideal of the individual member, able to choose leaders well and follow them diligently but critically. Hamilton in effect recognizes this point when she says of Xenophon's leadership that "he was able to convince them that he knew best and they *gave up their own ideas and followed him willingly.*"[14]

The best leadership is leadership of ideas and example. Xenophon always makes it a point to suffer more hardships than his troops. Good followership judges leaders critically, just as the Ten Thousand judged its officers, trying them for incompetence. Nevertheless, we must not pretend that all can be leaders. Most must "give up their own ideas and follow." This may be done critically and provisionally. The "loyal opposition" is a noble ideal. Nevertheless, there is a difference between leaders and followers that should not be glossed over or trivialized. "Every man a leader" is a lie, whether told by Xenophon or by Hamilton. In fact, both authors go on to contradict themselves, stressing the necessity of sound leadership and responsible followership. "For without leaders nothing fine can be accomplished in any field," says Xenophon (3.1.38).

The reason for this contradiction, or at least tension, has to do with how difficult it is to grasp the idea of the individual member: neither drone nor clone nor leader. It is as though we have no category for him, so we say one thing—"Every man a leader"—when we really mean another—"Every man capable of responsible group membership." That we cannot generally even

14. Edith Hamilton, *The Greek Way* (New York: Avon Books, 1958), p. 156, emphasis added.

say it right shows how difficult an idea it truly is, requiring an ability to hold two concepts at the same time, group and individual member. Ruderman suggests that Xenophon implicitly holds that there is a ruler and subject within each of us (or within each noble man). Political order results when these two parts get along well together, a state of "civic participation," what I have called "responsible group membership," depending as much upon the ruler as the subject in each.[15] Though I do not believe that Xenophon always adheres to this profound insight into man's struggle with his groupishness, he struggles with it courageously. Most moderns don't.

If this interpretation of *The Anabasis* is correct, the problem is not so much about leaders as about followers. It is about how difficult it is to be a mature follower, an individual member, and why there are so few. One reason is because being a mature follower is painful. Following a real leader means abandoning the hope that one might be saved by a superhuman one, who can overcome the tragedy of human life in groups, making out of us complete individuals and total groupies. In fact, followership is so painful that followers frequently make good leadership impossible. I surmise that there is a connection between this phenomenon in contemporary politics and in political theory.

"Run for President or Be a Normal Human Being—Take Your Choice"

Lloyd Grove points out that our presidential candidates are expected to lie and be inhuman.[16] Voters seem to demand this, treating any evidence of humanity, such as George Romney's insightful comment in the 1968 campaign that he had been brainwashed by Pentagon briefers in Vietnam, as evidence of instability. Similarly, Edmund Muskie's tearful defense of his wife (or was it just snowflakes in his eyes?) in 1972 fueled perceptions that he was a candidate out of control. But while voters seem scared of human candidates, they don't seem to want superhuman ones either—candidates who exhibit superhuman mastery, competence, control, intelligence, and decisiveness. Who would argue that any of the candidates in the 1992 presidential race displayed these qualities? Rather, what are wanted are inhuman candidates, robots and sleek liars. Why? Especially since voters seem to fear such candidates, such as Bill Clinton in 1992 and Gary Hart in 1988. "The character issue," it has come to be called.

In order to answer this question, it will be useful to consider the gaffe that so often seems to destroy candidates. Characterizing the gaffe as inad-

15. Ruderman, "Rule of a Philosopher-King," pp. 140–141.
16. Lloyd Grove, *Washington Post*, 29 March 1992, C1–2. This and the next paragraph draw upon Grove's piece.

vertent truth telling, Michael Kinsley defines it as the candidate's departure from the script in order to say what is really on his mind or otherwise opening a window on his real character. From this perspective, Ronald Reagan rarely committed a gaffe, as his errors, which were constant, never revealed himself. But perhaps this required the collusion of many voters as well, an agreement not to see the emptiness and confusion within. So too with the new Nixon in 1968. Presumably many who voted for Nixon would never have bought a used car from him.

Bion argues that the leader is generally an empty vessel, not a strong personality but an empty one, whom followers can fill up with their own projections. This doesn't quite fit Ross Perot, who appears to have a strong personality, or at least a markedly paranoid one, the other key psychological characteristic of the leader, according to Bion.[17] Perot appeals because he offers leadership without the leader: no policies and no personality, only the promise of pure leadership for its own sake. With such a leader voters need not engage his personality, his reality, and all the work it takes to make contact with it. Nor need they confront his policies and positions. Perot's 30-minute "infomercials" were no exception. Delivering too much information too quickly, on charts that couldn't be read, the infomercials served to convey the impression of mastery (Machiavelli's appearance of leadership), not to educate or define the candidate. Important in themselves, policies and positions serve as markers, indicators of the reality and substance of the leader. Especially in large grouplike entities, where people can't know the leader personally, policies and positions serve to circumscribe the leader's boundaries, defining his core by proxy, so to speak, so that people might know it. To trivialize policies and positions makes a totem of leadership for its own sake, testimony to the power of the fantasy of the missing leader, leadership without the leader.

Why are voters so attracted to obviously inhuman candidates, ones who never reveal themselves and increasingly their policies in public? (The governor of Maryland recently stated that certainly he had a position on abortion. He just wasn't prepared to tell what it was.) The psychoanalytic theory of the group suggests an answer. In the regressed and undeveloped small group, members assiduously ignore the leader, treating his interventions as irrelevant intrusions. It is as if they don't want the leader to exist and don't want to be reminded of his presence. In fact, the group members don't ignore the leader at all; they only ignore the person who is in the position of leader. Ignoring the person who is leader, the small group divides up the

17. Bion, *Experiences in Groups,* pp. 177, 67, 121–122.

leader into pieces, so that each may have a part, thereby remaining in unconscious union with the ideal leader. The most important leader is the leader who is not there. Something like this seems to be going on in American politics. Many voters don't want a human leader because it would be necessary to confront him as a person, which means to confront reality, including the reality of voters' feelings about leaders. Instead, voters would rather collude with inhuman leaders. The unspoken contract runs something like this:

We shall only elect leaders who lie to us and who never show us themselves, which means never commit a gaffe. But only because they never commit a truth. This way we shall be safe in our cynicism and won't have to change, as we might if we had a real human as a leader. If we had a human leader, we would have to begin to confront our true feelings about leaders, especially how much we hate and fear them and how desperately we need them. Instead, we shall collude with inhuman leaders, accepting their lies, as long as they ask nothing from us. This way we will not have to confront the fear that as a nation we have nothing to give anymore, that we are all used up, broken into a million pieces, a depressed and fragmented group. By choosing inhuman leaders, we shall protect the fantasy that someday a superhuman leader might save us. A real human for a leader would be just too much reality to bear: that not only must the group work very hard, but that there is no superhuman leader waiting in the wings. The real drives out the ideal and so causes us too much pain.

Such a contract reflects the belief, so common among groups, that leaders must be corrupted before they can be confronted. On a radio talk show a caller said that he admired Perot's refusal to state his positions. Other leaders have said one thing and done just the opposite, the caller continued. That citizens might expect leaders to tell them the truth and hold them accountable was apparently an incomprehensibly high aspiration. Instead, citizens can only collude with their leader, corrupting him so that he lacks the moral authority to make demands on them, demands that only adults could fulfill.

The alternative to collusion with the missing leader is encounter with a real one. Only this encounter makes group development possible, for all the reasons mentioned. Only this encounter allows members to reclaim parts of themselves previously devoted to maintaining the missing leader within the group. Hence only this encounter allows members to enter into the social contract that I have proposed. Leaders who tell the truth, revealing themselves and their policies, can further this process. But only when truth and self-revelation are not defined as gaffes. Now, however, we see why they are. Not only does the hope for the superhuman leader require the inhuman leader to save his place in line; behind the inhuman leader stands the fear of the malevolent leader, Locke's marauding patriarch, who cannot be confronted, so best that we not know him at all. Voters demand an inhuman leader, in order to save a place for the superhuman leader while protecting them from the malevolent leader. This is the best way to interpret Bion's pairing group, which idealizes the pair whom, members fantasize, will produce a child to save the group.[18] Not the sexual pair, but the pair that is the inhuman leader coupled with the malevolent leader, both holding a place for the superhuman leader, is the most important pair in the group.

It is not a political columnist and not a political theorist, but a political cartoonist, Garry Trudeau, who has grasped this truth with the figure of "Skippy," George Bush's evil twin, that crazy, vicious, demented, invisible double of the former president, who stands for all the things we fear about leaders but can hardly let ourselves know, except in the light touch of the cartoonist, who is not to be taken seriously anyway. Or perhaps we do let ourselves know; witness the cover of *Time* magazine (April 1992) that featured a terrifying negative photographic image of then candidate Clinton to illustrate its cover story on "Why Voters Don't Trust Clinton." But we tell ourselves in such subtle ways that we need not face what we know—or rather fear: that the current (as of 1992) president of the United States is a monster, a marauding predator such as Locke wrote of, who would halt at nothing to quench his lifelong lust for power.

Citizens' relations with leaders are complex, and if voters deeply fear their leaders, they also love them, still another reason why voters seek to destroy them. Group life is nothing if not ironic. Winnicott argues that the parent becomes real to the child only after the child has sought to destroy the parent but failed. Until then, the parent is not fully distinguished in the child's mind from the child's fantasies of parent as one imperfectly under his control, a flawed extension of the child. Because the child experiences the parent as an imperfect extension, the child rages, destroying the parent in fantasy a thousand times. It is by surviving in reality, not taking revenge but resisting the attempted destruction, that the parent becomes real to the child, an object in the external world to be used to further the child's development, not to confirm its fantasies.[19] Presidential candidates are not parents, but something similar seems to have occurred between Clinton and many voters, in which Clinton's ability to resist the repeated attacks on his character without self-destructing or becoming vengeful allowed voters to come to terms with his reality and so transform their paranoid fear into more realistic concern. *Interpretation isn't always a matter of saying what seems to be going on under the surface.* It may be much more subtle, an unconscious communication between followers and leader of which neither is aware. Many

18. Ibid., p. 151.
19. Winnicott, *Playing and Reality*, p. 94.

voters seem to have in effect asked candidate Clinton to allow them to try to destroy him, to which he agreed, so that his strength might be measured against their fear and rage and not be found wanting. This too is interpretation.

Political Theory and the Limits of Politics

If voters demand an inhuman leader, political theorists ignore leadership altogether, evidently because they are mortified and shamed by the eagerness of citizens to be led. Hitler, Stalin, Pol Pot, Jim Jones—the list of leaders who have captivated their followers, leading them to their destruction and often the destruction of others, only begins with these infamous names. The same names raise the possibility that man is not merely a herd animal, but a "horde animal" as Freud called him, a follower of leaders. Unfortunately, the studied refusal of political theory to confront the problem of leadership and followership does not make it go away. As in the small group, the missing leader is reproduced in the relationships within the group that the political theorists write of. The group itself becomes the inhuman leader coupling with the malevolent one. Unfortunately, the group is sterile. Out of this union of leaders comes nothing, just more dramas.

C. B. Macpherson argues that because Hobbes overlooked the unifying forces within society, particularly social class (the self-interest of the bourgeoisie), he assumed that only a leviathan could hold nascent capitalist society together.[20] Political theory has yet to come to terms with the implications of Hobbes's oversight. Since Hobbes, political theory has been so concerned with the problem of the tyrannical leader, be he an individual or a class, that it has failed to reckon fully the costs of holding society together by relying upon unifying forces within the group, forces whose toll on individuality are generally greater than that of the most malevolent leader. Which is why Rousseau's sovereign group is the worst tyrant of all. Does this mean that self-governance, as it is called, is not worth the risk or the price? Not at all. But political theory should not fail to reckon the cost of what is in many respects a tragic choice. Political theory might do this by exploring the meaning of self-governance, a term that is quite literally meaningless except when applied to individuals one by one, the governance of the self. In groups, self-government is not self-government at all. It is instead a particular relationship between leaders and followers, in which followers take their responsibilities seriously while not abandoning their status as individual members, able to criticize and evaluate their leaders.

20. C. B. Macpherson, Introduction to *Leviathan*, p. 55.

This is a real ideal, one that neither modern nor contemporary political theory has addressed. Because, I think, the balancing act is so complex: to be an individual, a group member, and a follower all at once. An individual member. It's a lot to ask and a lot to juggle, members resolving the tension by going to extremes: isolated member, the groupie, the disciple. All at once, the point of the cross diagram and the schizoid compromise. Most groups and individuals never get the balance right, most never come close, and none get it right for very long. But it is a real ideal, one that political theory, because it is removed from the actual day-to-day balancing act, has the luxury to confront. Which makes it doubly unfortunate that it hasn't. Like the regressed and undeveloped small group, political theory drives the missing leader into the group itself, so that the relationships within the society characterized by political theory are dramas that act out the missing leader.

From Pufendorf's exploitation of imbecillitas and indigentia, in which the need and weakness manifest in the idea of a missing leader are themselves used to bind the group, to Rousseau's transformation of the group into tyrannical sovereign, chapter 4 analyzed the way in which traditional political theory acts out the missing leader. Chapter 5 was concerned with a similar phenomenon among contemporary theorists. Barber reflects this way of thinking in *Strong Democracy*, where he states that "complete self-government by an active citizenry would leave no room for leaders or followers" (p. 238). This is not only an unrealistic ideal but a dangerous one. With no leaders and no followers there is only the group. Postmoderns wisely rebel against this ideal, but in such a way as to reproduce in their narratives the lack of individuality they decry, as the ideal of difference replaces individuals. As though there could be relationships without individuals to have them. Group theory, only apparently less concerned with individuals than liberals and postmoderns, turns out to appreciate individuality best.

A possible objection to my argument, both in this chapter and throughout the book, is a version of Macpherson's criticism of Hobbes. The entities that political theory is concerned with, civil societies and nation-states, are not grouplike entities, but at best groupslike entities, composed of many groups. Thus, political leadership is not so important as I have made out, even if leadership is important. The leadership of mothers, fathers, corporate leaders, community leaders, religious leaders, educational leaders—all these are important and fill in most of the gaps that I have found in the missing political leader. Political theory's ignorance of political leadership reflects the fact that we do not live in a totalitarian society but in a pluralistic one composed of numerous and overlapping groups and leaders. This missing leader is not really missing at all. He is just dispersed into lots of leaders in lots of groups, which is what a pluralistic society is about. The task of democratic political leadership is to coordinate these groups, not to be a big daddy.

The argument of Theodore Lowi's *The End of Liberalism,* discussed in chapter 5, is sufficient to dismiss this objection. None of the issues with which leaders need to be concerned, such as the need to make and explain choices, distribute value (as it is called in the political science literature), exercise moral suasion, and educate citizens, is any less important when citizens are divided into tribes. On the contrary, these activities become even more important, as conflict of tribes is generally even more fratricidal than conflict of individuals. Just as the absence of the patriarch doesn't eliminate patriarchy, so the absence of the leader doesn't eliminate the problem of leadership. It just drives the problem into the relationships within the group itself, including the relationships of tribes, making them that much more difficult to identify and solve.

"Group rights" is a complicated and touchy notion, no more easily discussed or defined than "political correctness." Whether group rights exist, whether they are even comprehensible or ought to be protected, cannot be addressed here. Nevertheless, group psychology can shed light on the issue. Group rights became a hot political issue with the nomination of Lani Guinier to head the civil rights division of the Justice Department in the spring of 1993. At the heart of the controversy was Guinier's rejection of what she called "simple-minded notions of majority rule" in favor of an outcomes approach, democracy being evaluated in terms of what she calls "proportionate interest representation," in which the outcome is fair if it reflects the interests of the various groups affected. To be sure, Guinier is not writing about every election but about those in districts with a history of discrimination against minority groups, a distinction not always appreciated by her critics. Nevertheless, there is a sharp difference between her view and that of Senator Joe Lieberman of Connecticut, who argues that the Voting Rights Act exists to protect the individual right to vote, not a group's right to an outcome.[21]

Although it stresses the empirical primacy of the group, a group-psychological approach lends little support to the notion of group rights. On the contrary, the group-psychological approach points out that the individual's worst enemy is usually his own group, the way in which it demands his individuality as a cost of group membership. If group rights are valued because one believes that this is the best way to protect the individuals in them, the argument that groups generally do a poor job of protecting their

21. *Washington Post,* A10, 4 June 1993, quoting articles by Guinier in the *University of Michigan Law Review* (1991) and *Harvard Civil Rights—Civil Liberties Law Review* (1989).

members' individuality is a powerful objection. If, however, group rights are valued because one believes that the group has an ethical value above and beyond that of the members' self-development (not an absurd position, akin to arguments about the preservation of minority cultures), then the group-psychological approach is not a decisive objection—except to the extent that it requires the supporter of group rights to recognize that group rights and individual rights are not only not identical but are often antithetical. Not always, of course, for individuals need groups as I have argued all along. The psychological theory of groups can help us think more clearly about issues like this, but it cannot solve them. Just what one would expect.

Are These the Proper Concerns of Political Theory?

One might agree in principle with my analysis and still hold that I have not identified the proper concerns of political theory. This would be the position of those like Judith Shklar, who in "The Liberalism of Fear" argues that politics is properly concerned with just one thing: protecting the freedom of individuals to make as many decisions as possible about their lives. The greatest barrier to this freedom, she argues, is systematic fear of cruelty and torture, pursued not just by tyrants but by virtually all powerful governments, as well as public bodies and corporations. "Systematic fear is the condition that makes freedom impossible, and it is aroused by the expectation of institutionalized cruelty as by nothing else."[22] A corollary for Shklar is that the proper subjects of politics are not reflective and discursive persons. Neither are the proper subjects friends and enemies, nor patriots and soldier-citizens, nor the individual members of whom I have written. The proper subjects of politics are the weak and the powerful, the task of politics being to protect the former from the worst depredations of the latter (p. 27). Shklar thus rejects the view that liberalism lacks an adequate theory of the self. More precisely, she argues that it hardly matters. "For political purposes liberalism does not have to assume anything about human nature," except that people differ a lot in their personalities and little in their abhorrence of pain and suffering (p. 35).

Shklar's is an attractive argument, probably the most effective that can be directed against mine. Not so much that I am wrong, but that it hardly matters, at least as far as political theory is concerned. What people fear and desire, love and hate, is in the end simple and powerful enough that all the subtleties and details, all the speculation about unconscious motives and

22. Judith N. Shklar, "The Liberalism of Fear," in *Liberalism and the Moral Life,* ed. Nancy Rosenblum (Cambridge, Mass.: Harvard University Press, 1989), 21–38, p. 29. All page references to Shklar in this chapter are to this essay.

group dynamics, hardly matter. Protect individuals from predators, be they individual or collective, and let them find their happiness in their own way. This is what liberalism is about, and Shklar's argument, a more serious version of Oakeshott's because she acknowledges fear and power in a way he never does, is its best defense.

Nevertheless, she is mistaken. Her argument, too, is based on splitting: that political theory can separate itself from the horrid details and subtleties just by being harshly realistic. It is a great temptation and a clever move, employing reality itself as a defense. Instead of retreating into abstraction, as postmodernists do, or into the magic of the unifying power of words, as the participationists do, Shklar turns to reality itself, as though knowing and stating clear and simple truths would eliminate the need to study them more carefully. As if we could simplify reality by simplifying ourselves. To be sure, it is the first obligation of every intellectual to state the simple truth, so that we do not forget it in the details. But this should not become an excuse for ignoring more complex truths or hypotheses, especially when these bear upon our ability to do something about these simple truths.

Just as Shklar argues that modernism (defined as a mixture of natural science, technology, industrialization, skepticism, disenchantment, nihilism, and atomistic individualism) and liberalism are not conceptually related but only historically associated, so one might argue that schizoid individualism has nothing to do with liberal individualism. One could readily have one without the other. But this is only logically true. Psycho-logically they go together, as liberalism is not just a political idea but a relationship of the individual to the group that leads the individual to split himself so as to be groupie and isolate at the same time. Reality is whole, by which I mean that the relationships that constitute it (for that is how I have defined reality, according to the principle of group-theoretic materialism) are not readily divided into social, economic, emotional, psychological, political, and the like. We may divide our ideas about reality, but when these ideas fail to correspond to the interwoven complexity of the relationships, they will fail. In political theory this failure takes the form of political theories that split off a dimension of reality in order to handle it more readily but, in so doing, become irrelevant, a mere academic exercise. Simplification, then, is not *just* simplification: it is wishful thinking, as though reality could somehow be confined as readily.

Shklar fails to recognize how the liberalism of fear undermines itself as it fails to address the isolation, meaninglessness, and economic vulnerability that produce the schizoid individual. One who is terribly susceptible to group pressures and hence vulnerable to anti-liberal movements, even as these movements have come to take on ostensibly nonpolitical form, such as mass culture—what Lasch calls the "culture of narcissism" and what Herbert Marcuse calls the "one-dimensional society." In a dim way this is what Pateman is getting at in *The Sexual Contract*. The abstract, rational, universal individual whom she identifies with men is actually the alienated, schizoid, and repressed group member, man or woman, cut off from others except as his or her relationships can be expressed in rational, formal-legal terms. Such relationships, Max Weber tells us, culminate in a world of icy polar darkness, an iron cage. But the inhabitants of such cages don't always sit quietly; they rage. Political theory should be concerned with identifying the types of leadership most supportive of the ideal of individual membership and the types of institutions that could foster the development of this leadership, particularly in large grouplike entities. In addressing these issues, political theory would be writing a social contract worthy of the developed group: a social contract that would *see* the individual rather than merely contain him—in iron cages or categories such as liberalism, which assume that everything that is not liberal can somehow be confined to "psychology."

Constitutional Liberalism and Strong Leadership

Constitutional liberalism combined with strong leadership is, I believe, the institutional form most supportive of the ideal of individual membership. It is the institutional form most likely to realize and maintain the social contract I propose. By "constitutional liberalism" I mean not merely a formal system of rules that establishes and regulates the state, but a substantive doctrine that embodies the provisions of limited government for an ethical purpose: to protect the individual, because it is the individual who is the highest standard of value, an end not a means. Constitutional liberalism protects the individual not just from the state and its leaders, but also from the group, dampening the tendency of the grouplike entity that is the state to oscillate along the axes of the cross diagram (chapter 3). Constitutional liberalism, understood as institutions such as a Bill of Rights and limits on the executive, legislature, and democracy itself (for example, protection of minorities against majorities), provides a background of interpretation that can help contain the grouplike entity within the central square of the cross diagram. It is only here that groups can listen to leaders.

Constitutional liberalism covers a lot of territory. One might argue, for example, that the social contract can never be realized under corporate capitalism, as the contract concerns the reappropriation of parts of the self alienated in the group, and capitalism is by its nature about alienating workers' skills. In chapter 5 I suggested that Marx's argument in *Grundrisse* regarding the exploitation at the heart of the so-called free labor contract may be seen as an instance of the social contract I propose. And so it may; for while Marxism is obviously incompatible with constitutional liberalism, forms of socialism and workers' control (even that studied by Pateman in Yugoslavia some years ago) are not. As Charles Lindblom demonstrates in *Politics and Markets*, there are more ways to organize the relationship between economy, society, and state than are dreamt of in most political philosophies.

It will not pay to pursue this level of detail further here. To do so is not only unnecessary but would be inappropriate. I am proposing a social contract, not a blueprint. The point is that constitutional liberalism is no code word for capitalism, even if they are historically associated. My guess is that the institution of private property (which is, of course, compatible with socialism) is important, acting as buffer between individual, group, and state. Or at least it once was, providing an aristocrat like Cincinnatus or Jefferson with a standpoint (and, more mundanely, a source of income) from which to assert his individuality against the demands of the state. But times change. Private property was no barrier to the National Socialists in Germany; it may even have lulled the upper middle classes into thinking they could immunize themselves against the carnage. Private property is, in any case, a detail, albeit an important one. It can be argued over fruitfully only when we are clear about the basic principle it is to serve, that of connecting the individual to society while separating him from it. It is here that individual and group development intersect. Let the argument begin: over private property and even over whether constitutional liberalism is the best or only way to institutionalize the social contract. It is not institutions but principles and facts that are the alpha and the omega: the value of individual development and the fact that it requires group development.

Strong interpretive leadership is the other implication of a group-psychological approach to politics. Lincoln's Gettysburg address is an exemplary piece of interpretive leadership according to *Lincoln at Gettysburg: The Words that Remade America*, by Garry Wills. Employing the rhetoric of the Greek revival and transcendentalism to reinterpret American history, Lincoln makes the Declaration of Independence, which calls all men equal, the primary document, rather than the Constitution. Reinterpreting a grouplike entity's history to reconstitute its boundaries is a classic act of interpretive leadership. Whether it is an act of *responsible* interpretive leadership depends upon whether this reformulation is based upon scapegoating, the creation of a demonic other to contain the evil that threatens to explode one's group.

Lincoln was a responsible interpretive leader, resisting this tendency in the midst of bloody civil war. So too were Churchill, Roosevelt, and Havel.

Not all interpretive leadership is or should be from the top down. Interpretive leadership begins in families, as parents interpret the anxieties of their children, perhaps by telling fairy stories, so helping their children to internalize and integrate anxiety. Families, churches, synagogues, schools, newspapers—all the associations that Tocqueville writes of—are the proper locus of an interpretive leadership that operates from the bottom up. Consider how similar, yet different, this is from the usual arguments about participation. It is similar in recognizing that a consumer politics, the civil privatism that Habermas and others worry about, invites the corruption of leaders and followers alike. Participation matters, but the participation that matters most is participation in encountering, evaluating, selecting, listening to, and following interpretive leaders. Groups can't lead themselves. The ideal is Xenophon's Ten Thousand, in which members express their individuality through the high standards to which they hold their leaders, as well as the alacrity with which they follow good ones. Thucydides captures this ideal when he characterizes the pride of the Athenian democrats not just in terms of their love of freedom but in terms of the demanding standards to which they held their leaders (*History*, III. 37–38).

This is how freedom must be expressed in groups. It is not the most important way. The most important way is still the individual's freedom to say "No, I won't go along, no matter what." But it is terribly important. Freedom is not just nay saying, but also yea saying: to the right things and the right leaders. The goal of constitutional liberalism is the creation of a political and social environment in which associations of interpretive leadership and followership may emerge and flourish—for the sake of the individuals in them, individuals who need developed groups to become developed individuals. A single, large, grouplike entity, the state, is insufficient. Learning how to encounter leaders so as to make realistic demands on them, neither idealizing nor devaluing their contribution, requires real contact with real leaders, not just with their images in the media. Participation in associations is indeed the training ground of democracy, as long as we understood this training properly. For most it will be training in creative and responsible followership, what it is to be an individual member.

This formulation takes the truth of republicanism seriously while avoiding its flaws. Its flaws are the inapplicability of republicanism to large, complex, diverse societies, its tendency to ignore man's war with his own groupishness, and hence its tendency to idealize the sacrifice of individuals to the ideals of civic virtue. The truth of republicanism is that the human excellences are so intrinsically social and relational that they must be practiced with others to be realized. This is the truth of group theory as well. To be generous, courageous, loyal, friendly, loving, compassionate, trusting, liberal, wise, self-disciplined, and just requires the intimate companionship and cooperation of others, without whom none of these excellences matter. Each of these virtues is relational. Yet each can belong only to individuals and can be developed only when there is distance between and among individuals. This, in turn, I have argued repeatedly, requires leadership. It is my hypothesis, and hope, that associations of interpretive leadership and followership are the best place to educate and practice republican virtues. This will, of course, not always be the case. Much depends upon the ability of the culture to resist the corrupting effects of economic decline, the way in which fear seems to make luxury goods of all the virtues. What I am sure of is that republicanism is not an alternative to associations of interpretive leadership and followership, but the best instance of them. Machiavelli knew this truth too.

Constitutional liberalism should not be confused with the liberal pluralism that Lowi writes of. Under constitutional liberalism, responsibility travels up. Society may be composed of associations of interpretive leadership, but the political unit is the individual—one who stands in a formal, constitutionally designated relationship to leaders whose responsibilities are spelled out. Responsibility is a crucial but unacknowledged dimension of interpretive leadership. The most important problem faced by members of small groups is making contact with the reality of leaders: who they are and aren't, what they can do and what they can't. Groups attribute responsibility to leaders for things they couldn't possibly have done and fail to hold leaders responsible for what they do. Taking the responsibility appropriate to the role, no less and no more, is the single most important thing that leaders can do to help members come to terms with their reality as leaders. Institutions can help insofar as they locate responsibility in offices and roles whose duties are clear and whose relationships of authority are spelled out, generally in a hierarchical form. In the end, constitutional liberalism and strong interpretive leadership are not two different strategies for group development but part of a single strategy by which the individual is separated from the group by connecting him to the reality of leaders, so that he may return to the group as an individual member.

Epilogue ❋ The Wolini

The Wolini lived in the Amazonian rain forest on the border between Venezuela and Brazil, a day's walk from the "river of rains" that empties into the Orinoco. One of the world's most isolated indigenous peoples, the Wolini recently became extinct. Guns, disease, and the new towns of the settlers did not destroy the Wolini, as they have so many other native peoples. The Wolini, whose name means "the real ones," or "the natural ones," destroyed themselves. This is the story of their self-destruction and the birth of the New Ones, an offshoot of the Wolini that has managed to survive and prosper.

The group was all to the Wolini, of whom only about 200 remained when I came to know them a number of years ago. Living together in a single longhouse in the vast tropical forest, the Wolini are distinguished in the anthropological literature by the way in which they name their children, as well as by the absence in their language of the first-person singular pronoun "I." Formed by the coming together of a dozen families many generations ago, the Wolini were known to each other by a combination of birth order and family name. Lowan, for example, was the third (Lo) child to survive to one year of age in the Wan family. Most anthropologists who have studied the Wolini comment on this system but miss the point. The Wolini do not have a unique system for naming their children; they lack the concept of a proper name altogether. Lowan is not really a proper name, as it does not designate an individual; it merely designates a member's place in the tribal group. Lowan may say, "Lowan did this and thinks that" (how the Wolini refer to themselves in the absence of the first-person singular), but the statement is not really comparable to the statement, "I did this and think that."

It is more akin to the statement, "The part of the group which is located here in Lowan did this and thinks that."

The longhouse of the Wolini was a variation of the typical longhouse pattern found among many indigenous peoples. Constructed of a timber frame with walls and overhanging roof of thatch, it was about 150 feet long and 20 feet wide, with a few small windows on each side. Located in a modest clearing created by the felling of trees for the house, it had a communal kitchen at one end, with the cooking fire just outside the door. Inside the longhouse was undivided, a single large room broken only by timbers supporting the walls and the roof. On the packed earth floor about 200 Wolini lived, loosely divided into twelve areas, corresponding to the twelve families. Within each area a member could call his own just the space occupied by his large grey blanket, his only possession apart from a wooden bowl from which he had his meals. While the Wolini were ostensibly patrilineal, their children would frequently wander from family to family, changing their name accordingly and finding refuge with whomever would have them. Since the food was grown by the entire community and distributed through the communal kitchen, there was no economic incentive to hold onto one's children or to exclude the children of others. It hardly seemed to matter. At mealtimes the Wolini lined up in an orderly file outside the communal kitchen with their bowls, returning to their blankets to eat

Life in the longhouse was difficult for the Wolini, who lived in a vast forest but crowded themselves into a single, dim room. Their way of life affected almost every aspect of their existence, from their system of names to their vocabulary—or rather, the concepts with which they apprehended their world. Living in a dense forest of tall trees frequently shrouded in mist and fog, they lacked the concept of a horizon. They spoke instead of a patch of brightness amongst the trees. Unlike a horizon, however, this patch was not something a man could move toward, not something that could represent a limit that might be breached, only to find another limit in the distance. The patch of brightness was inaccessible, unconnected with what went on down below. This was, I thought, a perfect metaphor for their lives.

Living under such close conditions, much social regulation—or rather, self-regulation—was necessary. The Wolini had few formalized rules and a thousand informal ones. Wolini children were simply not allowed to cry. At the first whimper, the mother (or, not infrequently, another adult or older sibling) would cover the child's nose and mouth until it became virtually unconscious from lack of air. The child learned quickly to cry silently. Of all my experiences among the Wolini, the one I remember most vividly was children with tears streaming down their faces making not a sound. The children's play was also remarkably restrained, both within and outside the longhouse, with little laughing, running, and screaming and lots of quiet play with tops, dolls, and the like. Not only did I never see two children fighting, but I never saw two adults, including married couples, fight openly, verbally or otherwise. Instead, they would exchange sly pinches and punches, which, judging from the expressions on their faces, could be quite painful. Among the Wolini anger and joy were both rigidly repressed, the consequences engraved in their stiff, tense, wooden bodies. Headaches and chronic stomach complaints were common, a muscle-relaxing massage the most cherished ritual between friends. Sexual relationships and marriage were, as might be expected, also rigidly controlled, and I will write about them later.

Not every Wolini observed all the norms all the time, most of which concerned the subordination of the individual to the ideal of the perfectly unified group. Punishment was necessary and could be brutal. The usual practice was for a group of young men to approach a malefactor in the middle of the night, throw a blanket over him, and whisper a warning. If there was a next time, they would do it again, beating him severely through the blanket. Several of the Wolini bore permanent marks from these reprimands, including deformed arms and legs from bones that had been broken and grown together crookedly. It was not my impression that these enforcers were some sort of Wolini youth gang; they seemed to be acting on behalf of the entire community. The injured were generally consoled by their "blanket-neighbors," as they were called, but never was the justice or injustice of the attack discussed. Condolences were offered as one might offer condolences to the victim of a lightning strike or other natural disaster.

The longhouse of the Wolini had a second level, a loft, much like a hay loft, extending over the communal kitchen and about one-fourth of the length of the longhouse. Reached by a straight ladder, one could stand on the edge of the loft and see almost all the Wolini. In one corner of the loft lived Wolan, their leader, direct descendent of the founding Wolan family. (The Wolini insist that they are not named after the Wolan family; Wolini, meaning real or natural ones, has, they claim, an independent derivation.) Wolan occupied the only private room in the longhouse; his meals were left outside his door by a servant woman, who would return to pick up the empty dish. The Wolini could go days without seeing Wolan, when suddenly he would appear at the edge of the loft for all to see, a frail old man. Sometimes, if the people were busy, he might not be noticed for several minutes. Then suddenly the Wolini would fall silent, as Wolan silently held the gaze of 200 pairs of eyes for perhaps ten minutes before returning to his apartment. His word was law, absolute, but his word was seldom heard, although much—everything really—was done in his name. Not just the traditional things, but anything out of the ordinary as well. The first season that I was with the Wolini the rains came early. The harvest of yams and barbasco was still in the ground and in danger of rotting. Quickly the entire community mobilized, the word going out that Wolan had ordered that every man, woman, and child drop what he or she was doing and devote full time to the harvest, a strategy to which the Wolini owed their survival. Wolan was never seen, however, none seeming to know who had received the original order. Dimono (the second son of the Mon family) heard it from Ungono (the first son of the Gon family), Ungono from Lowan, and so on.

Wolan was a fascinating character, and I heard many stories about his life. Once, just days before he disappeared into his apartment for the last time, I asked him about these stories, and he sat me down and told me one about his walks with the man he called Fa-ter Too-mas and his return to the Wolini. The rest I have pieced together from the stories I heard about Wolan from several Wolini, all of whom loved to tell stories about him. Wolan, it seems, was the only Wolini to have lived outside his tribe. It happened many years ago, when Wolan was a young man. Member of a Wolini hunting party, Wolan became separated from them, wandering alone in the forest for days. Eventually he was picked up by a neighboring tribe, the Eurfeyo, who did not treat him kindly. In effect, he became the slave of his rescuers, doing their dirty work, such as stripping the carcasses of the animals they had killed and eaten for the last ounces of fat and gristle, from which the tribe made poultices and other remedies. Several times Wolan attempted to escape, but he quickly became lost and was soon recaptured, only to be treated more harshly than ever. Where at first he had slept in a corner of the hut of the man who had found him, soon Wolan was tied up at night with the half-dozen goats maintained by the tribe. All knew that Wolan would eventually escape or die trying. In either case, the Eurfeyo would be left with nothing. So they decided to sell Wolan into slavery to one of the fierce cannibalistic tribes that lived downriver from them. One way or another, this tribe would know what to do with Wolan, and the Eurfeyo would at least gain something in the exchange.

One morning not long after, several Eurfeyo set out with Wolan to the land of the Aranago. Trussed up and laid out in the bottom of a dug-out canoe like one of the goats the Eurfeyo occasionally sold to the Aranago, Wolan had even less chance of escape. But it was spring, and the river was running high. Anxious to get rid of their cargo, who made the Eurfeyo intensely uncomfortable, they ran rapids they should have portaged. What was it about Wolan that made them so uncomfortable? First of all his gaze, which seemed to focus about five feet behind the one he looked at. And while they could lay him face down or cover his eyes and so avoid the gaze, they couldn't avoid being affected by the way he held his body, tense and distant but not rigid, as though they were no different from the goats among whom he was forced to sleep. So the Eurfeyo paddled faster and faster, recklessly running rapids they had never run before, even when the river was low. They weren't lucky. Not far from their destination the canoe smashed broadside against a rock and split in two. One Eurfeyo was killed outright as his head collided with a rock, another was drowned, and the third made it to shore, though what happened to him after that is unknown. After being carried by the current for some distance, Wolan's trussed-up body was deposited on a sandy shore where the river bends west and fans out into a broad alluvial cone.

Half drowned, bruised, and broken from having smashed into dozens of rocks, Wolan had survived. But, for the rest of his life, Wolan never knew whether he had been lucky. Not because of what had happened to him but because of what was about to happen—an experience so rich, powerful, and disturbing that he struggled for the rest of his life to come to terms with it, sharing it with his blanket-neighbors, who loved to hear the story, just as we love to go to a horror movie, out of the pleasure of experiencing terror at one remove. But, while they loved to hear his story, his blanket-neighbors were so far from understanding it that they could not help Wolan make sense of it. Because of this story and the way it had so obviously transformed him, they made Wolan their leader for life. For they couldn't really share it with him.

Wolan's bonds had been loosened by his brutal ride down the river, and he had had no difficulty slipping them. But he was half dead and would have died had not the missionaries who lived in a hacienda near the river discovered him and taken him in. Slipping in and out of consciousness for days, Wolan woke up on white sheets in a white room, with sun streaming through the window. He thought he had died and gone to the land of the misty treetops, where it was said that the spirits of the Wolini lived like parrots in the highest branches of the tallest trees. For this is how the Wolini imagined the afterlife, though they did not imagine it frequently. Or at least, they did not talk about it much, having no rituals or prayers designed to gain access to it—perhaps, I suspected, because it was an image of freedom too threatening to confront, as though death and freedom were one. It took some time for Wolan to become convinced that he was not dead. The presence of strange men in dark clothes speaking in a strange language while touching him gently—this did not convince him. What convinced him was the tremendous pain he felt when they pulled on his arm and leg, trying to set each so that the bones would not grow together crooked. This was something Wolan could understand, having seen the same thing among the Wolini when one had broken a limb and having felt in his own bones the silent fear and pain of the one whose limb was being set. What Wolan could not understand is why a people would make a religious ritual out of setting broken bones, choosing as an icon a man whose every limb seemed broken, so that his body had to be laid out on a tree to be straightened. For, as he slowly recovered and began to walk around this huge house, Wolan saw this icon everywhere.

Wolan spent months with the missionaries of the Orinoco. He ate their food, which he never learned to like, sharing, after a few weeks, their table with them, learning to use the tiny metal spears that they ate with. He even shared their religious rituals, in which they bent their bodies as though they had been beaten and spoke in what he recognized was yet another language. But he never learned their language, neither their secret ritual language nor their everyday language. He only learned one word, which he would remember all his life, Fa-ter Too-mas. This was the name of the priest with whom he came to share long walks along the river, whose narrow sandy shore stretched for miles, the dense jungle never more than a few yards away.

Something profound had happened on these walks, although Wolan could never say what it was, even as he puzzled about it for the rest of his life. They did not speak the same language, and while each would occasionally point to an object and make the sound for it in his own language, neither remembered the other's word. Because it didn't matter. Their communication was deeper, rooted in the way in which each would gaze into the other's eyes, while mirroring the other's posture or the pace of his walk, only to suddenly shift his gaze, carriage, and speed. Not just to escape for a moment the spell cast by the other, but to challenge him: to see if the other could and would keep up, to see how far the other could be left behind and how fast he could catch up. It was as if they were dancing in the depths of the river or in the tops of the trees. It was radiant, wonderful, and it took Wolan the rest of his life to figure out what it was all about. For as exceptional as Wolan was, he had no vocabulary with which to conceptualize the experience and no cultural tradition or resources in which to express it. To me he communicated the experience in what can only be called a pantomime ballet, in which he played both roles, coupled with a story about teaching his grandson to hunt. I cannot be sure that I have truly captured the meaning of Wolan's experience, but it was clearly transformative—

deeply moving, almost religious, and utterly incomprehensible to the Wolini. Actually, not utterly incomprehensible. They could understand enough of his experience to know that it was in some way awesome, the changes in Wolan rendering him *aidos,* both blessed and cursed. They could not understand enough to learn from it, however. Instead, they made him their leader.

Wolan remained with the missionaries of the Orinoco for months. The walks with Fa-ter Too-mas continued, as wonderful as ever. But Wolan was becoming restless, something Fa-ter Too-mas could feel in his bones. Recently, Wolan had taken to veering off into the jungle during some of their walks, remaining there until the next day, when he would rejoin Fa-ter Too-mas on his next day's walk. Neither said a thing, acting as though the day's absence was a matter of moments. But both knew it was time for Wolan to leave. Both knew too that while Wolan must leave, he would never find his way home alone. So one day, on what turned out to be one of their last walks together, Fa-ter Too-mas drew Wolan a map in the sand, showing him in what direction and for how long to walk upstream. Fa-ter Too-mas gave Wolan something else as well, a tiny piece of metal shaped like, but much smaller than, the miniature spear Wolan had learned to eat with. This tiny spear seemed to float in its own container, always pointing in the same direction. These gifts were apparently enough; with them Wolan made it back to the Wolini. Something I would never have believed possible for a man of Wolan's notorious lack of direction, a man who could get himself lost just yards from the longhouse, the subject of many jokes among the Wolini. It may have been this, more than anything else, that made Wolan *aidos* among his people. He was a holy fool, accomplishing a journey many times longer and more arduous than the best hunters and trackers of his tribe had ever attempted.

Wolan never spoke of his journey home, just as he never spoke of his leave-taking from Fa-ter Too-mas, except to say that one day shortly after receiving his gifts, he veered off into the jungle and never returned. Perhaps Fa-ter Too-mas still waits for Wolan to rejoin him on his walks, half expecting Wolan to walk out of the jungle where he walked into it some forty years ago. I know, or rather sense, that Wolan expected until his last days to be able to rejoin Fa-ter Too-mas on his walks. Sometimes I felt it was all he ever really cared about in his whole life. While Wolan never spoke of his return journey, one thing is known about it (by me alone), and one can be surmised. What is known is that Wolan kept the compass that Fa-ter Too-mas gave him. For Wolan took me to the spot near the longhouse where he had buried it upon returning to the tribe and dug it up, now rusted beyond use but not beyond recognition.

Wolan was made chief shortly after his return. An inspiration to his people, almost all Wolini life is organized around his sayings and his wishes—or rather, around what the Wolini imagine are his sayings and his wishes. For in recent years, particularly, Wolan has become more and more withdrawn, so that he only occasionally appears before his people, standing silently on the edge of his platform for a few minutes before returning to his room. This, though, has not diminished his power. Or at least, the Wolini seem quite content to organize their life around the sayings of Wolan while never hearing him say anything. He has so much on his mind, the Wolini explain, the fate of his people. About this the Wolini are at least partly right. Wolan had a lot on his mind.

For all their commitment to the group, the Wolini could be remarkably selfish. I noticed this at harvesttime, when each seemed to compete with the rest to do the least work—or rather, to get others to do more. Not that the shirkers would stand around talking and joking instead of working, a charming if improvident pastime. There was none of this. Instead, each would feign hard work while intentionally accomplishing very little, sometimes unearthing a tuber and covering it right over again. Frequently a Wolini would not very carefully conceal a yam or barbasco in his clothing, going off into the woods as though to relieve himself. There he would bury the tuber. Wrapped carefully in leaves, it would remain edible for several months, so that the hoarder might enjoy it at his leisure. Several Wolini even had their own private mini-gardens deep in the forest. This was, of course, a gross transgression of every value the Wolini possessed.

Striking was the way in which everyone knew what was going on but no one said a thing, as if the practice of hoarding did not exist. It was as though a Wolini could assert himself only by withholding from the group—an act so threatening to individual and group that it could not be acknowledged. I never heard a single Wolini mention this practice, other than to make remarks about "going to the woods," a phrase that ostensibly referred to the act of elimination but, accompanied by a sly smile, meant something quite different—not a private act, but a deeply selfish one, in a world in which no other expression of self seemed possible.

Like peoples everywhere, the Wolini have their rituals, the most important being the harvest sacrifice called the *Wolangesenko,* or gift to Wolan. Some, though, said the term meant the "gift of Wolan," but whether they meant a gift of his or the gift of Wolan of himself was not clear to me. The ritual began in the dark of the night, as small pieces of soft bark, several inches square, were passed around the longhouse to each of the approximately 65 adults who comprised the Wolini. On the backside of this bark the symbol of the man or woman to be ostracized was inscribed with a fingernail. While the Wolini did not have a written language, they possessed rudimentary written symbols denoting numbers from one to ten and the names of the Wolini families. Given the way in which the Wolini named their members, this was enough to single out any individual for sacrifice. Toward morning the inscribed chips were returned, and someone or some committee (I never found out which) totaled the votes. I had expected that the results would be announced in some way, perhaps by Wolan himself, in tones of solemnity and awe. But this is not how the Wolini worked. Instead, the name of the ostracized one was whispered around the room, from one blanket-neighbor to the next, so that by first light all but the victim seemed to know.

This, of course, was what made it so terrifying. Not to know was not to be connected to the group anymore. For this is all that happened to the victim. But it was enough, enough to cause his death within a matter of weeks. Thus it was that the victim was neither expelled from the longhouse nor tied to a tree, his throat slit and him left to bleed to death, as the Wolini did when butchering an animal—images that I had associated with ritual sacrifice. Instead, the victim was simply ignored. Utterly and completely. No one would look at or talk to him; no one would stand close to him in the food line. His wife and children removed themselves to another family, and his blanket-neighbors turned their backs on him. Even his name was taken over by the next in line. He didn't exist anymore, to others or to himself. What had Danwo, for this was the sacrifice's name this time, done to deserve this? Like every sacrifice before him, Danwo had stood out from the group, expressing his individuality outside one of the few ways the group would tolerate, such as hoarding food. Recently Danwo's father, with whom he had always hunted along with several other relatives, had died, and Danwo had subsequently taken to hunting alone. This was enough to make him a marked man. Not just because he went out alone, but because he was obviously grieving so deeply for a particular individual, a special one.

Why, I wondered, had this not happened to Wolan upon his return? Surely he had stood out, more than any Wolini ever. Unlike the scapegoat, however, Wolan had become involuntarily separated from his tribe. But not just this. Whereas most scapegoats, such as Danwo, were obviously terrified by their separation from the tribe, Wolan had remained in what can only be described as a state of religious ecstasy for months. Whereas Danwo at first made numerous hysterical and halting attempts to connect with the Wolini, going so far one night as to embrace one of his blanket-neighbors, refusing to let go, so that the Wolini were forced to physically separate them, Wolan didn't seem to know or care that others were present, talking quietly to himself for weeks after his return. Whereas Danwo, after these first attempts, quickly fell into a state of lassitude and withdrawal from which he never recovered, Wolan was filled with a manic energy that seemed to infect all those around him. Within weeks Danwo was dead, his body discovered one morning 100 meters from the longhouse, on the edge of the forest. Several Wolini simply dragged his body into the woods and left him there. There was no funeral ceremony. Or rather, the funeral had been conducted weeks before, when Danwo was ostracized. Within weeks of *his* return, on the other hand, Wolan was made leader.

By then, Wolan had been leader for years, a source of inspiration to his people. But he was an old man now and fell seriously ill. At first the group refused to acknowledge this. Food left for him piled up outside his door, and "Wolan says" continued to organize the group. But not for long, as one morning Wolan managed to crawl on his stomach to the edge of the loft and silently look out over his people. All the Wolini could see of him was his sick little head sticking over the edge, at the sight of which they fell into the deepest despair. After a while Wolan managed to crawl back into his apartment, from which he never came out alive, though he clung to life for months.

During this time the destitute Wolini made a fateful error which would ensure their annihilation. The soil of the Amazon is rich and fertile but is only a few inches deep and readily depleted, so that every few years the Wolini must abandon the plot they have been working and clear another, deeper in the forest. Over the past two years the yield of yams and barbasco had fallen precipitously, and all knew that the present plot would not support another harvest. Yet plant and harvest this plot they did, as they were too demoralized and exhausted to undertake anything new. The result was a disaster, a harvest yielding at best four months' worth of food, with eight months standing between the Wolini and the next harvest. With no reserves, the Wolini knew they would starve, and they knew when, unless they decided to feast now and starve earlier. It did not occur to the Wolini to sacrifice half the tribe to save the rest. For better or worse, probably better in this case, this is not how they thought. Or at least not how they thought out loud. In public. Possibly the existence of private hoards of food misled some Wolini into thinking they could survive the famine that would carry away the others. In fact, none survived; the private stocks were depleted within weeks, by "owners" and trespassers alike.

Wolan finally died, apparently forgotten by the group in its misery, until his body began to stink so vilely that it could no longer be ignored. Shocked back to reality the Wolini held an elaborate funeral fit for a chief. Or rather, they tried to hold such a funeral, only to see it fall apart in disgrace. Years before, Wolan had instructed the Wolini how to bury him. His head and limbs were to be neatly severed from the body, so that each piece might be buried separately, in the shape of an extended body, the head buried slightly above the torso, the arms slightly to the left and right, and so on, as though burying a huge, superhuman form. This was, said some Wolini, the point. To portray the body image of the chief, outlined in small stones on the forest floor, even bigger in death than in life. Others said it was to make sure the chief was really dead, or that all the praise and suffering on his behalf would not somehow restore him to life.

The Wolini never completed the funeral ritual. Wolan was laid out before the front door of the longhouse, Wolini standing in a semicircle several members deep around the corpse, the ones at the back craning their necks and pushing forward to see it. The first, or un, members of the twelve families crouched low over the body, several taking out knives with which they quickly severed the head and limbs from the body. But as they were doing this, other Wolini surged forward, engulfing the body, submerging it under their own bodies. Soon one Wolini could be seen emerging from the pile of bodies with a piece of Wolan's arm, then another with a piece of his leg, still another with Wolan's head under his arm. Off each ran into the forest with his treasure, but what each did with his piece of Wolan I have never learned. Ate it? Buried it like a stolen yam? Left it for the animals and bugs? In any case it was several hours before the Wolini staggered back into the longhouse, the exaltation that had possessed them now completely gone. Rather than incorporating the fallen leader into the group, the dispersal of the *disjecta membra* of Wolan seemed to have rent the group, shattering its wholeness and unity forever, nothing remaining to hold its members together.

The unity of the group, the belief that they would starve together as they had lived together, was the only comfort the Wolini had known recently. Now this too was shattered; each member would simply starve, one by one. Too bereft and guilty to choose a new leader, the Wolini did the only thing they could think of, mounting a special observance of the *Wolangesenko* months ahead of schedule. For the Wolini the group may have been invaluable and indivisible, but the individual member was expendable if his exclusion would allow others to huddle more tightly together, the alienation of one heightening by contrast the sense of togetherness of those remaining.

The night of the selection ritual was especially tense, with lots of whispering and scurrying around. It was a wonder anybody slept, and many didn't. The Wolini were so desperate, as well as so angry, that they might have chosen anyone. Shortly after first light it became apparent that it was Sowan who had been chosen. As his blanket-neighbors turned their backs on him, his wife and two daughters silently arose, each carefully stepping around the edges of the blankets of his neighbors, to take up life with another Wolini family across the longhouse. No one spoke to Sowan, though several Wolini standing nearest to him in the food line appeared to whisper his name while shyly glancing at him. This may have made all the difference in the world. Unlike Danwo, Sowan continued to use his own name in talking to his blanket-neighbors and others. Or rather, in learning to talk to himself. For no one responded to Sowan, even as several no longer turned their backs on him. Deprived of his own name and having no concept of the first person pronoun "I," Danwo, like every sacrifice before him, had quickly become a nonperson, even to himself. How could he even know that he existed if he had no way to talk to himself? Not only did Sowan continue to use his old name, but this had the effect of preventing anyone else from taking it, as the one who would ordinarily have taken it over refused to do so, afraid that he would be sacrificed too. Afraid, that is, that he would be confused with Sowan. For no two Wolini ever had the same name.

Upset, pale, distraught, Sowan nonetheless did not fall mortally ill. On the contrary, he continued to live his life, talking to himself as once others had talked to him. Soon others began to talk to him, in whispers at first, in the middle of the night, then more openly. Soon the space around his blanket became crowded, as several Wolini from across the longhouse moved closer, in order to listen to his stories—the same stories that had gotten Sowan into trouble in the first place. For this was his offense, the reason for his sacrifice: making up stories or telling new versions of old stories that had never been told before. One story that he told was especially beloved by his growing cadre of listeners. But, perhaps "beloved" isn't quite the right word. The story captivated and entranced his listeners, though none could say why. It was a story about the origins of the Wolini, why they became the people they had become.

Originally, according to Sowan's story, there was only one small tribe in the huge forest, the Ur-tribe. These predecessors of the Wolini lived freely in the forest, the men and women hunting, fishing, and gathering together. Parents and their children lived together in grass huts arranged in a circle around a communal fire, and everyone had his own name, even the children. One day a strange animal appeared at the edge of the forest, about 30 yards from the clearing in which the huts were located. It was like nothing anyone had ever seen before. From their descriptions it sounded to me like a huge wild dog, ugly, reddish brown, and mottled with mange or some other disease of the skin, so that patches of fur were mixed with scabrous skin. While it is hard to be sure about the details, the beast made an enormous impression on them. For all its fearsome appearance, the beast was not unfriendly, allowing the children to feed it scraps of fatty meat and eventually allowing the children to pet it. It was never friendly; never did it wag its tail (if it even had one) or slobber over the children as dogs do. But it did not run away either, calmly standing about halfway between forest and village as the children would dare each other to run up and touch it, which they did, quickly running back to join their group a few yards away. Soon the children were playing with it, or rather, playing all around it, falling all over it, as the beast stood or sat on its haunches, tolerating everything in its good-natured way, even the toddler who bit its ear.

At first the parents paid little attention. While even this Edenic forest had its dangers, they were few, and the parents were accustomed to allowing the children to play by themselves all day under the guidance of the older children. Soon, however, the parents noticed that something strange was going on. A delegation of men was sent to investigate, and the animal loped off into the forest before they could come near. The men had seen enough, however, to know that they had never seen anything like it. They had seen enough, in other words, to be scared. The children were ordered not to go near the beast, and a party of the best hunters was sent to track it down and kill it. They never found it, but all seemed well. The parents took turns watching over the children more closely, and the beast did not return—at least, not for a while. Soon, however, something far worse happened to the tribe. Its children began to disappear. Not all at once, but sporadically, one this month, another the next, still another two months later. For a tribe of several hundred, in which every member was at least acquainted with every other, this tragedy struck deeply at every member. Its happy, for the most part healthy, and joyous children were the pride of the tribe, treated like the natural resource they were, cherished but allowed to grow in their own time and in their own way. At first the disappearances were inexplicable, and then the tribe remembered the beast. Soon new reports of the beast filtered in, as members remembered seeing it in the evening mist on the edge of the forest on the very night that a child disappeared.

The children were confined to the huts and the circle formed by them, always watched over by several adults, even during the day. The adults sent out hunting parties to destroy the beast and tracking parties to recover the remains of the children. None were ever found, nor were any signs of struggle. While sightings of the beast continued, the hunting party never got close, though they caught a glimpse of the beast from time to time as it ran through the forest. The disappearances continued until almost two dozen children had been taken. The parents were inconsolable, the tribe disconsolate. But this was not the worst thing. The worst thing was the way in which the tribe, which had lived together for so long and so well, began to destroy itself in grief and rage. Parents blamed each other for being insufficiently vigilant, and they blamed older children for not watching over the younger ones. The women blamed the men for not killing the beast, and the men blamed the women for allowing the missing children to slip away in the middle of the night, for that is when the disappearances occurred. And families began to blame each other, as the families with children who had disappeared charged that the children who remained encouraged the beast by leaving scraps of food for it, calling to it in the middle of the night, and so forth. It was as if the only way the tribe's grief and fear could be contained was to transmute it into conflict and strife, one part of the tribe fighting the other to get it to take responsibility for all the sorrow and suffering.

Slowly the tribe began to fragment, as families who had not yet lost any children left the group and moved deeper into the forest. To escape the beast, they said; but what they feared is that the black magic of the beast had somehow contaminated those who had lost a child. And those who remained came to experience themselves as somehow polluted, impure, huddling closer together in the stasis of their shame and grief. It is these families who became the Wolini, drawn together closer and closer, as though they could create their own black hole, from which nothing could escape. And they succeeded, creating a world from which no individual children could escape and into which nothing foreign could enter, not even the light from above.

Sowan's auditors listened to this story many times, most desiring to hear it again and again, instead of a new one. Eventually, they began to debate its meaning among themselves. Quietly at first, in whispers in the middle of the night, and then with increasing fervor. What really happened to the children? Nothing, said one, a man of a secular cast of mind (no matter how much they pretended, the Wolini were not as identical as all that). A couple of children may have wandered off into the forest, but the story of the beast is no more than a legend, used to cover up the fact that it was petty rivalry and jealousy among the leading families of the tribe that led to its division. This, and the fact that as the tribe became more prosperous, it began to neglect its children, even as it idealized them more. Another auditor disputed this, believing in the literal truth of the beast, holding that somewhere, deeper in the forest, lived a tribe of lost children led by a beast, children who never grew up and a beast who never dies. And while not one claims to have seen this lost tribe, several of Sowan's auditors claim to have recently seen the beast standing at the edge of the forest in the deepening dusk, apparently hoping that a child might come out to play with it and so fall under its spell. But Wolini children don't go out to play anymore and haven't for some time.

Striking was that even the most secular of Sowan's blanket-neighbors believed the myth to be a noble lie, literally false, but figuratively true. Not the beast in the forest, but the beast within every man, the beast of fear, greed, need, arrogance, and rage will destroy the tribe unless it huddles together so tightly that no individuals are left, no individuals to feel these things. A painted image on one wall of the longhouse shows two jaguarlike animals trapped together in a hunting net that is being pulled more tightly together by Wolini hunters. It's a compelling image, the animals wrapped about each other like the yin–yang symbol of Chinese philosophy. Only, unlike the black and white Chinese symbol, the painting was luminous, the only colorful thing in the longhouse. Upon asking about it, I was told that as the net begins to close upon a pair of animals, they always begin to fight each other and will continue fighting until the net is drawn so tight that they are trapped in a cocoon, or womb, in which no movement is possible. Only then do they stop trying to kill each other, when they are exhausted and half dead.

Sowan and his companions—for that is what they had become—did not just tell stories to each other. They also began to talk about survival— how the Wolini would survive until the next harvest. Soon this became the prime topic of conversation. And then one morning they were gone, about two dozen of them. Vanished, along with their blankets and bowls. The Wolini who remained were awestruck. Nothing like this had ever happened before. Had the beast whom they had been telling stories about, for by now every Wolini had heard the story, whispered from blanket-neighbor to blanket-neighbor, dragged them all away? Soon, however, the Wolini who remained began to piece together another story, in which Sowan and his companions had decided that their survival depended upon leaving the longhouse, to live off the forest until the next harvest could be sown and reaped. This they did, leaving in the wee hours to seek their future in the forest. One Wolini claimed to have seen them walk single file into the forest, the full moon casting pale shadows behind each of the two dozen.

The group of men and women who followed Sowan into the forest did not have an easy time of it. Taking almost no supplies, they spent most of their first months foraging for edible plants and trapping small animals, living together under a thatched lean-to. But they survived the winter season and planted early, Sowan having cleverly taken a few yams and barbasco with him for rootstock. Even more cleverly, he did not tell anyone else about this trove until planting time, lest it be eaten in the first desperate weeks. It seemed so symbolic, this theft of rootstock, but what exactly did it symbolize, I wondered? Was Sowan some sort of Prometheus of the Amazon? Not exactly. The theft symbolized, I decided, the way in which a totalitarian group contains within itself the seeds of its own destruction, defining every act of self-expression as hostile to the group and making it so. In such an environment, individualism is bound to be deviant, antisocial—such as hoarding food rather than using it as a resource for living. Yet, it seems to me that the New Ones, as they came to call themselves, took a more positive lesson from the Wolini as well, though they did not yet know it. Differentiation, the creation of a space for individuals within the group, must be differentiation *from* something, even if it is the forced unity of the group. The unity of the Wolini, deeply flawed, nonetheless provided a starting space for this development, even as it threatened to crush it. It provided something to rebel against, something for the New Ones to define themselves by contrast with. Once, that is, they could get a little distance from it; which means once they took the terrifying first step of walking off into the forest.

The first harvest of the New Ones was abundant, the virgin soil rich and fruitful. They had survived almost two seasons (one year) now. Already children had been born, and several more were on the way. Still, the New Ones were troubled, not wanting to reproduce the way of life they had left behind but having no model on which to build a new one. Nor were they a bunch of indigenous idealists, out to create a perfect village. They were survivors, having left the Wolini not so much as an act of rebellion as out of recognition that to stay would have meant starvation. As it did. The Wolini perished that winter.

The New Ones chose as their leader Sowan, the one who had preserved the rootstock that assured their survival. Yet, this is not why they chose him, nor because he told wonderful stories, though that was part of it. Nor was Sowan the best hunter of the group, nor the best gatherer, and certainly not the hardest-working farmer. Sowan was chosen because of his moral example, particularly the way he learned to talk to himself when no one else would talk to him. This, these exiles from the Wolini intuited, they would have to learn to do for themselves as a group. During the first season away from the longhouse the New Ones nearly perished. One faction wished so badly to return to the longhouse that it sabotaged any activity likely to win the survival of the New Ones, talking loudly in the forest while hunting the fallow deer, for example. Several New Ones simply wandered off into the forest and would have died had Sowan not sent others to track and fetch them. Sowan understood their loneliness, sharing his hope for the future with them, and so helping them to contain their sorrow. Sowan made no speeches and had no long-range plans, at least that he could articulate. He was, however, steadfast in his belief that the New Ones had done what they must to survive. Regretting that it was necessary but apparently harboring few doubts that it was, Sowan told the group a new version of the Wolini founding myth, the story of the beast and the children—a version that combined the contributions of some of his auditors back in the longhouse. In so doing, he was able to connect then and now. The radical break was not a total one.

There really was, said Sowan, a beast who made off with the children of the Ur-tribe. But the beast didn't kill them. He took each child gently in its jaws, causing it to fall into a deep and dreamless sleep. Carrying and dragging the child all night, the beast brought the child to a clearing in the jungle next to a limpid pool formed by the confluence of two streams. There the beast would care for the child, feeding it from its teats until it learned to forage with the others. Which didn't take long, as the land to which he brought them was lush, filled with tropical fruits, the pool teeming with fish. Still, the children took up most of the beast's time, until it figured out that older children might care for the younger, and that is when the beast began to carry off older children as well. It was hard work, for the older children were wary and much more difficult to drag through the forest. Some missed their parents and tried to return. So the beast had to watch over them closely. Soon, however, the children formed their own society, the older ones caring for the younger ones and each doing his job. The beast was happy, and so were the children. While some still missed their parents, for most it was enough. Even today the careful traveler in the forest may hear the children playing, catching glimpses of them as they hide behind the trees, waiting for the traveler to pass before resuming their lives.

The beast and the children were happy, but the parents were not. The tribe fought among themselves, family against family, just as the original legend has it. Only the founding legend is wrong on one important point, said Sowan. The tribe did divide, but it did not separate into those who left because they feared their children would be taken and those who stayed because they had already lost their children. This was not the point at all. Many who left had already lost their children, and many who stayed had not lost any. The tribe divided into those who valued their children all the more because there were so few and wanted to have many more and those who decided never to conceive and bear more children, as their loss caused so much pain.

Those who decided to have more children left in order to begin a new life elsewhere in the forest. Eventually their children and children's children and children's children's children populated the forest, the seed from which all the tribes of the forest sprang, including the Eurfeyo and the Aranago. And what of those who remained? They could not escape nature, even their own nature, no matter how hard they tried. So of course they had more children. But they didn't have many, and they were so scared of losing them that they gave their children no real names, so that when one was lost he would not be missed. He could not even be searched for, as no one would even know what to call him. Those who remained became the Wolini. This was Sowan's story, one of many that he told that first year, stories that kept the New Ones alive. Not just by giving them hope, but by helping them mourn their loss. While they had left the Wolini in order to save their lives, the New Ones were still very attached to them, their escape from the longhouse a wrenching dislocation. Sowan helped them experience this loss by telling a story about it, so helping the New Ones give their loss a meaning which could be shared.

At first the New Ones kept their old names, third child of the Gon family, fifth child of the Wan family, and so on. Gradually they abandoned this practice as the families that gave these names their meaning had been left behind. Since members had never thought of these designations as personal names to begin with, but more like placeholders within the Wolini, it was not difficult for the New Ones to let their old designations fall into desuetude, for that is what happened. But what to call themselves? Soon members came to take the names of birds, animals, and plants around them, such as Blue Parrot, Forest Deer, Tree in Mist. But, having no experience with the idea of a personal name and the identity that it represents, many took the same name, Honeybadger being much more popular than Tapioca Plant, for example. The result was actually greater conflict and confusion, at least at first, each member delighting in his new identity, each deeply resenting its appropriation by others. Such a problem had never arisen before, each having had no identity to lose.

At night the New Ones would sit by the communal fire, around which there were now more than a dozen thatched huts located in a rough circle. All great storytellers now, the New Ones would exchange embroidered tales of the day's events and distribute the tasks of the next day. It could get quite confusing, as when Honeybadger would say, "Honeybadger believes that the New Ones should plant less barbasco and more yams next year," only to find three other members named Honeybadger violently disagreeing with him, furious at having their own positions misrepresented, none being overly fond of yams either. Disagreements over what to do, difficult enough in themselves, became disputes over the misrepresentation of another's beliefs, a much more fractious issue. Not merely what to do, but the integrity of the speaker, as well of those he claimed to speak for (if he did), were at stake in every dispute. The result was disputes that went on for hours, becoming more heated and confusing as they wore on, until finally no one knew who believed what about anything. The group was exhausted.

It was thus that the first-person singular pronoun was born, so that Honeybadger might say "I believe that" and so differentiate himself from all the rest, including all the other Honeybadgers. The "I" was no easy concept for the New Ones to grasp. At first many believed that "I" was just one more proper name like Honeybadger, not understanding how it could shift around the group so quickly, from one member to another. Was a person's name just a momentary possession, until someone else took it away? Even more confusing, sometimes it seemed as if the whole group had the same name, I, taking turns in using it as though it were a rare and valuable possession. Or perhaps everyone had two names, I and Honeybadger or I and Birdsong, shifting back and forth to confuse the group, as the hunter Danyo covered himself with musk to fool the shy fallow deer. Soon enough, however, the New Ones learned that the I belonged to whoever was speaking, being passed on to the next speaker much like the communal wine gourd was passed around the group when the New Ones sat by the fire. This is why what we call the first-person singular pronoun came to be called the speaker's name or the speaker's voice by the New Ones, something all might possess but only one at a time.

With the speaker's voice a member could separate himself from the group, distinguishing himself from all the others, after which he would give up his I to another in the group, knowing, or at least hoping, that he could in time get his I back from the group. Of course, it wasn't always that easy. Some New Ones felt that even to hear the word I was an obscenity, an insult to everyone else, a verbal attack on the unity of the group. One compared it to that terrible experience that all remembered, but none dared recall, in which one of the Wolini ran off with Wolan's head into the forest. Others liked the I too much, refusing to give it up, refusing to recognize anybody else who used the name, treating it as if it were his own personal property. Soon the I became such a source of conflict that it was proposed that only

Sowan could use the speaker's voice, and penalties were proposed for anyone who took the speaker's name in vain. But Sowan said that he had been given too many I's, I's that didn't belong to him.

Sowan understood something the others did not. The point of the speaker's voice is not to make leadership easier, though it has that effect. It is to make self-revelation possible. With the speaker's voice I may show myself to others and so come to know who I am. Not just because self-revelation allows me to know myself as I am mirrored in the eyes of others, though that is part of the story. But also because in speaking for myself I must make a public commitment as to who I am. Potentially I may be many things, but in publicly revealing myself to be one thing, that thing that I am becomes more real. Not just to myself but to the group as well, as what I am becomes available to it, no longer hidden among all the other members. It is ironic. The greatest act of selfishness, to take the name of the speaker's voice, is also the greatest gift to the group. But might members not just pretend to reveal themselves? Of course, and most group life is about that. But if the group can come to share freely the speaker's voice, the members will have an incentive for genuine self-revelation. With the help of the group the members can become what they claim to be, which is really what each member wants most of all. And when members are what they claim to be with the help of the group, group development occurs, as the group does not depend upon suppression of individuality to hold itself together. Instead, the group is held together by mutual recognition, each depending on the group as an arena in which to realize himself.

Sowan intuitively grasped many of these things. But this is not what he said. What he said is that if the members would not take back their I's, he would be willing to own the speaker's voice for a little while, as long as he was free to lend it out to anyone who wanted to borrow it. But they would have to pay him for it, he added. "What must we pay you?" asked Tall Tree. "An extra portion of meat, perhaps, or a piece of colored cloth?" "Much more than that," replied Sowan. "You must give up forever the name you had among the Wolini, the name that says you are nothing more than your place in the group." No one took Sowan up on his offer, at least not at first. The New Ones loved their new names but had not thought that they would really have to choose between old and new. Hardly anyone spoke in public for days. Then several of the more daring members borrowed the speaker's voice for just a little while, and then for just a little while longer. Soon after, most of the members were using the speaker's voice, some more than others of course. Sowan never demanded his payment. But he didn't have to. He was paid in full, as the old names were never heard again among the New Ones.

The New Ones still had much to learn about the I. Infatuated with it, they entered into an agony of difference, each seeking to distinguish himself from all the others. Some decorated themselves with the feathers of birds and the pelts of animals. Others painted themselves with mud. Still others sought to distinguish themselves by speaking their own private language, only to find that a tongue spoken by one was really no language at all. Soon groups of three or four formed, so that each might have someone with whom to speak his language. But this meant that all but one would have to give up his private language for another, and none was willing to do this. The result was an Amazonian equivalent of the Tower of Babel, everyone talking and no one listening, as none understood a word the other was saying. Sowan saw all this and was sad. So he called the New Ones together, delivering for the first and last time in his life a little speech.

To be an I, said Sowan, is not just about being different. Anyone can do that. Pile mud on your head and howl at the moon. That's different, but it's not being an I. To be an I is to develop one's gifts. But gifts are only gifts when they are given, shared with others. A gift that isn't given is nothing. If you have a gift as a hunter, develop it and share its bounty with the New Ones. Then you will be an I. If you have a gift as a weaver and dyer, develop it and be prodigal with the New Ones. Not because the gift really belongs to the New Ones. It doesn't. It really belongs to the giver. It's his gift, remaining with him always. But because the gift means nothing to the giver, it doesn't even exist unless it is given away. Be generous with your gifts, so that you may come to own them. Then you will be an I. You will become your gift.

The New Ones listened to Sowan in silence. After one of Sowan's stories the New Ones would talk among themselves, elaborating upon it, repeating favorite lines, and acting out some of the favorite characters among themselves. But after Sowan's speech there was only silence. Still, it seemed to make a difference. While the mutterings of private languages could still be heard around the village, more New Ones could be seen practicing their gifts, competing with each other (for the New Ones were nothing if not competitive) to give the most and the best gifts. Soon there was more meat on the table, more beautiful and colorful cloths were available, and the harvest was more plentiful. Not only did the New Ones prosper, but they seemed happier and more fulfilled. At least, in most things.

Not everything, however. Sexual relationships, especially, troubled the New Ones. Among the Wolini, sexual relationships were rigidly structured and ritualized, so that they would not disrupt the close life of the group, 200 men, women, and children living together in a large room with no walls and no privacy. Marriage was neither a union of love nor an institution by which to raise children, largely a communal undertaking. Marriage was a way of regulating sexual competition and jealousy in a claustrophobic world in which both could be enormously disruptive to the entire group. The norms, sanctions, and rituals surrounding sex and marriage among the Wolini were complex, but the basic principles were simple. Marriages were arranged by the older women of each of the twelve families. In order to discourage sexual experimentation, marriage took place in early adolescence between young men and women of different families. Divorce was a virtual impossibility for either party, adultery being met with severe sanctions, including expulsion. The Wolini term for marriage, *mailon,* which roughly translates as the containment of sex, captures their thinking on the subject. Why the Wolini put up with all this is best explained by their whole way of life, though it shouldn't be overlooked that a Wolini would never expect to live with his spouse in any case. Their life was communal, marriage strictly a way of controlling sexual conflict and desire within the group.

Released from the confines of the longhouse, sexual relations among the New Ones were promiscuous and demanding, as men and women learned to love and need each other and so demand a fidelity that lacked any institutional support. Sexual desire, competition, envy, fear, and jealousy infiltrated almost every aspect of group life, as discussion and distribution of tasks around the communal fire were complicated by these emotions. Imagine what can happen during a group discussion over whether to devote more resources to hunting or farming when the speakers are having sexual relations with each other's consorts.

Various solutions were considered by the New Ones. Mist in the Forest proposed a version of the Wolini marriage contract, the only answer to sexual conflict that they knew. It was Forest Deer, however, who captured the emerging consensus, at least among the men.

Sex is destroying the New Ones, setting man against man, woman against woman, and man against woman. Soon we shall be worse off than the Wolini, who at least did not perish over something as silly as sex. For the good of the group I propose that the women live together in a large hut. From there they will be escorted by the eldest woman of our tribe to the huts of the men, who will peacefully and quietly decide among themselves which woman is to sojourn with which man. Sexual desire is more deadly to the unity of the New Ones than any poison. Just as we do not poison our hunting arrows until we are ready to shoot them so that no one might be accidentally hurt, so we must keep men and women separate until they may safely come together.

Finally a woman spoke up, and this is what she said:

I have taken my own name, Birdsong, and given up my Wolini name, learning to share the I with the men as well as the women. I do not want the speaker's voice just for myself or just for women. But the New Ones must never forget why we worked so hard to learn the speaker's voice—so that no one might hide behind the group and so speak in the name of another without his consent. You, Forest Deer, have forgotten this. The next thing we will be hearing from you is that the trees in the forest also wish the women to live together, or at least the male trees do, and that you are their voice too. Unless I hear every tree give its consent, you shall not be their voice, and unless I hear every member give his or her consent, you shall not speak for the group either.

Birdsong's speech made a great impression on the New Ones, transforming an unproductive dispute between the tribe of men and the tribe of women into a discussion of individual and group. Even those New Ones still hostile to that obscenity called "I" came to see that it is not the speaker's voice that poses the greatest threat to the group. It is posed by one who refuses to take the name of "I," who speaks in the name of the group when what he really means is "me and those like me." Those who hide behind the group voice, Birdsong added, turn the group into a giant animal that either consumes its members as though it were devouring its own carcass or causes its members to flee for their lives. Once the New Ones learned all this—and it took some time—their solutions to sexual conflict within the group began to show respect for actual men and women. If a man and woman declare their relationship openly before the group, the New Ones eventually decided, then they would acquire a new status called "a pair." Still individuals, as well as group members, their new status signified only— but this is nonetheless a lot—that the other group members would respect the sexual and emotional bond between them, until one or both declared publicly that the bond was broken. Jealousy, adultery, and sexual competition were hardly eliminated by the group's recognition of the pair, but most found it an improvement.

The invention of the pair erected a boundary between couple and group that served the interests of both. Not only did this boundary insulate the couple from the insensitive intrusions of the group, which idealized love but could never appreciate lovers. But the group's recognition of the pair's status actually bound the couple to the group, as anyone is bound by the recognition of another. From pairs came some of the most creative contributions of the group. Not so much unique new ideas (these remained the work of individuals), but a renewed energy for group life that did not demand more from the group than it could give. To ask from the group more intimacy and warmth than it can ever provide, the New Ones learned, is a major source of discontent, anger, and frustration in group life, the source of endless conflicts. Satisfied in some of their deepest personal needs, many couples actually found more energy for, and interest in, the group. Members still resented the pair, but many found their jealousy of the satisfied couple offset by the vitality such couples brought to the life of the group. This vitality is embodied in the children born of the pair, children who will continue the life of the group, but it extends to other aspects of group life as well. Through the pair, the group too found a new lease on life.

Seasons passed, the harvest continued to be fruitful, the soil here richer and deeper than where they had come from. Soon they would have to clear another plot of land still deeper in the forest. But for now their big problem was what to do with Sowan, whom they had virtually imprisoned with their worship, out of hope that he might save them from the hard work yet to come and fear that he could not and so must be prevented from trying. Some wished to build for Sowan a special hut where he might be fed and adored. Others, in what amounted to the same thing, wanted to make of him a gift to the beast of the forest, in the hope that it might gently carry him off—or not so gently, if that's what it took. Finally, in a stroke of collective genius it was decided to create for Sowan a special title, Distinguished Imaginer of the People, setting him to work teaching the children, of which there were now a number, the history of the New Ones. Since this history was perforce brief, Sowan created many beautiful myths out of his distinguished imagination, some so compelling that they were told and retold for generations.

Leadership of the New Ones was never again held by a single man or woman, being passed around according to the needs of the group and the skills of its members, as when Danyo, the group's best stalker, was called upon to organize the increasingly ambitious hunting and trapping expeditions. The New Ones could not, they found, do without leaders. But the leaders they needed were the ones who could do best the things that needed to be done. And since the group needed many things done and no one member could do them all best, the group chose as its leader the one who could best do the task at hand. Then they followed. Sometimes they even followed Sowan, especially in times of doubt and crisis, when his special ability to imagine the group was needed. Then Sowan would tell the group a story about itself, much as he told the children, and for a little while the group would feel whole again, warmed by his idea of them as they were warmed by the communal fire.

The New Ones had learned much. One day they would write it all down, a constitution for the New Ones. But not for some time, as they were still figuring things out. It seems to me that they got the order right. Writing it down is not as important as feeling it—feeling the paradoxical way that individual and group need and use each other, an experience so subtle and complex that unless one is deeply familiar with it, one is liable to simplify and distort the experience in the very act of writing it down, so that when one comes back to the text, the experience that gave it meaning is lost. The New Ones would remain close to experience for a long time. For they believed in it.

Works Cited

Alford, C. Fred. "Mastery and Retreat: Psychological Sources of the Appeal of Ronald Reagan." *Political Psychology* 9, no. 4 (1988): 571–589.

———. *Melanie Klein and Critical Social Theory.* New Haven: Yale University Press, 1989.

———. *Narcissism: Socrates, the Frankfurt School and Psychoanalytic Theory.* New Haven: Yale University Press, 1988.

———. *The Self in Social Theory: A Psychoanalytic Account of its Construction in Plato, Hobbes, Locke, Rousseau and Rawls.* New Haven: Yale University Press, 1991.

Appleby, Joyce. *Liberalism and Republicanism in the Historical Imagination.* Cambridge, Mass.: Harvard University Press, 1992.

Bacal, Howard, and Newman, Kenneth. *Theories of Object Relations: Bridges to Self-Psychology.* New York: Columbia University Press, 1990.

Barber, Benjamin. *Strong Democracy: Participatory Politics for a New Age.* Berkeley: University of California Press, 1984.

Barker, Ernest. Introduction to *The Social Contract,* by Rousseau. New York: Oxford University Press, 1948.

Baumgold, Deborah. "Liberal Individualism Reconsidered." In *Liberals on Liberalism,* ed. Alfonso J. Damico, 151–166. Totowa, N.J.: Rowman and Littlefield, 1986.

Bellah, Robert, Madsen, Richard, Sullivan, William, Swidler, Ann, and Tipton, Steven. *Habits of the Heart: Individualism and Commitment in American Life.* Berkeley: University of California Press, 1985.

Bentley, Arthur. *The Process of Government.* Chicago: University of Chicago Press, 1908.

Berns, Laurence. "Thomas Hobbes." In *History of Political Philosophy,* 2d ed., ed. Leo Strauss and Joseph Cropsey, 370–395. Chicago: Rand McNally, 1972.

Bion, Wilfred. *Experiences in Groups.* New York: Basic Books, 1961.

Bollas, Christopher. *The Shadow of the Object: Psychoanalysis of the Unthought Known*. New York: Columbia University Press, 1987.

Borch-Jacobsen, Mikkel. "The Freudian Subject." In *Who Comes After the Subject?*, ed. Eduardo Cadava, Peter Connor, and Jean-Luc Nancy, 61–78. New York: Routledge, 1991.

Brodbeck, May. "Methodological Individualisms: Definition and Reduction." In *Readings in the Philosophy of the Social Sciences*, ed. Brodbeck, 280–303. New York: Macmillan, 1968.

Burns, James MacGregor. *Leadership*. New York: Harper and Row, 1978.

Connolly, William E. *Identity\Difference: Democratic Negotiations of Political Paradox*. Ithaca, N.Y.: Cornell University Press, 1991.

de Tocqueville, Alexis. *Democracy in America*, ed. Richard D. Heffner. New York: New American Library, 1956.

Dinnerstein, Dorothy. *The Mermaid and the Minotaur: Sexual Arrangements and the Human Malaise*. New York: Harper Colophon Books, 1976.

Faguet, Emile. *Dix-huitième siècle*, 43d ed. Paris: Société française d'imprimerie et de librairie, n.d.

Feyerabend, Paul. *Against Method*. London: New Left Books, 1975.

Filmer, Sir Robert. "Observations on Mr. Hobbes's *Leviathan:* or his Artificial Man—a Commonwealth" (1652). In *Patriarcha, or the Natural Powers of the Kings of England Asserted and Other Political Works*, ed. Peter Laslett. Oxford: Oxford University Press, 1949.

Frazer, Sir James George. *The Golden Bough*, abridged ed. New York: Collier Books, 1950.

Freud, Sigmund. "The Antithetical Meaning of Primal Words." In *The Standard Edition of the Complete Psychological Works of Sigmund Freud*, ed. James Strachey, 24 vols., 11:155–161. London: Hogarth Press, 1953–1974.

———. *Civilization and its Discontents*, trans. James Strachey. New York: W. W. Norton, 1961.

———. *Group Psychology and the Analysis of the Ego*, trans. James Strachey. New York: W. W. Norton, 1959.

———. *Totem and Taboo*, trans. James Strachey. New York: W. W. Norton, 1950.

Geller, M., and Krantz, J. Introduction to *Group Relations Reader*, vol. 2, ed. A. Colman and M. Geller. Washington, D.C.: A. K. Rice Institute, 1985.

Gilligan, Carol. *In a Different Voice: Psychological Theory and Women's Development*. Cambridge, Mass.: Harvard University Press, 1982.

Girard, René. *Violence and the Sacred*, trans. Patrick Gregory. Baltimore: Johns Hopkins University Press, 1977.

Group for the Advancement of Psychiatry. *Us and Them: The Psychology of Ethnonationalism*. New York: Brunner/Mazel, 1987.

Grove, Lloyd. "Run for President or Be a Normal Human Being—Take Your Choice." *Washington Post*, 29 March 1992, C1–2.

Guntrip, Harry. *Schizoid Phenomena, Object Relations and the Self.* Madison, Conn.: International Universities Press, 1992.

Habermas, Jürgen. *Legitimation Crisis,* trans. Thomas McCarthy. Boston: Beacon Press, 1975.

Hamilton, Edith. *The Greek Way.* New York: Avon Books, 1958.

Havel, Václav. *Open Letters: Selected Writings, 1965–1990,* ed. Paul Wilson. New York: Vintage Books, 1992.

Hegel, G. W. F. *Phänomenologie des Geistes.* Hamburg: Felix Meiner Verlag, 1952.

Hinshelwood, R. D. *A Dictionary of Kleinian Thought.* London: Free Association Books, 1989.

———. *What Happens in Groups.* London: Free Association Books, 1987.

Hobbes, Thomas. Introduction to his translation of Thucydides' *History.* In *English Works of Thomas Hobbes,* ed. William Molesworth, vol. 8, xii–xxxii. London: Bohn, 1840.

———. *Leviathan,* ed. C. B. Macpherson. Harmondsworth, England: Penguin Books, 1968.

———. *Philosophical Rudiments Concerning Government and Society* (English version of *De Cive*). In *English Works of Thomas Hobbes,* ed. William Molesworth, vol. 2. London: Bohn, 1840.

Horkheimer, Max. "Authority and the Family." In *Critical Theory,* trans. Matthew J. O'Connell et al., 47–128. New York: Seabury Press, 1972.

Jaques, Elliott. "Social Systems as Defence Against Persecutory and Depressive Anxiety." In *New Directions in Psycho-Analysis,* ed. Melanie Klein, Paula Heimann, and R. E. Money-Kyrle, 478–498. London: Tavistock, 1955.

Johnston, David. *The Rhetoric of Leviathan: Thomas Hobbes and the Politics of Cultural Transformation.* Princeton, N.J.: Princeton University Press, 1986.

Kavka, Gregory S. *Hobbesian Moral and Political Theory.* Princeton, N.J.: Princeton University Press, 1986.

Kinder, D. R., and Fiske, S. T. "Presidents in the Public Mind." In *Political Psychology,* ed. M. Hermann, 193–218. San Francisco: Jossey-Bass, 1986.

Laclau, Ernesto, and Mouffe, Chantal. *Hegemony and Socialist Strategy: Toward a Radical Democratic Politics.* London: Verso, 1985.

Lasch, Christopher. *Haven in a Heartless World.* New York: Basic Books, 1979.

Laslett, Peter. Introduction to *Two Treatises of Government,* by John Locke. New York: New American Library, 1965.

Leakey, Richard, and Lewin, Roger. *People of the Lake: Mankind and its Beginnings.* New York: Avon Books, 1978.

Lifton, Robert Jay. *The Nazi Doctors: Medical Killing and the Psychology of Genocide.* New York: Basic Books, 1986.

Lindblom, Charles E. *Politics and Markets: The World's Political-Economic Systems.* New York: Basic Books, 1977.

Locke, John. "Some Thoughts concerning Education." In *The Educational*

Writings of John Locke, ed. James Axtell, 111–325. Cambridge: Cambridge
University Press, 1968.

———. *Two Treatises of Government,* ed. Peter Laslett. New York: New American
Library, 1965.

Lowi, Theodore J. *The End of Liberalism: The Second Republic of the United States,*
2d ed. New York: W. W. Norton, 1979.

Machiavelli, Niccolò di Bernardo. *The Prince* and *The Discourses.* In *The Portable
Machiavelli,* ed. and trans. Peter Bondanella and Mark Musa, 77–166,
167–418. New York: Viking Penguin, 1979.

MacIntyre, Alasdair. "The Idea of a Social Science." In *The Philosophy of Social
Explanation,* ed. Alan Ryan, 15–32. Oxford: Oxford University Press, 1973.

Macpherson, C. B. Introduction to *Leviathan,* by Hobbes. Harmondsworth,
England: Penguin Books, 1968.

———. *The Political Theory of Possessive Individualism: Hobbes to Locke.* Oxford:
Oxford University Press, 1962.

Mansbridge, Jane. *Beyond Adversary Democracy.* New York: Basic Books, 1980.

Marglin, Stephen. Review of *Stone-Age Economics,* by Marshall Stahlins. *New
York Review of Books,* 19 July 1984.

Marx, Karl. *Grundrisse: Foundations of the Critique of Political Economy,* trans.
Martin Nichols. In *The Marx–Engels Reader,* 2d ed., ed. Robert Tucker,
221–293. New York: W. W. Norton, 1978.

Miller, David, Coleman, Janet, Connolly, William, and Ryan, Alan. *The
Blackwell Encyclopaedia of Political Thought.* Oxford: Basil Blackwell, 1987.

Morgenthau, Hans J. "Love and Power." In *The Restoration of American Politics,*
7–14. Chicago: University of Chicago Press, 1962.

Neumann, Franz. *The Democratic and the Authoritarian State.* New York: Free
Press of Glencoe, 1957.

Nisbet, Robert. "Rousseau and Equality." In *Rousseau's Political Writings,* ed.
Alan Ritter and Julia C. Bondanella, 244–260. New York: W. W. Norton,
1988.

Norton, David L. *Democracy and Moral Development: A Politics of Virtue.* Berkeley:
University of California Press, 1991.

Oakeshott, Michael. *Rationalism in Politics and Other Essays,* new expanded ed.,
ed. Timothy Fuller. Indianapolis: Liberty Press, 1962.

Ogden, Thomas. *The Primitive Edge of Experience.* Northvale, N.J.: Jason
Aronson, 1989.

———. *Projective Identification and Psychotherapeutic Technique.* Northvale, N.J.:
Jason Aronson, 1982.

Palmer, R. R., and Coulton, Joel. *A History of the Modern World,* 2d ed. New York:
Knopf, 1962.

Pateman, Carole. *Participation and Democratic Theory.* Cambridge: Cambridge
University Press, 1970.

———. *The Sexual Contract.* Stanford, Calif.: Stanford University Press, 1988.

Pocock, J. G. A. *The Machiavellian Moment: Florentine Political Thought and the Atlantic Republican Tradition.* Princeton, N.J.: Princeton University Press, 1975.

———. "Virtue and Commerce in the Eighteenth Century." *Journal of Interdisciplinary History* 3, no. 2 (1972): 119–134.

Pufendorf, Samuel. *Samuel Pufendorf's On the Natural State of Men,* trans. and intro. by Michael Seidler. Lewiston, N.Y.: Samuel Mellen Press, 1990.

Rawls, John. *A Theory of Justice.* Cambridge, Mass.: Harvard University Press, Belknap Press, 1971.

Rousseau, Jean-Jacques. *The Confessions,* trans. J. M. Cohen. Harmondsworth, England: Penguin Books, 1953.

———. *The First and Second Discourses,* trans. Roger Masters and Judith Masters. New York: St. Martin's Press, 1964.

———. *La Nouvelle Héloïse,* trans. Judith McDowell. University Park: Pennsylvania State University Press, 1968.

———. *The Social Contract,* ed. and trans. Charles M. Sherover. New York: New American Library, 1974.

Ruderman, Richard. "The Rule of a Philosopher-King: Xenophon's *Anabasis.*" In *Politikos II: Educating the Ambitious. Leadership and Political Rule in Greek Political Thought,* ed. Leslie Rubin, 127–143. Pittsburgh: Duquesne University Press, 1992.

Sandel, Michael. *Liberalism and the Limits of Justice.* Cambridge: Cambridge University Press, 1982.

Saxonhouse, Arlene. *Women in the History of Political Thought: Ancient Greece to Machiavelli.* New York: Praeger, 1985.

Schochet, Gordon. *Patriarchalism in Political Thought.* Oxford: Basil Blackwell, 1975.

Shklar, Judith. "Jean-Jacques Rousseau and Equality." In *Rousseau's Political Writings,* ed. Alan Ritter and Julia C. Bondanella, 260–274. New York: W. W. Norton, 1988.

———. "The Liberalism of Fear." In *Liberalism and the Moral Life,* ed. Nancy Rosenblum, 21–38. Cambridge, Mass.: Harvard University Press, 1989.

———. *Men and Citizens: A Study of Rousseau's Social Theory.* Cambridge: Cambridge University Press, 1969.

Singer, Irving. Introduction to *The Nature of Love,* vol. 1, in *The Philosophy of (Erotic) Love,* ed. Robert Solomon and Kathleen Higgins, 259–278. Lawrence: University Press of Kansas, 1991.

Spillius, Elizabeth. "Some Developments from the Work of Melanie Klein." *International Journal of Psycho-Analysis* 64 (1983): 321–332.

Starobinski, Jean. *Jean-Jacques Rousseau: Transparency and Obstruction,* trans. Arthur Goldhammer, intro. by Robert Morrissey. Chicago: University of Chicago Press, 1988.

Steiner, George. *Antigones: How the Antigone Legend has Endured in Western Literature, Art, and Thought.* Oxford: Clarendon Press, 1986.

Strauss, Leo. *The Political Philosophy of Hobbes,* trans. Elsa Sinclair. Chicago: University of Chicago Press, Midway Reprint, 1984.

Sullivan, William. *Reconstructing Public Philosophy.* Berkeley: University of California Press, 1986.

Tarcov, Nathan. *Locke's Education for Liberty.* Chicago: University of Chicago Press, 1984.

Turquet, Pierre. "Threats to Identity in the Large Group." In *The Large Group: Dynamics and Therapy,* ed. L. Kreeger, 87–144. London: Maresfield Reprints, 1975.

Vaughan, C. E. *The Political Writings of Jean-Jacques Rousseau,* 2 vols. Oxford: Basil Blackwell, 1977.

Volkan, Vamık. "Narcissistic Personality Organization and 'Reparative' Leadership." *International Journal of Group Psychotherapy* 30 (1989): 131–152.

———. "The Need to have Enemies and Allies: A Developmental Approach." *Political Psychology* 6, no. 2 (1985): 219–247.

Warren, Mark. "Democratic Theory and Self-Transformation." *American Political Science Review* 86, no. 1 (Mar. 1992): 8–23.

Wells, Leroy, Jr. "The Group-as-a-Whole Perspective and its Theoretical Roots." In *Group Relations Reader,* vol. 2, ed. Arthur Colman and Marvin Geller, 109–126. Washington, D.C.: A. K. Rice Institute, 1985.

White, Stephen K. *Political Theory and Postmodernism.* Cambridge: Cambridge University Press, 1991.

Wills, Garry. *Lincoln at Gettysburg: The Words that Remade America.* New York: Simon and Schuster, 1992.

Winch, Peter. *The Idea of a Social Science.* London: Routledge and Kegan Paul, 1958.

Winnicott, D. W. *Holding and Interpretation.* New York: Grove Press, 1986.

———. "Mirror-Role of Mother and Family in Child Development." In *Playing and Reality,* 111–118. London: Routledge, 1971.

———. *Playing and Reality.* London: Routledge, 1971.

———. "Primary Maternal Preoccupation." In *Collected Papers: Through Paediatrics to Psycho-Analysis.* New York: Basic Books, 1958.

Wolin, Sheldon. *Politics and Vision: Continuity and Innovation in Western Political Thought.* Boston: Little, Brown, 1960.

Wood, Gordon S. *The Creation of the American Republic, 1776–1789.* New York: W. W. Norton, 1969.

———. *The Radicalism of the American Revolution.* New York: Knopf, 1992.

Young, Iris Marion. "The Ideal of Community and the Politics of Difference." In *Feminism/Postmodernism,* ed. Linda J. Nicholson, 300–323. New York: Routledge, 1990.

Index

A. K. Rice Institute, 2, 26, 45
Abstraction: individual as male and, 141;
    political theory and, 139, 148–49; Rawls's
    individualism and, 135–40. *See also*
    Language
Aggression: enactment of missing leader
    and, 60–61; ritual sacrifice and, 31
Alienation, of parts of self, 147–48. *See also*
    Schizoid compromise; Splitting
Anthropology, 1. *See also* Wolini story
Anxiety: autistic-contiguous position and,
    29; Bion's basic assumptions and, 59; first
    minutes in Tavistock groups and, 27, 90;
    interpretation and, 71–72. *See also* Fear
Appleby, Joyce, 21; *Liberalism and Republi-
    canism in the Historical Imagination,* 145,
    146
Aristotle, 155, 161
Attunement, 50, 51–52, 60
Autism, 105
Autistic-contiguous position, 65–66, 67, 68.
    See also Regressed group
Autonomy: as goal of expansive democracy,
    122; need for leadership and, 5, 133–35;
    in state-of-nature rhetoric, 78, 81, 95–96,
    105–07

Bacal, Howard, 52
Balbus, Isaac, *Marxism and Domination,* 129
Barber, Benjamin: civil privatism and, 118,
    120; sexual conflict and, 141; *Strong
    Democracy,* 115, 123, 124–25, 176
Barker, Ernest, 107

Baumgold, Deborah, "Liberal Individualism
    Reconsidered," 86, 87
Bellah, Robert, 118, 119, 120; *Habits of the
    Heart,* 115, 123
Bentley, Arthur, 18, 130
Berns, Lawrence, 86
Bion, Wilfred: basic assumption groups and,
    56–58; group mentality and, 14–15, 16;
    leadership and, 172; pair as locus of hope
    and, 30; splitting and, 53
The Blackwell Encyclopedia of Political Thought
    (Mill, Coleman, Connolly, & Ryan, eds.),
    154–55
Bollas, Christopher, 54n
Borch-Jacobsen, Mikkel, 39
Burns, James MacGregor, *Leadership,* 153–54
Bush, George, 76, 164, 174

Capitalism, 180–81
Carlyle, Thomas, 155
Catholic University of America (Washington,
    D.C.), 26
Child-rearing, 102n
Churchill, Sir Winston, 71, 162, 182
"Civic liberalism," 127
Civic submission, 81, 82, 83–85
Civil privatism: definition of, 118–19; indi-
    vidualism and, 116–20; participation as
    solution to, 118; as schizoid compromise,
    115, 118
Civil society, and state-of-nature theory, 88,
    109, 140
Clinton, Bill, 171, 174–75

Coleman, Janet, 154

Collusion: in sexual stereotypes, 144–45; between voters and inhuman leaders, 172–74

Communitarianism, 115; "expansive democracy" and, 121–22; individual-group conflict and, 4, 5, 8, 9, 10, 20; leadership and, 155; metaphysics of presence and, 131; Rousseau and, 107–10. *See also* Rawls, John

Competence. *See* Creativity; Individuality

Competitiveness: identification with leader and, 37, 38; sacrificial leader and, 28

Compromise, and individual-group conflict, 5, 20, 124, 130

Concepts. *See* Ideas

Confession, function of, 33–35

Conformity, and American individualism, 116–17

Connolly, William, 115, 130, 132, 133, 134, 154; *Identity\Difference*, 8–9, 121–22, 127, 128, 131–32

Constitutional liberalism, with strong leadership, 11–12, 74, 180–83

Consultant-leader: developed group and, 68; group conflict over soul of, 56–57; identification with, 37–40; interpretive task of, 23; regressed group and, 66; sacrificial leader drama and, 28, 30–31. *See also* Leadership

Contextualization, false, 3, 4

Contract, idea of, 146–47

Corruption, 165, 166, 167

Creativity: identification with goals of group and, 94; projective identification and, 51; sex as symbolic of, 36–37. *See also* Individuality

Critical thought: group dramas and, 23–24; regressed groups and, 42

Cross diagram, 73, 120, 149, 176, 180

Culture. *See* Grouplike entities

Cynicism, and Pufendorf, 83–85

Czechoslovakia. *See* Havel, Václav

Death, fear of, 85, 89, 92. *See also* Despair, deadness, and hopelessness drama; Sex and death drama

De Beauvoir, Simone, 144, 145

Dedifferentiation. *See* Deindividuation

Defenses: Bion's basic assumptions as, 59; against desire to merge, 106–07; interpretation of, 24; in regressed group, 65; sex and death as, 35

Deindividuation: postmodernism and, 130; regressed group and, 66, 87; sacrificial leader drama and, 29; Tocqueville and, 117–18; withholding of recognition and, 40

Democracy: expansive, 121–22, 124; leadership and, 76, 165–66, 182; liberal pluralism and, 132–35; Rousseau and, 110–11, 112

Dependency, 55, 82

Depressive anxiety, 59, 64, 165, 169

Derrida, Jacques, 131

Despair, deadness, and hopelessness drama, 32–35; enactment of missing leader and, 62; Pufendorf's cynicism and, 84–85; sex and, 36; undeveloped group and, 68

Developed group: characteristics of, 68–70; rarity of, 68, 69–70; social contract and, 150, 180

Development, idea of, and political theory, 142–44

Difference principle, 135–37

Differences: complex, 42–43; liberal pluralism and, 134; metaphysics of presence and, 129–30; postmodern political theory and, 9; Rawls's communitarianism and, 135–37, 138–39; regressed group and, 66, 106, 120–21; Rousseau and, 109–11; sexual, as primary, 43–44; valuing of individuals and, 121. *See also* Conformity; Individuality; Tribal warfare drama

Dinnerstein, Dorothy, *The Mermaid and the Minotaur,* 144

Doublespeak, 109

Doubling, 84–85

Dramas: concept of group fantasy and, 44–46; emotions in, 53–54, 56–59; types of, 27–28. *See also* Missing leader, group enactment of; *specific types of dramas*

Ego ideal, and leadership, 167

Emergence, 14, 15–16

Emotions, in group dramas, 53–54, 56–59

Enemies: group need for, 41–42; within, 165

England, 72

Epistemology, 6

Equality, and individualism, 117–18

Erikson, Erik, 43, 153

Evasive thinking, 3–5, 25

"Expansive democracy," 121–22, 124

Experiences in groups: basing of political theory on, 3–12; despair, deadness, and hopelessness drama and, 32–35; leadership and individuality drama and, 37–40; origin of concepts in experience and, 21–22, 23–24; readers' lives and, 9–10; sacrificial leader drama and, 28–32; sex and death drama and, 35–37; Tavistock groups and, 2–3, 9–11; tribal warfare drama and, 40–44; types of dramas in, 27–28. *See also* Group development

Explanatory individualism, 15–16

Externalization: group-sanctioned targets and, 41–42; leadership and, 161

Faguet, Emile, 107

Family: civil privatism and, 119, 120; interpretive leadership and, 182; state-of-nature theory and, 80–81, 90–91, 101–03, 105, 143. *See also* Mothering; Patriarchy

Fear: failure of leadership and, 72; of malevolent leader, 173–74, 178; motivation and, 85, 89, 92, 94, 112; pairing and, 35; patriarchal authority and, 96–97; Pufendorf's sociability and, 82, 83; schizoid compromise and, 52–56; sexual collusion and, 144–45; of total dependency, 55; of work and development, 169. *See also* Anxiety

Filmer, Sir Robert, 90, 95, 96–97, 101

Frankfurt school of critical theory, 119

Frazier, James, *The Golden Bough,* 31

Freedom: civil privatism and, 119–20; expression of, in groups, 182; of leader, 38–39; Locke's state of nature and, 97–98, 101; as only concern of political theory, 178–79; Rousseau's state of nature and, 105–09

Freud, Sigmund: *Civilization and its Discontents,* 152; concept of projection and, 48; group psychology and, 12, 14, 15, 16, 38–39, 40, 166; leadership and, 38–39, 151–52, 166, 175; role of love in groups and, 34–35; sexual conflict and, 141, 145; *Totem and Taboo,* 31, 57, 59

Gaffe, 171–72

Geller, Marvin, 58

General will, 110–11, 112

Generative violence, 31

Gilligan, Carol, 141, 154; *In a Different Voice,* 143

Girard, René, *Violence and the Sacred,* 31

Glacier Metal Company, 125–26

Goals of individual vs. group, 33. *See also* Individual-group conflict

Gould, Carol, *Marx's Social Ontology,* 129

Government: expectations of, 158; liberal pluralism and, 133–35; origin of, in Locke's state of nature, 100–103. *See also* Grouplike entities

Grotius, Hugo, 80

Group: idea of, and conformity, 117; instability of emotional life in, 58–59; organization of, 13; primacy of, and political theory, 3–12, 18–19; response to members and, 50–51, 55–56; as term, 12–13. *See also* Experiences in groups; Groupishness, man's war with own; Individual-group conflict; Tavistock groups

Group-as-a-whole perspective, 58–59, 130

Group development: autistic-contiguous position and, 29, 65–66; interaction with individual development and, 113–14; need for leadership in, 5, 64–65, 152–54; oscillations in, 72–75; political theory and, 70–72, 113, 147–48, 178–80; positions in, 65; process of, 70–71; recovery of lost selves of members and, 56, 144, 146–49, 165; role of leadership in, 60–61, 64–65; sacrificial leader drama and, 29–32; sexual differentiation and, 142, 143–46; work required for, 101–02, 109, 143–44. *See also* Developed group; Leadership; Regressed group; Undeveloped group

Group fantasy, 44–46, 125–26; leadership and, 159–60; liberal pluralism and, 133–35. *See also* Dramas; *specific types of dramas*

Groupie, as term, 8

Groupishness, man's war with own, 4; metaphysics of presence and, 129; need for confrontation with, 113; political concepts as relationships and, 17–25; unsolvability of individual-group conflict and, 4–5, 109. *See also* Individual-group conflict

Grouplike entities: policies and positions and, 172; political leadership and, 176–77; political theory as, 17–25; role of institutions in, 73–75; small groups and, 12, 13–14; as term, 13

Group member, as term, 86–87

Group mentality, 14–15, 16

Group-psychological materialism, 17–25; concepts of political theory and, 17–20; metaphysics of presence and, 129–31; social theorists and, 20–24

182–83; Havel as, 163–66; Lincoln as, 181–82; Philopoemen as, 160; political candidates and, 174–75; Xenophon as, 169–70
Isolation: conformity and, 117–18; regressed group and, 66–67, 116; schizoid compromise and, 53; state-of-nature theory and, 79, 87, 106

Jaques, Elliott, 125–26
Jealousy, 38, 40
Johnston, David, *The Rhetoric of Leviathan,* 78

Kant, Immanuel, 141
Kavka, Gregory, 85
Kerr, Clark, 119
Kinsley, Michael, 172
Klein, Melanie, 48, 59, 64
Kohlberg, Lawrence, 153
Krantz, James, 58

Labor, and social contract, 147–48, 180–81
Laclau, Ernesto, 123
Langer, Suzanne, 154
Language: participationists and, 122–23, 124, 126, 143; postmodernists and, 123–24, 128–29, 131; self-transformation and, 122–24. *See also* Rhetoric
Lasch, Christopher, 120, 180
Laslett, Peter, 95, 101
Law, 38, 40, 97–98. *See also* Natural law
Leadership: appearance of, and Machiavelli, 159–63; constitutional liberalism and, 11–12, 74, 180–83; developed group and, 68–69, 149–50; devouring of the leader and, 39, 57, 60–61, 97, 111; effectiveness of, 72, 76; good vs. bad, 152, 155, 162, 167; group denial of importance of, 37–38; group structure and, 13; Hobbes's sovereign and, 91–95, 152, 175, 176; holding function of, 60–61; by interpretation, 23, 70–71, 74–75, 153–54, 183 (*see also* Interpretive leader); limits of politics and, 175–80; in Locke, 95–103, 157; Machiavelli's story about Philopoemen and, 160, 162–63, 168; narratives about, 163–75; as necessary for group development, 5, 64–65; Oakeshott and, 157–59; oscillations in group development and, 73; as patriarchal category, 143; political theory and, 5, 11, 12, 76, 152, 154–55, 167–68; relationship with the led and,

166, 167, 174–75; in Rousseau, 103, 110–12, 176; in Tavistock groups, and politics, 75–76; traditional political theory and, 5, 11–12; women's voice in issues of, 143; Xenophon's *Anabasis* and, 168–71. *See also* Consultant-leader; Interpretation; Missing leader, group enactment of; Sacrificial leader drama
Leadership and individuality drama, 37–40, 63
Liberal individualism: group development and, 17; methodological individualism and, 86; Rousseau and, 107–10, 112. *See also* State-of-nature theory, traditional
Liberalism: fear and, 6; individual-group conflict and, 4, 5, 9, 10, 20; modernism and, 179–80. *See also* Constitutional liberalism, with strong leadership
Liberal pluralism, 132–35, 183
Lieberman, Joe, 177
Lifton, Robert Jay, *The Nazi Doctors,* 84–85
Lincoln, Abraham, Gettysburg address, 181–82
Lobbying, 121
Locke, John, 104, 143; communitarianism vs. individualism of, 107–08; denial of psychology of groups in, 98–99, 100–103; *First Treatise on Government,* 95–96, 103; leadership and, 95–103, 157; *Second Treatise on Government,* 96–100, 101, 102, 148; social contract and, 107–10, 148; state of nature according to, 97–100; *Thoughts Concerning Education,* 102
Love: enactment of missing leader and, 59–60; identification and, 43; of the leader, 38, 101, 151–52, 174; role of, in groups, 34–35; threat of romantic pairing and, 35–37. *See also* Identification; Sex
Lowi, Theodore, *The End of Liberalism,* 133–35, 177, 183

Machiavelli, Niccolò, 155; *The Discourses,* 160; *The Prince,* 159–63; story about Philopoemen, 160, 162–63, 168
MacIntyre, Alasdair, 23–24
Macpherson, C. B., 85–86, 175, 176
Malinowski, Bronislaw, 21
Mansbridge, Jane, 120
Marcuse, Herbert, *One-Dimensional Man,* 119, 180
Marriage contract, 147
Marx, Karl, 45–46, 148; *Grundrisse,* 138, 147

individual-group conflict and, 4, 5, 8–9; language and, 123–24, 128–29, 131–32; liberal pluralism as implication of, 132–35; psychology and, 6–7
Power: in Hobbes's state of nature, 88, 90, 92; of leaders, protection of, 159–60, 162, 170; in Locke's state of nature, 102–03; in Rousseau, 109; sexual conflict and, 140–41; social contract and, 147
Presidential candidates, 171–75
Primal horde, 59
Principle of sociability, 82
Private property: civil privatism and, 118; constitutional liberalism and, 181
Projective identification: acting out the missing leader and, 47, 48–52; concept of, 48–49; effects of, 51–52; group response to members and, 50–51; interpersonal pressure and, 49–50
Psycho-babble, 21–22, 34
Pufendorf, Samuel, 78–85, 176; cynicism of, 83–85; *De officio*, 78–79; human weakness and, 79, 81–83

Racial difference, 44
Rage, 32–35, 62, 83
Rape, 35
Rawls, John, 141, 148; difference principle of, 135–37, 138; *A Theory of Justice*, 115, 135–40; total community and, 137–39
Reagan, Ronald, 167, 172
Reality, and political theory, 1, 3–5, 18, 25, 178–80
Reason, 2, 141
Recognition: desire for power and, 89–90; difference and, 106–07; individuality and, 38–40. *See also* Responsiveness
Regressed group: critical thought and, 42; differences and, 66, 106, 120–21; Hobbes's state of nature and, 87–91, 94, 109; Locke and, 99–100, 102, 109; participationism and, 120–21; as position in group development, 65–67; Rawls's communitarianism and, 135, 136, 140; Rousseau and, 69, 105, 106, 107–10, 111
Religion, 33, 34
Republicanism, 182–83
Responsibility: fear of, 144–45; leadership and, 164, 165, 166, 183; liberal pluralism and, 134–35
Responsible group membership, 170–71
Responsiveness: maternal, 50, 60; projective

identification and, 50–51; schizoid compromise and, 54–55. *See also* Recognition
Revolution, concept of, 22–23
Rhetoric: participationists and, 122–23, 124; state-of-nature theory as, 77–78, 87. *See also* Language
Rice Institute. *See* A. K. Rice Institute
Ritual sacrifice, 31–32, 34–35. *See also* Sacrificial leader drama
Roles: developed group and, 68–69; enactment of missing leader and, 62–64; Hobbes and, 86–87, 89; state-of-nature theory and, 83. *See also* Projective identification
Role suction, 50, 89
Romantic love, 21
Romney, George, 171
Rousseau, Jean-Jacques: individuality and, 109–11; *La Nouvelle Héloïse*, 113; leadership and, 103, 110–12, 176; popularity of, 107–10, 112, 125; *Second Discourse*, 1, 2, 103–06, 107, 108–10; *Social Contract*, 34, 107, 111–12, 148, 166; state of nature according to, 104–07
Rubin, Gayle, 140
Ruderman, Richard, 169, 171
Ryan, Alan, 154

Sacrificial leader drama, 28–32; enactment of missing leader and, 61–62; Hobbes and, 85–95; regressed group and, 66; tribal warfare drama and, 64; undeveloped group and, 67
Sandel, Michael, 115, 148; *Liberalism and the Limits of Justice*, 129, 135, 137, 138–40
Saxonhouse, Arlene, 141
Scapegoating, 2, 28, 29–32, 164. *See also* Sacrificial leader drama
Schizoid compromise: acting out the missing leader and, 47, 52–56; definition of, 52; developed group and, 69–70, 176; group enemies and, 42; grouplike entities and, 13, 20; identification with leader and, 37; interpretation and, 72; metaphysics of presence and, 131; personal baggage and, 53; problems with, 52–54; Rawls's communitarianism and, 135; regressed group and, 66, 116; in Rousseau, 107–10; solutions to individual-group conflict and, 4–5, 19–20, 72–73, 125; split-off emotions and, 53–54; state-of-nature theory and, 79, 92–93, 94, 103, 106;